# SWALLOWING A BITTER PILL

# SWALLOWING A BITTER PILL

## How Prescription and Over-The-Counter Drug Abuse is Ruining Lives

### —My Story—

*Cindy Rae Mogil-Cooley*

Prescriptions Anonymous, LLC
Naples, Florida
Second Edition

## SWALLOWING A BITTER PILL

Copyright © 2019  Cindy Rae Mogil-Cooley

Prescriptions Anonymous, LLC
Naples, Florida

Cindy Rae Mogil-Cooley

All rights reserved. No part of this book may be reproduced or transmitted in any form, or by any means, electronic or mechanical, including photocopying, recording or by any information storage and retrieval systems, without the prior written permission from the author.

ISBN - 978-0-578-55485-3

10 9 8 7 6 5 4 3 2 1

Second Edition

Printed in the United States of America by
Serbin Print Marketing & Publishing, Sarasota, Florida

# Author's Note

This book is based on my research, interviews, and experiences with dual diagnosis, prescription, and over-the-counter drug addiction and recovery, as well as the experiences of others struggling with this potentially destructive disorder. In order to protect privacy, fictitious names and identities have been given to some individuals in this book, and otherwise identifying characteristics have been altered. For the purposes of simplifying usage, the pronouns his/him and her are often used interchangeably.

The material in this book is intended to provide information and raise awareness about prescription and over-the-counter addictions. This book serves only as a supplement to, not a substitute for the thorough and professional care of a licensed physician, psychologist, therapist, psychiatrist, addictionologist, and other professionals at an addiction treatment facility.

# TABLE OF CONTENTS

| | | |
|---|---|---:|
| Foreword | | ix |
| Acknowledgments | | xiii |
| Chapter One | My Story | 1 |
| Chapter Two | Addiction | 11 |
| Chapter Three | Denial | 31 |
| Chapter Four | Admitting the Problem | 45 |
| Chapter Five | Getting Help | 61 |
| Chapter Six | Diagnosis | 97 |
| Chapter Seven | The First Thirty Days | 123 |
| Chapter Eight | Facing Life Without Abusing Rx Drugs | 149 |
| Chapter Nine | Relapse | 171 |
| Chapter Ten | A Family Disease | 205 |
| Chapter Eleven | Recovery and the Family | 227 |
| Chapter Twelve | The Peace of Recovery | 247 |
| Epilogue | | 257 |
| Appendix I: Questions and Answers | | 273 |
| Appendix II: Resources | | 295 |

# Foreword
## by Angela Cornell, M.D.

I have been a practicing psychiatrist since 1980, after graduating from Emory University in Atlanta, Georgia, and a Certified Addictionologist specializing in addiction medicine since 1992. Substance-addicted patients have come to me for help from all socioeconomic levels and all racial, ethnic, and gender backgrounds. From the barely educated to Ivy League PhD's, from day laborers to the most highly-regarded executives, my patients come from all walks of life. Yet all of them are confronted by the same roadblocks of ignorance and helplessness when they first try to face their addictions. Perhaps those patients for whom struggles with addiction and attempts to recover are hardest are healthcare professionals. For them, access to drugs, especially prescription drugs, is incredibly easy, and they are often lulled into believing that their high levels of education and professional experience should protect them from temptation or prepare them to quit at the first sign of dependence.

Physicians, nurses, pharmacists, dentists, and other healthcare professionals number among those most at risk for addiction to prescription medication. These professionals, like others who suffer from addiction, often try to explain away their drug abuse with excuses like: I was stressed/afraid/tired/overworked/in pain; my husband/partner/boss/children/parents expected too much from me, and I couldn't meet their expectations; I couldn't relax; I didn't have time to think/I didn't think/ I couldn't think. The difference between these professionals and those who do not work in the medical field is that healthcare professionals don't need to make doctor appointments, don't need to persuade first one doctor then another across town to write out prescriptions; they can simply wait until their colleagues look the other way. It's easy. The irony is that despite being surrounded by other trained healthcare professionals, these individuals feel the same as most people dependent on drugs do: absolutely alone, helpless and, yes, ignorant when the practice of self-medication evolves into a self-destructive habit.

It is in response to the needs of all persons addicted to prescription and over-the-counter medication that Cindy Rae Mogil-Cooley, a professional healthcare provider and Addiction Recovery Coach, who struggled with her own addiction to prescription drugs, founded Prescriptions Anonymous in 2001 in Atlanta, Georgia, at that time the only Addiction and Family Recovery Coach and support group in the country. Since 1998, this support network group has not only survived but thrived because of Cindy's diligence and dedication. She knows, as do I, how difficult it is to confront a group of strangers and confess not only one's difficulties, but one's need for education and support. For this reason, she has written this book, a lay person's guide to prescription and over-the-counter pill addiction. Cindy draws on her personal experiences and the experiences of others who are fighting daily to recover from the mental, emotional, and spiritual poverty that defines drug addiction. In this book, Cindy extends a much-needed invitation to all people who could be on the path to recovery if only someone would point the way. She's pointing the way. I, too, invite you to come along.

*Angela Cornell, M.D.*

# Acknowledgements

Among my many blessings was being led to Letitia Sweitzer. Her insightful editorial skills, generosity, vision, and guidance made our collaboration a joy. Her devotion to this project and respect for my work is evident throughout this book; I will forever be grateful.

I especially would like to thank those who shared their personal stories of recovery. Though many have chosen to remain anonymous, I would like to thank in particular the following who were identified by first name only: Michael, Kevin, Pat, David, Shawna, Carol, Brandon, Logan and Tom.

I thank Dr. Angela Cornell for her wisdom, compassion, and ability to both pull me from the depths of despair and help me find the courage to embrace recovery without fear.

Special thanks to the following people who generously lent time and expertise, thus making this book possible: J. Bertram Solomon, Jr., B.S., D.C.; Floyd P. Garrett, M.D.; Nan H. Davis, R.Ph., M.S.; and Pharmacists Anonymous.

A word of sincere thanks to my family for their support and love. God has blessed me with a family that has taught me to believe in myself and never give up what I know is right.

A special thank you to my friends; Becky Staples-Rutledge, Kathy Blackburn, Donald Leach, Cathy Nadeau, Cheryl Bean, Michael Hemmer, Lisa Commery, and Patch Adams, M.D. of Gesundheit Institute who have seen me through it all with their support and encouragement to complete my novel and continue my efforts to combat the prescription and over-the-counter addiction epidemic!

To my son, Lucien, with loving appreciation for his sense of humor, support, encouragement, and his ability to lift my spirits when I need it the most. I dedicate this book to you with all my love.

# >>> 1

# My Story

I recovered from my 20-year addiction to controlled substances and over-the-counter pill medications in 1997. Remembering my own painful journey through addiction to sobriety and health, I felt compelled to write *Swallowing A Bitter Pill*, published in 2001, to offer information and hope to others trapped in the tragedy of addiction. Today, almost two decades later, the need for new information and renewed hope is even more urgent.

According to the Center for Disease Control, there were more than 72,000 drug overdose deaths in 2017 alone. The sharp increase in overdose deaths over previous years has been caused by a steep rise in deaths related to fentanyl and fentanyl analogs (synthetic opioids) with nearly 30,000 overdose deaths. It is now more urgent than ever that this crisis be addressed actively and relentlessly. I again feel compelled to share what I have learned and continue to learn about addiction and recovery, along with new information and renewed faith that recovery is possible. While I feel wiser now than when I first wrote my story, because of my recent years of experience as an Addiction Recovery Coach and Family Coach, my own story is still as painful to me as it was when I first wrote it. More important, it still fills me with the hope I want to pass on to others suffering with addiction. Here it is:

*The number of times I drove under the excessive influence of prescription drugs is too great to count. The ease with which I obtained Demerol injections from different clinics and emergency rooms is frightening. I'd drive home afterward knowing my mind was so impaired I could hurt or kill myself or someone else with my car. I had reached the point of no return, and I wasn't sure I cared anymore. I felt alone, misunderstood, severely depressed, and hopeless.*

*While driving home on the highway one day, something strange happened. Numbness besieged my face, neck, and arms, paralyzing me with fear. Though I was only ten miles from home, at that moment I had no idea where I was. Confused and disoriented, I managed to call my husband on my cell phone to tell him I had taken a wrong turn and couldn't find my way back home. It was the first time I had ever told him I needed help for anything. Sitting in my car in the emergency lane, a shaking hand holding the cell phone to my ear, I could barely understand my husband's directions. Frightened and in tears, all I could think about was, how could this have happened to me? I felt certain I could never reveal to my husband what was really going on. We had been together for nine years, and he never suspected that I was anything but a well-adjusted, happy, normal adult. After all this time, how could I tell him that my "friends"—the prescription pills I abused to numb emotional pain—were now my predators?*

*When family and friends and even doctors first learn of a person's prescription medication addiction, they often ask incredulously, "How did you ever get into this mess?" They seem ready to accept that celebrities in big cities with their grow-up-too-fast, jet-set lifestyles can easily fall prey to such problems, but a regular person like you? It couldn't happen* to them, they think—you can hear it in their voices—so they can't imagine how it happened to you. Well, it can and does.

For some people, hereditary traits, environment, and family structure interplay to create a susceptibility to addiction. One common precursor to addiction is emotional pain. For many people, emotional pain begins in early childhood. That's what happened to me. My emotional pain took root when I was only ten years old.

Shortly after my tenth birthday, I was molested at an ice-skating rink. One night while playing tag with friends, I jumped over a high snow bank at the end of the ice rink to hide and avoid being tagged out of the game. A young man who had joined the game skated over to the bank after me where no one could see. As I lay there in the snow, he climbed over the bank and rolled right on top of me. Surprised and frightened by his sudden presence, I lay there in stunned silence. I tried to squirm my way out from under him, but he grabbed my arms so tightly I couldn't move. Then he began touching my chest. I tried to tell him to stop, but I couldn't get the words out. Almost as quickly as it started, he abruptly let me go, telling me to never reveal to anyone what had happened or I would suffer the consequences. I pretended like nothing happened, afraid of what he might do to me if anyone found out. The next night, I reluctantly went back to the ice rink with my friends. Again, the young man caught me by surprise, and the nightmarish event repeated itself. This time I could not keep quiet. I began to cry and in a small voice begged him to stop, but he refused. After what seemed like a lifetime, he took his hands off me and once again threatened to hurt me if I told a soul. I walked home in fear and shame as tears flowed down my cheeks in the cold, windy night. Thankfully, I never saw him again, but the effect he had on my life was profound.

I never told my parents or my sisters about the young man or what he had done to me because I thought they would be angry at me. I didn't *want to be scolded or told that it was my fault. I was afraid my family would make me feel worse about myself than I already did. Over the next three years, I survived life and my parents' divorce by withdrawing from the world and becoming extremely shy, sensitive, and insecure in the process.*

*One day, a classmate approached me and handed me a little blue pill. She told me she could see I was often sad, and the pill would make my world a better and happier place to live in. I couldn't wait to take this "happy pill." I found out much later that the pill was an amphetamine, often called "speed." When I took the pill, I felt carefree, numbed, rid of all my uncomfortable emotions and feelings. I liked feeling that way. Through that drug, I had found a place to which I could escape from my fears and loneliness. I was fourteen and a freshman in high school. I continued using speed regularly until my junior year in high school. One day my mother approached me, saying she suspected I was on drugs. I felt so guilty and ashamed for disappointing her that I abruptly stopped taking my "happy pill." She never asked why I had taken the pills, and I certainly never volunteered any information about my emotional state.*

*Ten days after my eighteenth birthday, I was driving my car on my way to pick up a girlfriend so we could enjoy a night of laughter and dancing. To my surprise and shock, a pedestrian darted out into the street, seemingly unconcerned about the busy oncoming traffic. As the man came to a deliberate stop in my lane, I realized in that split second that he didn't appear to have any plans to get out of the street nor would I have time to avoid colliding with him. My heart pounded as I slammed on the brakes as hard as I could, silently praying for a miracle to prevent a terrible accident. My worst fears were realized when suddenly I saw a slim body collide with my left fender, then roll across the hood as the car skidded sideways. I remember the frightened look on his face as he rolled off my hood and landed face down on the sidewalk. Despite my own shock, I immediately sprang into action. Jumping out of my car, I screamed out for someone to call for an ambulance. When I reached the young man's body, I ripped off my jacket and gently placed it under his head. The young man died three days later of massive internal and brain injuries. He was only twenty-one years old. He was discharged from a drug rehabilitation facility earlier that day. For reasons unknown he relapsed that night and committed suicide using my car as his deadly weapon. His name was Andrew.*

*Even though I was not found to be at fault for the accident, the tragedy caused me to isolate myself again from my family and friends. The guilt I felt consumed me. I couldn't sleep, eat, or talk to anyone. Seeing my despondency, my mother became fearful that I might try to commit suicide. She turned to my father for help, and they decided it would be best for me to live with him. I felt abandoned by my mother. I was so distraught I wasn't able to make any decisions for myself, so I went along with whatever they decided. Counseling was never an option approved by my mother or father. They both felt I didn't need outside help from anyone and could heal my own emotions. To them, this was **just** a car accident, and I needed to move on with my life. But I just couldn't. I couldn't even look at myself in the mirror, and I didn't know how much more guilt I could endure. I wasn't even sure I would be missed if I died. Isolation, devastation, and severe depression took over my life for the next five years.*

*My stepmother, however, saw how much pain I was in and suggested that I might seek help through counseling to talk out my feelings. This would be my first encounter with therapy. I didn't have a clue how I could talk to a stranger, but it was a chance I needed to take. My life depended on it.*

*The County Health Department therapist walked in, introduced himself and blurted out, "So why are you here?" As I nervously stared* at the floor, I gave him a short story of my past, not fully understanding how to respond to such a broad question. When my forty-five minutes were up, he said to me in an insensitive tone, "You need to forget about your accident. You said it yourself: The accident wasn't your fault. If you keep telling yourself you can't forget or forgive yourself, then you never will get on with your life. Here, try a prescription called Valium. It should help you feel better."

Without hesitation, I started taking Valium along with high doses of the sleeping pills he also prescribed. I felt lightheaded. I liked the sensation of carefree thoughts and the floating effects the drugs had over me. I didn't experience fear, worry, guilt or depression. In fact, I didn't have any feelings anymore. I simply enjoyed the peace.

After a few weeks of what I felt was "useless therapy", I stopped making appointments. I knew what I needed to do to feel better: take enough pills to blot out the painful, shameful feelings, and memories. I enjoyed numbness and didn't want to come back to reality, not for a long while anyway. I was able to manipulate the receptionist and nurses at the counselor's office to refill my prescriptions about six times before I was told I needed to make another appointment.

The ease with which I could get prescriptions and refills from other healthcare providers surprised me. I decided I didn't need help from the county therapist or anyone else. I had made a new friend, and it came in the form of a pill. It would be there when I needed it to be, any time, any place—to comfort, to calm, to numb. My world turned into manipulation: I lied to my husband, family, friends, and coworkers. Over the next twenty years I manipulated doctors, dentists, therapists, emergency room personnel, pharmaceutical drug representatives, and friends to get an array of different pills. My pills of choice were, Darvon, Elavil, Demerol, Haldol, Darvon, Percocet, Percodan, Vicodin, Xanax, and Ativan, to name a few. The healthcare providers I manipulated were *prescribing medications based on symptoms I made up to get the drug I wanted and needed. An accompanying performance would usually convince them they were doing the right thing by writing my preferred prescriptions. As my tolerance to pills grew so did the number of pills I took daily, sometimes up to fifteen or more a day. I started taking my pills the minute I woke up, with no preferences to what kind of pill I took. I had pills for breakfast, lunch, and dinner. I took a few more pills for sleep. I replaced food with pills and eventually mixed them with alcohol to speed up the effects. My weight dropped from 124 to 104 pounds within five weeks, and I still didn't think anything was wrong.*

*I perhaps reached my lowest point while working at a cardiology office after eighteen years of experience in the healthcare profession. One day the doctor asked me to prep a patient for a Treadmill Stress Test. We used the treadmill to monitor the patient's heart rate at different speeds while he walked on the moving platform. As the treadmill's speed was increased, the patient became short of breath and began experiencing chest pain. The cardiologist ordered me to stop the treadmill immediately. Because I was high on pills, however, I couldn't locate the stop switch quickly enough and the patient fell off the platform. Fortunately, the cardiologist was able to catch the patient so that he didn't fall to the floor. The patient was shaken but luckily not hurt during the ordeal. I couldn't explain my behavior—my failure—to the cardiologist or the patient, let alone forgive myself for my actions. That day I knew I had a real problem.*

*I found a new therapist Angela Cornell, MD who, realizing I was in danger of overdosing or committing suicide, saw me in her office the same day. She admitted me involuntarily into the drug rehabilitation hospital for drug overdose, anxiety, suicidal thoughts, and severe depression. In Georgia, laws required a mandatory 72-hour suicide watch while I was detoxing from controlled substances, suicidal thoughts, and alcohol. I was in the treatment facility for only ten days based on health insurance rehabilitation guidelines. I still denied that I had a serious problem. Nevertheless, I adhered to their rules. Finally, on the eleventh day, I was released.*

*Relapse came quickly. Within two months I was back to my old habits manipulating doctors any way I could to maintain my supply of pills. One day, I noticed tingling in my arms and numbness in my jaw. I called my therapist to tell her. Again, fearing I had overdosed and might be contemplating suicide, she told me to return to the hospital. I refused to go. However, without my knowing it, she dialed 911 and called for an emergency paramedic to come to my house. I had previously mentioned to her that my husband had a gun in the house, so she told emergency medical services I might be armed and dangerous. While I was still talking with her on the phone, the doorbell rang. I put the phone down and answered the door. There stood three police officers with their guns drawn asking, "Do you have a weapon in your hands?" I said, "No," and held up my empty hands as proof. I was put into the ambulance with police escort and brought back to the same drug rehabilitation facility where I had previously been. I finally admitted I was powerless over my addiction and needed help. I wasn't in denial any longer.*

*Withdrawal, however, does not make a pretty story. My discomfort ranged from physical pain like headaches and aching muscle to emotional pain including wild mood swings, the strong urge to use drugs again, and suicidal thoughts. Withdrawal doesn't mean just getting off the drugs, giving up the "high" or pleasurable feelings. It also means facing life. When I was on drugs, I was able to mask my problems and hide from reality. Once I was off drugs, trauma from my past were still there awaiting me. Now I had to deal with all the hurt, guilt, pain, shame, anger, and loss that had made me turn to drugs in the first place. Feeling pain meant I was returning to reality again, and it was a frightening place in which to be. To be vulnerable to other people after being shielded for years from whatever personal pain I had to face was beyond hard and unbearable. Then on top of that pain, I was now afraid of being judged harshly as a recovering addict. If I had had the strength for all this, I wouldn't have been on pills in the first place! I had to decide if I wanted to live more than I wanted to die. I had to find self-respect and to love myself. If I couldn't find purpose and goals for myself, it would be hard not to relapse. If I didn't love myself, then pills would always be predators waiting for me to experience a moment of weakness.*

Since then, I have learned how to keep promises to myself and to always be truthful, honest, and open-minded. I will always be a recovering addict, meaning I must use safe and healthy choices wisely. These insights have come to me the hard way. I can only keep these precious gifts that I have gained through recovery by sharing them with others. That is the reason I founded Prescriptions Anonymous in 1998, a non-traditional recovery program and website-based support network for people addicted to or in recovery from controlled substance abuse, and the reason I wrote this second edition of my book. I'm working as a Nationally Certified Addiction Recovery and Family Coach, focusing on staying in recovery for aftercare treatment or seeking help for a current addiction. Giving back to others in need has been the greatest gift I could give to an individual or families seeking recovery and understanding.

I only ask that you "pay it forward" one day to someone else who needs your help, encouragment and support.

## >>> 2

## ADDICTION
### *"How did I get into this mess?"*

All the people who have joined Prescriptions Anonymous, the group I founded in 1998, have distinctive yet disquietingly similar stories about how and why they became addicted to controlled substance prescriptions and/or over-the-counter drugs.

Kevin is a salesman, and his story, like mine, illustrates decades-long addiction rising out of a need to escape some lasting childhood hurt.

**Kevin's Story**

*I was a very shy and insecure child by the age of three or four. Something happened at that age between my father, brother, and me. I cannot recall the details, but I vividly remember the result. I sat on the couch in our living room and thought, "I will never let myself get close to anyone because I will be hurt." And I didn't.*

*By the time I reached fifteen years old, I had begun to experiment with street drugs. With them, I found a way of covering up my fear of being close to people. By retreating into my fantasy world, I would not worry about other people at all. I drank sporadically but developed an affinity for marijuana. I was playing "Russian roulette" with my own life, not thinking about the consequences. I loved the senseless feeling of being high. At twenty-one, while I was away at college, I broke into a liquor store. I was arrested and charged with a felony. My parents, however, paid for a good lawyer, who got me off with just probation. I remember wondering, since there were no consequences for my actions, what else can I get away with?*

*All through my twenties I abused opioid painkillers and depressants, including over-the-counter medicines, just to get high. They were cheaper than street drugs, and they were legal. After I'd quickly built up a tolerance to these, I needed stronger and higher doses of medication. I broke into my friends' homes to steal pills while they were gone. My conscience never bothered me; it never once told me this was wrong! I was in control, or so I thought.*

*I took all kinds of pills, drank liquor, smoked pot, sometimes all at the same time, without thinking about what I was doing to myself. I had developed a habit and didn't realize I would have to confront my demons one day. I frequently got sick from pills and alcohol poisoning until I passed out. My body was physically wearing out and shutting down. It was a miracle that I didn't die from all the binges. Depression developed, but I still somehow managed to put on a performance of being focused and normal while at work or with friends and family. My friends who saw me drink never voiced their concerns over my consumption, or they just chose not to say anything. And it quickly became apparent that very few people get concerned if they see you putting a pill in your mouth!*

*Through manipulation and lies, I persuaded my dentist to write opioid painkiller prescriptions for fake toothaches. I never paid any attention to the instructions from my dentist or the ones that came with the medicine. I often consumed at least twice the amount prescribed.*

*My life was empty. Isolation and depression ruled me. I kept to myself outside of work and home. Most of my hours were dedicated to getting high, alone. I remember thinking, what a waste! But I couldn't stop, and I didn't know how to ask or look for help.*

*I met my wife when I was thirty-eight years old. We were like two peas in a pod. We both enjoyed drinking and partying, although her drinking was not as chronic as mine. After we were married, the pressures of marriage, home ownership, and being a stepfather began to weigh heavily on me. At forty-one, I changed jobs, and we moved closer to my work. We also had a son of our own by this time. With so many mounting pressures, my anxiety became uncontrollable. I was illegally taking prescription painkillers now, but my wife never suspected that I might be addicted to pills. If she had suspected, she would have done something about it, but I had her convinced that I was all right.*

*Once I went to my dentist with a legitimate problem, for which he gave me opioid painkillers. These ran out after a few days, so I had to get "creative." I returned to him and lied about the severity of my toothache from a root canal he had done. After a month, he would no longer give me any more pills or refills, so I went to my wife's dentist, who, for a while, became my "Dr. Feelgood." If I asked for painkillers, he would prescribe them without question or hesitation. Over the course of three months, he wrote between fifteen to twenty prescriptions for Percodan.*

*One day, even "Dr. Feelgood" refused to write any more prescriptions, so again I got "creative" and decided to write my own prescription. I took the prescription that the dentist had written for me, used white-out to cover up the old prescription, copied it, and then wrote out new prescriptions. I never felt guilty. I'd never thought about the consequences before, so why should I start now? It was a miracle pharmacists never caught on to my fake prescriptions in the beginning.*

*After twenty-five forged prescriptions, I got caught! While I was at work one day, a detective went to my house and spoke with my wife. She was stunned and could only listen in shock and amazement when the* detective pulled out all the forged prescriptions to show her. He was a kind man. He did not issue a warrant for my arrest but only told her he needed to talk with me.

My wife called me at the office and made up a story to get me home, fearing I might run from this problem if I knew what was happening. I'll never forget the shame I felt when my wife confronted me at home. In tears and anger, she asked, "How could you do this to us and this family?" For the first time, I was overwhelmed with fear and remorse. I realized I was inflicting the same hurt on those who loved me as I'd suffered as an abused child.

I obtained a lawyer, and he was able to talk the detective out of arresting me. He "took care of it"—familiar words to me, the same ones used when I was arrested as a teen. As a result of this crisis, I tried Alcoholics Anonymous and Narcotics Anonymous for the first time, but I felt I was wasting my time listening to everybody pouring out their stories of sorrow and grief. One week of meetings was all I could stand.

Soon I was going to dentists again, lying about tooth pain to get yet another supply of painkillers. I did this for a few months until my wife caught me with some pills. She threatened to leave me if I didn't get help. I tried Alcoholics Anonymous and Narcotics Anonymous again, for her, not for myself. Within a couple of weeks, I was forging prescriptions again with no end in sight. I was in a nightmare and couldn't wake myself up.

When I could no longer find a doctor to write prescriptions for me, I used fake names and new pharmacies to get my forged prescriptions filled. After three months of this insanity, I had exhausted myself and could not go on. I was killing myself, a slow death, and for the first time I was afraid of dying. I returned to my old therapist, admitted what I had done, and asked for help. There had to be a better way of life for me. My way was destroying all I loved, my family, and myself.

*Somehow I got the strength to tell my wife the truth of what I had done. Thankfully, she decided to stay with me. I have accepted the fact that I have a disease called prescription addiction as well as alcoholism and that my recovery requires a commitment from me and from my family.*

*I feel differently about recovery this time. Admitting my wrongs and making amends was my first step. I now have a sponsor and addictionologist that gives me the guidance and clarity I've needed for years.*

*I attend meetings every week at Prescriptions Anonymous and Alcoholics Anonymous to get the support and understanding I so desperately need. I learned that thousands of people die from this disease every year. I'm so grateful I found help in time and pray that others find help and support somewhere before it's too late.*

## Shawna's Story

*At the ripe old age of five, I underwent open-heart surgery. The surgery was successful, but what changed my life more than the surgery itself was the little opioid pill the doctor gave me afterward for pain. I have forgotten the pain, but I remember the pills. They gave me a wonderful, oh-so-happy feeling I had never felt before and could not have imagined. I did not want to give them up.*

*"Mommy, it hurts so bad!" I don't know how many times I uttered these words as a child. I remember there was a small merry-go-round outside of the children's ward. I begged my father to take me there one sunny afternoon. I asked him to push me faster and faster. Then I faked a pain in my chest. I knew that if I said I was hurting, they would give me some "stuff" to make me feel all nice and warm. Nurses and doctors came running. I can vividly picture my father's face as they listened for chest sounds. He was devastated, tears rolling down his cheeks, thinking*

*he was the cause of my pain. That was the beginning of a way of life, full of deceit, which still haunts me today.*

*As a young girl of ten, I was diagnosed with scoliosis, a curvature of the spine. The doctors took a "wait and see" approach for a couple of years, but it got progressively worse. Finally, I was fitted for a Milwaukee back brace. It was made of steel and hard plastic and enclosed my entire torso and spine. I hated it for making me so unattractive and a target for teasing. Thus, I was pleased beyond delight when, two years later, the orthopedic surgeon said that he needed to do surgery. I was thirteen. Little did I know just how excruciating spinal surgery would be. I remember it hurt to even move my fingers, my toes, or my mouth. I was in so much pain that I prayed to die. Several times I screamed until someone gave me morphine. Three days after my back surgery, my stomach began to bloat to the point that I looked nine months pregnant, even though I weighed only one hundred pounds. Doctors and nurses would come in and push on my stomach, asking me if it hurt. Even though it genuinely hurt, I would cry out in a much more dramatic way than was warranted. I was once again rushed into surgery. They were sure it was appendicitis. When they opened me up, they found my appendix to be in marvelous shape. So they kept cutting deeper and wider only to find an ovarian cyst the size of a grapefruit. They removed it and stitched me back up. The scar ended up spanning the entire stomach region. Not only was I recovering from spinal surgery, now I had to deal with staples all down my front. The doctors, knowing this, kept me completely doped up for a good month. Then they sent me home with enough narcotics to last a couple of months. I took them all!*

*I remember thinking at some point that I probably didn't need to keep taking the drugs, but since the doctor prescribed them, I did. My parents were always after me, "Shawna, do what the doctor says!" I had no idea that the pills were addictive, I only knew they made me feel better. I didn't even know what addiction was. My father should have known, but I was his little girl who could do no wrong. If I was in pain, he was going to make sure that I was taken care of. Who would've guessed that his "angel girl" would end up being a hard-core prescription drug addict?*

*When the drugs were gone, I was in a world of psychological hurt. I couldn't function. My mother would tell me to "quit moping around... and stand up straight!" I was in a black hole that I could not seem to get out of. I couldn't understand why. Why wasn't I like my six brothers and sisters? Why couldn't I be carefree like my schoolmates? I quickly learned to put on a face of confidence, even radiance. I knew what my parents and teachers wanted, so I gave it to them. I didn't want anyone to see my gut-wrenching depression and low self-worth. So I excelled for them. I performed regularly, winning awards for musical talent. I was the lead in school musicals and the solo voice in many choirs. I loved the art of drama because I could literally get out of myself for a while and become an entirely different person. In between productions, however, I would break down. I longed to be in that warm safe place again where I didn't have to think about anything.*

*During this time, I recalled what the doctor said to my parents after my last surgery, "Teenage girls get cysts all the time. But for some reason it's more painful for some. It looks like your daughter may be in this category. You'll want to keep an eye on her ten to fourteen days after her periods each month." That was a green light to me. I kept track of my period and, fourteen days to the day, I would feign horrible abdominal pain. My parents would rush me to the gynecologist, who would do a pelvic exam.*

*Ninety percent of the time they could go in surgically and remove a small cyst. This meant weeks of painkillers. Sometimes my doctor would ask me to ride out the pain, and he'd call in a prescription for sixty*

Vicodin. *This was fine by me. By the time I was eighteen, I had endured approximately twenty unnecessary surgeries. I felt truly evil for being so deceitful.*

Not everyone who becomes addicted to prescription drugs—or any substance—acquires the addiction as early as Kevin, Shawna, and I did. Not all pill abusers have suffered from childhood traumas or physical pain. Some, like Pat, first fell under the spell of prescription drugs in middle age.

## Pat's Story

*I didn't become addicted to any substance until I was over fifty. I didn't even like the floaty feeling my first prescription pills gave me. But I was, I now realize, addicted to power—the power I had over my husband as a care-giver. For twenty-seven years, I was married to an alcoholic who leaned on me to take care of everything, including the bills and paying for his tickets he acquired while driving under the influence of alcohol. I even made the important decisions in our lives, whether it was buying major appliances or deciding on the best schools for our children. This gave me tremendous power in the marriage. I liked the feeling of that power, the adrenaline high I felt over someone else, even when he turned from Dr. Jekyll to Mr. Hyde from drinking. When he decided to seek help through Alcoholics Anonymous, I was glad that he was trying to control and stop his drinking, but fearful for myself because I knew I would lose control over him and our lives would be changed.*

*He had an affair with someone he met at Alcoholics Anonymous and decided to leave our marriage for her. I felt relieved that I wouldn't be living with an alcoholic anymore, but, in losing my power, I was scared and alone for the first time in twenty-seven years.*

*A few months after the divorce, I went to see our family doctor, complaining of anxiety, depression, and tension headaches. She gave me a prescription for a thirty tablets of Fiorinal with Codeine, an opioid medication for the headaches. She never warned me of the addictive tendencies of the drug, nor did she instruct me on how to take them. She even gave me three refills!*

*Even though I didn't like them at first, after a few weeks, I came to love the little pills. I would count out my feel-good pills in the morning to make sure I had a full day's supply. I would have never dreamed that pills could become such a powerful part of my life. I not only had lost control over my ex-husband, but now I had lost control of myself. I no longer took my medication for pain, but for coping. They made my stressful day more bearable. They gave me a second wind. They made me excel, or so I thought.*

*I really thought I was on top of it all, staying in touch with reality. I was blind to the multitude of compulsive behaviors in my life like shopping, overeating and hiding in seclusion. Once my tolerance to the pills developed, it was virtually impossible for my friends or family to accurately gauge the extent of my dependence. I could appear completely normal during an extended part of my day.*

*One Friday I realized I didn't have enough pills to last through the weekend, so I decided to call in sick at work and made an emergency doctor visit. I perfected my "performance" in my car and in the waiting room, visualizing exactly what I'd say and how I would act to get my fix of pills. I even wore sloppy clothes, no make-up, and messy hair to look the part of a person in pain. It worked well. Too well.*

*Back at home, high under the influence of the pills, I had an accident. I stumbled into a tall piece of furniture and a one-hundred-pound metal light fixture fell on my head, causing a severe head injury. I managed to get to the phone to call 911. I needed surgery to stop bleeding inside my head. It was while I was recuperating in the hospital that I had to face up to my addiction.*

*After two days of not having any Fiorinal, I began to feel nervous, and soon my anxiety returned with a vengeance—classic signs of withdrawal. Because of my severe injuries, I was refused my Fiorinal, which I had brought with me to the hospital. I was told that, because of the other medications they were giving me, Fiorinal would hinder my treatment for internal bleeding. My withdrawal symptoms were becoming more noticeable to the nurses and my doctor. They suspected that I might be addicted to a substance.*

*I was ashamed and embarrassed about having to ask for help, but I had no choice. I was powerless, and I had to admit it to someone. At first, my doctor did not understand how or why I had gotten myself addicted to Fiorinal. It was difficult to be truthful with him, but, ever since the day I finally explained to him about my addiction, he has been a source of comfort, empathy, guidance, and support. He has directed me to people who could help me through my recovery.*

*I received my initial treatment through Chemical Dependency Services. This organization gave me the steps to recovery and offered support groups where I could talk freely about the anger and frustration I felt about my divorce. I've also learned about the co-dependency I practiced throughout my marriage. I am learning how to take care of myself for the first time in my life.*

*I once viewed alcoholics as having weak character; I had no sympathy for them. Now I know I was no better than my alcoholic husband. I am as sick as he was. Alcohol was just not my "drug of choice." I now understand, after all these years, the misery and pain my husband must have gone through.*

*I'll admit that some days I still try to talk myself into believing that my addiction was not really that bad. Denial pops into my still vulnerable mind. It has taken time for me to "wake up" and see how much of life I was missing. The deeper I get involved with real life, the less power my addiction has over me.*

*Recovery is a journey on new paths every day. I have found myself wanting to try them all, but, knowing I must be careful not to get lost along the way, I have finally found that right path. I would gladly share it with others. I call it freedom.*

Now that Kevin, Shawna, Pat, and I have told you how we got into the mess of prescription addiction, here is what the experts say about us and millions of others in the same boat. First of all, even though we may have been given our first addictive medication by someone else, perhaps medical professionals and perhaps for legitimate reasons, very soon we misused or abused the substance. The definition of medication abuse is the misuse of a prescription or over-the-counter medications in any way that is different from the instructions given by the doctor or printed on the label of the medication.

The most addictive medications, whether prescription or over-the-counter medication, fall into three categories: stimulants, narcotics and sedatives. Scientific research has shown that when these addictive or abusable drugs bombard the system, they change the biochemistry of the brain. In this way, drugs themselves cause addiction when they are taken often enough, for long enough, and in sufficient quantities. Some individuals are much more vulnerable to addiction than others, as with any disease, but even the less vulnerable can become physically addicted through use and misuse.

Joshua A. Gordon, M.D., PhD., director of the National Institute for Mental Health, explains it this way: "After ongoing infiltration over time, drugs insidiously shift the brain's circuitry until they have eventually usurped control of the brain's normal mechanism for regulating behavior."

Dr. Gordon likens addictive drugs to Trojan horses. In masquerade they enter the brain, but, as they wreak havoc with the brain's natural mechanism of regulating pleasure, the apparent gift becomes an agent of betrayal.

These drugs initially fool the brain into producing extra dopamine. Dopamine is the major chemical substance or neurotransmitter in the brain's normal reward circuit. The release of extra dopamine induces feelings of well-being or euphoria. Whereas short-term use of some prescription drugs increases dopamine levels, the brain, which tries to keep the body's chemicals in balance, physically adapts to chronic use by actually decreasing dopamine levels as well as the ability to produce it.

For the prescription addict, abuse often begins the moment a pharmacist fills a doctor's prescription. Instead of taking the medicine as prescribed, the abuser soon increases the amount and frequency without the doctor's knowledge or approval in order to get more of the desired effect. As the abuse becomes more frequent, depleted levels of dopamine result in both depression and craving—important elements of addiction and the key factors leading to relapse. This is how addiction happens and, as you can see, it is both physiological and psychological.

Floyd P. Garrett, M.D., Addictionologist at Emory University Hospital, complains of confusing terminology. He calls the physical addiction that Dr. Gordon describes "physical dependence." He contrasts this to "psychological dependence," a phrase that describes a dependence on something that is not necessarily physically powerful, on a placebo or sugar pill, for example. A person is psychologically dependent on something because he feels better with it in spite of no pharmacological changes. One could be psychologically dependent on a substance, on an activity such as thumb sucking, or on a lucky charm. Sometimes a psychological dependence is relatively harmless except that giving it up is problematic.

The term "addiction" Dr. Garrett reserves for that complex pattern of behavior characterized by "obsession with obtaining and using the drug; excessive, prolonged, and harmful use despite adverse consequences and the mental defense mechanisms of denial, rationalization, minimization, and justification." While many people beat dependencies by a period of abstinence or a gradual withdrawal, those who are vulnerable become addicted.

And who are the vulnerable? The vulnerable may be those individuals whose lives include emotional suffering as in the first story in this chapter. We must not discount, however, individual differences in physical reaction. Different drugs affect different people in different ways. Appropriate dosages are not always predictable. Who knows which people will be sensitive to which drug? I have talked to people who have undergone surgery, taken the pain pills afterwards, were grateful for the relief from pain, but say that the pills didn't alter their mood at all. "Percocet did nothing for me," I've been amazed to hear people say. Percocet did everything for me; that's why I took more and more.

Here's a well-expressed insight shared by one recovering addict:

*So many of us started taking the pills just to get a break from the pain. I don't know about you, but I never expected the sense of euphoria that comes along with it. I absolutely live for the first two hours after my pill kicks in. Sad thing is, I told my doctor this, and all he asked me is: "Would you prefer the pain?" I honestly don't know anymore.*

The addict is propelled from his first flirtation with misuse into a pattern of addiction and denial that leads to self-destruction. "The dangers posed by prescription drugs are not all obvious," says Heather Sweeten-Healy, Mental Health Program Manager for a rehabilitation recovery clinic in Detroit. "As users start taking larger doses, their tolerance to the drugs' effects increased, but the lethal limit does not. You're still functioning, walking, and talking on doses that would have knocked out a normal person, all the while inching closer to a dose that can kill you without warning".

Mood altering prescriptions and over-the-counter medications; abuse or misuse can hook anyone. The abuse of legal drugs occurs in a variety of ways, in all segments of our population, in all kinds of neighborhoods and workplaces. What level of abuse will have an addictive effect on you depends on your physical and emotional vulnerability to addiction. The lucky ones get away without addiction. But how many are unlucky?

Results from the 2014 National Survey on Drug Use and Health (NSDUH) indicate that about 15 million people aged 12 or older used prescription drugs non-medically in the past year, and 6.5 million did so in the past month. This issue is a growing national problem in the United States. Opioid prescription drugs are misused and abused more often than any other substance, except marijuana and alcohol. This growth is fueled by misperceptions about prescription drug safety and increasing availability. A 2011 analysis by the Centers for Disease Control and Prevention found that opioid analgesic (pain reliever) sales increased nearly four-fold between 1999 and 2010; this was paralleled by an almost four-fold increase in opioid (narcotic pain medication) overdose deaths, and substance abuse treatment admissions increased almost six times the rate during the same time period.

In 24 of the nation's largest cities and the counties that surround them, fentanyl-related overdose deaths increased nearly 600 percent from 2014 to 2016, according to county health departments nationwide. According to overdose records in those cities reviewed by The Washington Post, there were 582 fatal overdoses linked to Fentanyl in 2014, a number that soared to 3,946 in 2017.

In one regional report, crimes related to controlled substances included:

A woman being treated at a clinic, who had been charged by police with feeding her addiction to Fentanyl by forging prescriptions;

A healthcare professional charged with stealing sample medications while at work and calling in prescriptions to pharmacies to obtain her own controlled substance medications;

An ambulance driver charged with stealing painkillers while on the job from the patients he was transporting;

A social worker caught stealing pain medication from a cancer patient, telling police that no one would ever notice if one of the bottles went missing;

A mother charged with neglect after officials found out she was filling prescriptions for her sick child only to feed her own addiction and never giving the needed medication to her child.

"Sometimes, family members become actively involved in their loved ones' prescription drug abuse," says Frank Poloucek, Doctor of Pharmacy at the University of Illinois, Chicago. Family members give prescription drugs to their kids to calm them down or dope up their elderly relatives to keep them quiet. Poloucek calls such abuse "assault with a chemical weapon." Moreover, healthcare professionals such as physicians and nurses, studies show, are addicted to prescription drugs at about the same rate as the general public.

According to the Drug Enforcement Administration (DEA) prescription drug abuse is the fastest growing drug problem in the U.S. About 25,000 deaths in 2014 were due to controlled substance prescription drugs, and about 19,000 of those deaths were due to prescription opioids. Each day, an average of 46 people die of an overdose of opioids, and one person in the U.S. dies of an unintentional drug overdose every 21 minutes. Overall, 30% of drug misuse problems begin with prescription drugs. Use can start with a legitimate need such as opioids for a back injury, migraines, or an accident, but evolves into misuse and abuse. In 2014, a total of 10.3 million persons reported using prescription opioids that were not prescribed for them or using them for non-medical purposes such as getting high. Darren Orloff Founder and CEO of Pillars Recovery in Orange County California says, "the opioid epidemic has become a public health crisis with catastrophic consequences to the nation's public health as well as social and economic welfare." Pillars Recovery was created to be a part of the solution to this growing epidemic.

The Drug Abuse Warning Network (DAWN) collects data from hospital emergency rooms and coroners offices on deaths or injuries related to drugs and reports their findings to the DEA. From this information in 2011, DAWN estimates that about 2.5 million emergency department visits resulted from medical emergencies involving drug misuse or abuse. About half of these involved the non-medical use of pharmaceutical drugs. Between 2009 and 2016, emergency department visits involving overall misuse or abuse increased by 19 percent or by about 400,000 visits over the 2 years. In 2016, almost half of emergency room visits for misuse or abuse of pharmaceuticals involved pain relievers, which were most commonly opioids. Another class of drugs that has seen a rise in emergency room visits is stimulants used for ADHD.

The Substance Abuse and Mental Health Services Administration (SAMHSA) tracks substance abuse. This organization defines prescription drug abuse as the use of prescription pain relievers, tranquilizers, stimulants, or sedatives by a person who doesn't have a prescription. In 2014, 27.0 million people aged twelve or older used an illicit drug in the past month, which corresponds to about one in ten Americans. This illicit drug use in 2014 was higher than that reported in every year from 2002 through 2013. The estimate of illicit drug use for 2014 continues to be driven primarily by marijuana use and the non-medical use of prescription pain relievers. This includes 22.2 million current marijuana users aged 12 or older and 4.3 million people aged 12 or older who reported current non-medical use of prescription pain relievers. Columbia University states the earlier a young person starts to use any mood or mind altering substance, the greater the possibility of developing a substance abuse disorder.

According to Freedom from Chemical Dependency Prevention Works 100,000 students grades 6-12 surveyed database, students who used cannabis in 2016 when compared with those who did not, were:
> Thirty-one percent were less likely to get A's;
> Five times more likely to report feeling the need to also use alcohol or other drugs;
> Twice as likely to have trouble concentrating on important tasks;
> More likely to ride with an impaired driver (30 percent) than students who reported using alcohol (21 percent); and
> Two to three times more likely to engage in physically, emotionally and academically risky behaviors.

**The most commonly abused controlled substance prescription medications are:**
> Alprazolam
> Amphetamines
> Codeine
> Dextroamphetamine
> Diazepam
> Fentanyl (Duragesic)
> Hydrocodone (Vicodin, Hycodan, Lorcet)
> Hydromorphone (Dilaudid)
> Meperidine
> Methylphenidate
> Morphine (MS Contin, Kadian)
> Oxycodone (OxyContin, Percocet)
> Oxymorphone
> Pentobarbital

The abuse of prescription drugs is a particularly complex facet of America's drug problem because, unlike illegal drugs, convenient access to prescription drugs must be maintained for legitimate purposes. Prescription drug abuse is often overlooked because people think that, if a doctor prescribes the drug and a pharmacist dispenses the medication, it can't be abused. It is difficult for most people to understand that prescription drugs can be every bit as addictive, destructive, and craved as illicit drugs. I hope our personal stories have made this danger clear and helped readers understand how even ordinary people can fall into the trap of prescription addiction.

This chapter is intended to answer its title question "How did you ever get into this mess?" However, in order to give hope to all readers—those who are addicted, the families and friends of the addicted and the professional helpers—I want to remind you that the storytellers in this chapter went on to eventual recovery. There is real hope glimmering at the end of even the most difficult stages of the journey to recovery, as you will see. Statistically, a full 50 percent of those who decide to beat addiction succeed, the other 50 percent we pray they find recovery and peace. I hope reading this book will help you or someone you care about join the ranks of those fortunate individuals who have conquered their addictions.

## >>> 3

# DENIAL
### *"I don't have a problem. I'm in control"*

Denial is a game we addicts play with our family, friends, and associates. It is also a game we play by ourselves, like solitaire. We can play either functional or dysfunctional denial.

Functional denial occurs when you have convinced yourself that you know what's best for you because you can still function normally. You feel you are actually being more productive on the job or at home with pills than without. You have completely resolved in your mind that it is all right to take more pills than directed without consequences. You keep this to yourself so others won't ask questions. You feel that as long as you aren't slurring your speech, stumbling over the furniture, or falling down on the floor, you are still in control. You deny that drugs are in control.

Dysfunctional denial occurs when you have difficulty waking up or when you get up with a foggy mind in the morning, swallow stimulant pills before showering, then try to converse with your loved ones, not paying attention or caring about what they have to say. Despite all this, you think you are okay. Dysfunctional denial means barely remembering driving under the influence of pills.

If you didn't kill anyone, this was a good day! Dysfunctional denial means loss of control of your life. It can include loss of a job, divorce or separation, and isolation from friends. Days of happiness, a clear mind, and genuine caring for someone else besides yourself are now gone. Despite this, you continue to tell yourself and others you don't have a problem.

Whether functional or dysfunctional, denial has several levels. Some level of denial occurs even in healthy people. Most of us have trouble admitting that a problem we don't want to deal with exists, or we make excuses for what we know is our contribution to a problem. Healthy people deny up to a point; addicts deny way beyond health and reason. For prescription addicts, it seems to make sense to protect the one thing that has long been a constant in our lives—pills.

At one level, we flat out deny our misuse of prescription drugs. Have you heard yourself say any of the following lines, which you now know to be untrue?

> I'm not addicted to my prescription drugs or over-the-counter medicines.
> I'm not misusing or abusing prescription drugs or over-the-counter medicines.
> I can stop taking this controlled substance medication any time I choose.
> I don't try to hide any of my prescriptions or medications from family or friends.
> I take medicines as directed.
> I never mix mood-altering prescriptions with alcohol.
> I can function normally at home and work without mishap.

At another level of denial, addicts may not bother to hide their abnormal behaviors or symptoms because they don't recognize these signs as being unusual. For example, I used to go up to girlfriends and ask them for a pill or two from their prescriptions as casually as some people bum cigarettes. I didn't realize that I was doing anything out of the ordinary. If an addicted person's behavior has never gotten him or her arrested, then it must be acceptable, the reasoning goes. Such individuals are like speeders who say, "I don't speed" when they mean, "I have never gotten a ticket." And if a doctor hasn't identified their symptoms as dangerous, they're okay, right?

The emotional signals of addiction, including mood swings, isolation, boredom, unexpressed resentment and hatred, chronic depression, and dishonesty are usually recognized by family members first and later by friends and co-workers but rarely by the addict, who sees the negative emotions as just a normal part of a disappointing life. Physical symptoms of abuse are also frequently misinterpreted. The addict and even his doctors may see the physical symptoms but not connect them to drug abuse. These symptoms include liver or heart failure, frequent and lingering injuries, slurred speech, blackouts, decreased sex drive, and overall deterioration of physical and emotional health. Failure to connect these symptoms to prescription drug abuse may even get additional drugs prescribed, which further feed the addiction.

At still another level of denial, the addict is more conscious of the problem and so tries harder to hide it. At this level, misuse of prescription drugs requires "justification" or rationalization. The abuser of prescription drugs may say one of the following:

> Accidents can happen to anyone.
> I was so depressed, I only took an extra pill or two to calm down.
> I was more upset than usual. One more pill couldn't hurt.
> I still can't sleep...my over-the-counter medicine said take one or two pills at bedtime. What's wrong with one more?
> It's none of your business how many pills I take. I'm fine.
> I need to lose weight fast so I will still be attractive.
> Sample medications are free, so no one will miss a few.
> I can't bear the pain. I need an extra pain pill now. It's only an hour before the next dose is due.

Do any of these lines sound familiar? Justification comes so easy. I remember. If you feel you have to justify your use of medication, you are probably in denial.

Notice also that several of the rationalizations above describe a degree of discomfort as intolerable: "so depressed," "can't sleep," "more upset," and "I can't bear." Our minds can play such evil tricks on us! As prescription addicts, we will create or exaggerate a symptom in our minds in order to justify taking any type of mood-altering pill available in the house. Our sick minds will somehow tell us that the pain is worse than it really is in order to justify taking the pills. The deceit not only seems to justify the misuse of the drug, but the drug serves as a reward or reinforcement for the pain or discomfort so that subsequent pain or discomfort actually increases in frequency or intensity.

This sets up the next exaggerated pain, which is not long in coming. For example, an addict who takes a pill because she can't sleep is rewarding herself for the sleeplessness and the next night may toss and turn to get the same problem in order to justify the same solution. For people who enjoy the feeling of an altered mind, taking pills conditions the person to experience the symptom that requires the pill.

Finally, some people addicted to prescription drugs do see their own pattern of abuse fairly clearly. In fact, they have strong feelings of remorse and guilt over their out-of-control behavior with prescription drugs and nearly destroying lives, including their own. To ease these unpleasant feelings, they take more pills. It's the only remedy they have mastered. They don't have the courage to admit to others that they have a problem or to seek out help. In fact, lack of courage underlies all forms of denial.

To some extent, denial works for a while. Addicts have to be really desperate to see that something else works better.

People attending Prescriptions Anonymous or using the services of an Addiction Recovery Coach for aftercare treatment often recall the denial that earlier kept them from seeking help. "The idea of getting caught or being accused of abusing my prescriptions or over-the-counter medicines never played a part in my everyday scenario," one recovering person told me in our support group recently.
"The thought that one day I might need to face my 'problem,' if I had one, never crossed my mind," another admitted. "I would probably never seek outside interventions on my own because I believed I was still in control."

Another member in recovery shared his thoughts and memories. "At first I wasn't abusing my medications because I was taking them as directed. But when money problems and stress from issues with my family, wife, and kids became unbearable, I had such a strong compulsion to take extra pills for anxiety, something to stay calmer than what the usual dosage prescribed. I chose to take an extra three pills one day, then five, eight, ten and the cycle of misuse began. I justified my abuse to myself and did not tell anyone."

During an Addiction Recovery Coach meeting, a recently widowed woman sadly related, "I never recognized my denial until after I stopped abusing anxiety medication and sleeping pills. I used these drugs to help me sleep and cope after my husband died. I was allowed to receive as many refills as I wanted with just a little persuasion on my part. The doctors who prescribed the drugs never told me how addictive they are. They simply said I should take them as needed, so I ended up taking as much as I wanted as often as I wanted. It seemed okay at the time, because it was all legal, aboveboard, and approved by my doctors." The distinction of legality and doctor approval is a typical aspect of denial in the prescription drug addict. It leads her to falsely believe her problem isn't really a problem. After all, she is not some junkie on a street corner or doing drugs in a back alley. Her drugs are legal. Her doctor gave them to her. Thus, how could she be a "drug addict"?

Another member shared how denial contributed to her struggle with prescription drug addiction. "Denial for me meant refusing to believe the truth no matter what someone else said. I could justify my behavior and addictive habit to anyone, including myself. I self-medicated when I needed to, stopped or slowed down as I pleased, and thought this was fine. I refused to ask for help. I was too proud, very independent, strong headed, and thought I could take care of myself. I didn't want anyone telling me how many pills I could take. Pills were like trophies to me; I didn't want anyone else touching them".

I, too, denied my drug abuse even after I was in therapy. I had been severely depressed for months, and my therapist prescribed anti-depressant pills. I never said to my therapist that I had been misusing my pills for weeks because I didn't think that someone else knew what was best for me. It wasn't anybody else's business. Besides, I knew how much my body could tolerate.

Aside from spending time with others in support group meetings, now that I have several years of recovery from mood-altering substances, I frequent Internet chat rooms devoted to discussing medication addiction. For many of the faceless, often anonymous, chat room members, this forum is the first place they go to admit they have drug problems. Many will test the waters on chat sites to see how they might be criticized and judged by family and friends. Others are in recovery and working to stay clean. Through the shared stories of painful struggles with prescription addiction, one element is consistent throughout: denial. The expression of denial, past or present, shared in these virtual chat rooms sound similar to those heard in face-to-face support group meetings. For example, one woman felt her addiction to pills didn't make her a drug addict because "I am a white, middle-class woman. I had a well-paying job, a family, a home. I wasn't some person on the street living in the gutter."

Another man admitted to the group of Internet "chatters" that he was shocked when addiction caught up with him. Like all of us, he just never thought it could affect him. "My ex-wife had addiction problems. Not me. I always thought it could never happen to me."

Denial can be subtle. It may take a long time and a lot of soul-searching for a recovering addict to even identify some of his past actions as denial. One wealthy man admitted it was denial that led him to choose an insurance-covered detoxification program instead of a rapid detoxification program that was significantly faster. At the time, he explained the choice as frugality but has since realized he was really allowing himself several more months in which to abuse prescription drugs than he would have had if he had chosen the rapid program.

Though some expressions of denial seem pretty straightforward, others are more complex. One woman with whom I chatted on the Internet shared her story, which included multiple levels of denial.

"I used alcohol at one point, but I didn't really like the taste of alcohol so I was able to stop. Later, after I was diagnosed with migraine headaches, I began abusing Percocet prescribed to me. They made me feel good. I thought it was okay. After all, if it wasn't, why did my doctor give them to me?"

I immediately recognized the many levels of denial she was experiencing. First, she claimed, "I was able to stop." In reality, she didn't like alcohol, so she justified her use of pills with a false confidence in her level of self-control. With prescription drugs, she didn't see the abuse as a problem. After all, they made her feel good; she liked them. When she finally did see she had a problem, she placed the responsibility squarely on the shoulders of her doctor.

An admission of addiction combined with denial of the effect addiction has on others is another very common form of destructive thinking. Patti, a thirty-year-old woman who told me how she takes up to twenty pills a day, knows she is addicted and wants to stop, but assured me, "My family does not suffer from my abuse. I take care of my kids and I work." All I could think upon hearing her words was that I'd like to talk to Patti's husband, children, and co-workers to see what they have to say about her behavior and actions. I suspect her drug addiction has a huge impact on them, whether Patti wants to admit it or not. Furthermore, her young children may seem oblivious to the problem now, but if asked years from now, the long-term effects of their mother's addiction will likely be evident to them. Chances are very good that Patti's home and work environments are not as healthy and happy as she claims they are.

Denial seems to be obvious to an outsider and even to drug abusers themselves once they've quit. When wrapped up in one's own medication addiction, however, it is difficult to see or think clearly. Few realize they are in denial. Instead, the addict angrily dismisses responsibility for his actions and places blame on others. One of the easiest and most common targets for the prescription medication addict's blame is his doctor.

Thomas, who was still very much in the grip of denial, shared his feelings with our support recovery group. "I can't confront a doctor again, so I borrowed a prescription from a friend. Now it's almost gone. What am I going to do? I hold these doctors responsible. They give refill after refill until you are hooked. Why are doctors able to do this to people?"

Peter, who has yet to begin addiction recovery, agreed with Thomas, adding his own complaints about doctors. "They don't seem to ever want to take any of the blame. They don't always tell you when you get the pills to beware, that they are or can be addictive."

To some extent, both Thomas and Peter have legitimate complaints. Physicians do have the responsibility to fully explain to a patient not only possible side effects, but the potential for addiction of any drug they prescribe. Nonetheless, blaming others, whether they deserve it or not, is a dangerous form of denial because it diverts energy and attention from the addict's responsibility to move forward in recovery. It creates anger instead of hope. Someone else may be responsible for your addiction, but you are responsible for your recovery.

Anger at people who try to help an addict or obstruct his drug abuse often fuels denial. Yet it is a natural reaction for many to view those who try to help as villains. One young woman, Tiffany, told the support group about her pharmacist's attempt to intervene after she tried to refill her controlled substance within a few weeks of picking up her original controlled substance prescription. At the time, his actions made Tiffany furious.

"I submitted a prescription from a doctor who wasn't my regular family doctor. My pharmacist caught it immediately. I think he suspected I was an addict already. He pulled me over to the side of the counter and told me how dangerous and addictive these drugs are. Then he suggested that I might be an addicted to pills. I became irate."

Like all of who have suffered with prescription addiction, Tiffany was at a point when she wasn't ready to face her problem. And she certainly wasn't pleased to have someone else point it out to her. Happily, she finally got help and came to realize the pharmacist did what he did because he really cared about her well-being and, in fact, may have saved her life. She was finally so touched by his kindness and concern that she has since gone back to tell him of her recovery and thank him for his compassion.

Another kind of denial involves obstructive thoughts. I call this "but I can't" denial. I have great sympathy for those who say, "but I can't" because the basis of their reasoning is real. They say, "I know I'm addicted. I know it's ruining my life, *but I can't* go into treatment because..." The lists of reasons that follow usually sound legitimate. Whether they are financial constraints or childcare issues, they are real concerns that take priority over recovery for many people. Here are some examples of the "but I can't" denials I've been told throughout the years:

"My new doctor gave out controlled substance prescriptions freely until I mentioned to her that I felt addicted. Then she cut me off and told me I needed to go to a drug and alcohol rehabilitation facility to detox. I cannot go into detox because I have three kids in school."

"My wife stays at home with the kids, and I am the one who works outside the home. If I leave for treatment, then she and the kids will lose everything. I can't lose my job."

An even more prevalent reason than financial burdens or time constraints for many who use the "but I can't" excuse is the fear of public exposure. I have seen that fear expressed over and over in support group meetings and during Addiction Recovery Coaching discussions:

"I would really like to stop, but I live in a small town and am too ashamed to let others know about my problem. I can't go into the only treatment center nearby; everyone will find out. Besides, my husband and his family are prominent and well-known members of this small community. It would cause them great humiliation."

The fear of public scrutiny and condemnation is a powerful deterrent to seeking addiction treatment. Eve, a single working mother, provides another example of this fear. She told the group, "I can't risk tarnishing my image as a mother or employee by entering a rehab center. God knows I look at the place every time I drive by and wish that I could just walk in and say, "HELP ME!"

Any recovering addict can sympathize deeply with her fear. I have felt the same and did not overcome it on my own. Yet I know that sooner or later her drug addiction will tarnish her image much more than entering a drug rehabilitation facility would ever do. Besides, the self-respect she can gain through recovery will be much more real and joyful than the image she tries to project while addicted.

The previous examples of different type of denial were meant to enlighten. Anyone suffering with addiction likely sees him or herself in one or more of the stories shared. What addicts must do is forget "but I can't" thoughts. Telling yourself treatment is "not an option" is absurd. Consider the option you have chosen instead: abusing prescription or over-the-counter medications. Thinking, "I can't risk treatment" is dangerous. Consider the risks you have decided to take by abusing drugs: jail, sickness, disability, loss of family, job, and death. How could treatment possibly be riskier than that?

As for the cost of going into treatment or difficulties of finding childcare, these are certainly real concerns. However, there are many options to choose from, some more affordable than others, some providing more flexibility than others. Have you researched all of your options? Very few of those who use excuses like, "I can't take time off from work" or "I don't have anyone to take care of the kids" have actually explored the options that are available (e.g. leaves of absence, use of sick days, the cost of nannies vs. group childcare, company funded childcare). The cost of an absence from work or of twenty-four-hour childcare for a few weeks or months while you are in treatment is high, but probably minimal compared to the cost of your habit over a year's time. Think about what you spent on drugs last month. And what will you do about money and childcare if you end up in jail? Stop saying you can't. Forget "not an option." The fact is you can, as many have done. Including me. Parents, other relatives, or friends can sometimes help out with your children even if they don't live in the same state you do. Many companies offer leaves of absence, loans and credit card debts can eventually be paid off, and you can live on less for a while.

The first time denial begins to drop away is not the time to relax. Denial doesn't instantly disappear. Denial for prescription addicts must be peeled away in layers like leaves of an artichoke. The process is different for each person. For example, at first, you may admit your problem to yourself, but deny it to others—or the other way around. At some point, perhaps when caught in the act, you may admit your problem to others, casting off the tough outer layers of denial. But even then, you may secretly think you are different from other prescription addicts and deny the impact of your addiction on your life and the lives of those around you. Every layer of denial must be peeled away until they are all gone. It is not a quick or simple process. But it can be done.

If you have told yourself that you are finished with denial and are ready to be honest, but you haven't reached the point that you can tell someone else, try your story out on God or some other spiritual entity. As long as this higher power has meaning for you, speak to it. Get your feelings out. Enjoy sharing without interruption or criticism.

If you're not spiritual or are not quite ready for God, write out your thoughts in a journal or try your confession out on the most understanding, imaginary person you can fabricate. Practice your spiel in bed, in the shower, or in the car. It doesn't really matter where, just as long as it's peaceful, quiet, and safe from the scrutiny of others. Know that this imaginary person, like God, will understand and care. If you can begin peeling back the layers of denial, even just a little, you are ready to get help from an appropriate healthcare professional. This person—whether it be a psychologist, psychiatrist, social worker, addictionologist, addiction recovery coach, or support group sponsor—is a real human being who will talk to you in the same understanding way that you imagined and hoped for, someone who will talk to you in a way that gives you hope, guidance and support. An understanding healthcare professional and/or rehabilitation treatment facility is waiting to help you right now. Make the call. And keep reading.

>>> 4

# ADMITTING THE PROBLEM
*"That's when I knew I needed help."*

What makes people finally face the disease of pill addiction? One recovering pill abuser explains, "When I exhausted myself with pills and over-the-counter medicines and then became severely depressed, I had to make a decision whether to live or lie down and die."

"When you've gone so low in your life that up is the only direction you can go. When you're sick and tired of being sick and tired", responds another.

It's often said that you don't reach such a turning point in addiction until you have hit rock bottom. Yet "rock bottom" usually involves the loss of whatever is most important to you. Hitting rock bottom is different for everyone, but eventually you'll have one if your addiction continues to spiral out of control.

Sometimes addicts don't actually identify their "rock bottom" on their own. It may happen that a confrontation by a spouse or family member gets the person into treatment. Unfortunately for some, it may take an encounter with the police. If only it didn't come down to being forced to face their addictions, imagine the anguish these individuals and their loved ones could have avoided. No one wants to spend a night in jail or have their spouse threaten divorce, but for some, it takes such drastic measures to make them not only face their addictions, but jump-start their desire to live a clean and sober, drug-free life.

Any form of hitting rock bottom may propel you towards recovery. Each route has its own elements, its own twists and turns. But you don't have to wait until you hit bottom. Experiencing vicariously the turning points of others who have gone before you could inspire you to make changes in your life. Give it a chance!

Let's start with those who were forced to face their problem by others. Notice the common thread in each story: "I got caught, they demanded, I was forced, I lost my job, they gave me an ultimatum."

*I didn't start to pay the consequences until my husband noticed I was having memory problems and weight loss, as well as a personality change.* **He insisted** *I call my therapist and fill her in on all my self-medicating escapades.*

*My turning point came when* **I lost my job** *and found that* **others knew** *I had a problem.*

**I got caught** *eleven days ago by my fellow workers at the hospital. I was so embarrassed, but they did not call the authorities and have kept it pretty quiet. Actually, I felt very much relieved when this intervention took place.*

As the previous anecdotes reveal, the embarrassment of getting caught or the loss of a job can be the jolt one needs. Though pressure from friends or family may not force everyone to a turning point, a serious ultimatum might, as the next story illustrates.

*One afternoon, my father called* **demanding to know** *what was going on with me. Later that same day, my husband told me* **he was** *ready to leave me. They both told me to make a choice. My father hit home with the children and my husband. I knew I had to do something. I told my doctor, who referred me to a psychiatrist and addictionologist. That day I called and made an appointment. It was the best thing I ever did. Reality had hit me hard, I could lose everything I hold dear if I didn't get help.*

Another prescription addict who was turned around by her family's ultimatum shared the following story.

*My husband went behind my back and talked to a family therapist.* **They gave me an ultimatum**: *Either I checked into a treatment center or my husband would leave me and take the kids. I broke down and just wanted to die for putting my babies at harm. Luckily, I had great counselors at the treatment center, who helped me get in touch with my feelings and deal with life on life's terms. I also get great support from my involvement with Narcotics Anonymous and Prescriptions Anonymous. It helps knowing there are others out there who have lived and survived this hellish nightmare.*

The turning point for Kim came when the twenty-five year old was caught by someone less sympathetic than kindly employers or family members.

*Hitting my "bottom" was the night my home was searched by police who suspected I was dealing controlled substance drugs. This was not true; I was having a very hard time keeping a supply for myself.* **I was forced** *to go to an inpatient treatment center. There I prayed that God would help me and send caring people to my aid. God did send the caring people in support groups and the wonderful counselors at the treatment center where I got help I desperately needed.*

As Kim's account clearly reveals, those who don't respond to concerned family members or unhappy employers can expect more drastic interventions. Several support group members who went through experiences similar to Kim's shared with me the next shocking stories.

*My uncontrollable addiction was so strong that while inside the pharmacy I used to take a look at other people's prescriptions that were laying in the pick-up pharmacy hold bins and pretend I was the patient labeled on the bag. Without asking for ID they would give it to me.* ***I was caught*** *by the DEA soon after with heavy fines and a jail sentence.*

Another young woman finally got the message and got off light. She's now in recovery.

*I hit bottom when I lost a boyfriend, my job, my family's trust and was almost arrested three different times for falsifying a prescription. The third time, I was taken by officers to the police station. There they told me the severity of the offense (I had no idea it was Federal offense) and demanded that I obtain help. Today, I feel lucky to be where I am: clean, sober, and not in prison.*

Addicts forced into treatment often fail because they didn't make the decision to get help on their own and thus are unable to commit to recovery life changes. However, this is not always the case, as in the next story in which forced treatment led to an especially happy ending.

*Eventually, having worn out my welcome with just about every type of healthcare professional, I started calling in my own prescriptions.* ***I soon got caught.*** *Over the next three years, I spent a total of seven months in jail and went through three rehab programs. My turning point came after three and a half months in jail when I was sent to a state-run rehabilitation facility. It was truly a special place. There, I met a fellow recovering addict. When we were released, we decided to try living together. It has been two years since I got clean. I have a job I like* and a fulfilling relationship with my fellow recovering addict. We now have a six-month-old baby.

Joanna, a young woman with a successful career in the financial industry, also shares the story of her turning point.

***I was arrested*** *at a drugstore for trying to pass a forged prescription. I was taken to the city's police station, where I sat for several hours until I was transferred to the county facility. During that time, I was going through withdrawal and, even though I was facing a major felony charge, the only thing I could think of was getting drugs. I was released when a friend put his house up for bail. That day I made a decision that I could not live like that anymore. I was able to check into a detox hospital and went through hell for several days. During that time I was introduced to Prescriptions Anonymous. I was shocked to learn that other people actually had stories like mine! The most important thing I learned was that I was not alone! I recently celebrated my fifth year anniversary with my Prescriptions Anonymous Addiction Recovery Coach for outpatient aftercare support. I am very grateful to be alive today.*

The following story from a thirty-nine-year-old addict paints a vivid picture of how devastating and life-changing hitting bottom can be.

*One day, as I sat waiting for the doctor in an exam room—under the fake name I had been using—the door to the room opened and the police walked in.* ***I was arrested,*** *handcuffed, and led out of the doctor's office through a busy waiting room with everyone staring at me. They searched my belongings and found evidence of every doctor I had ever seen under the name I made up. Each prescription I received under my fake name from different doctors was a separate felony charge. I was booked on seven class C felony charges. I had never so much as had a speeding ticket before and now I was headed straight to jail. I spent six* *days in jail before I could see the judge and post bail. In jail, they don't care how sick you are due to withdrawal. I lost twelve pounds in three days from vomiting. I am now on supervised release, which means I have a case manager to whom I must report every week. I have to call the corrections department every day to see if I have come up for a random urine sample. This can happen up to three times a week. I cannot take pain medication unless approved and dispensed by medical professionals and also approved by my case manager at the corrections department for surgery or chronic health problems only. I just have to live with any other. I became addicted and broke the law, so now I must pay the consequences of my actions.*

As the previous stories indicate, it would be much better to make the decision to get help yourself instead of waiting for the police to come knocking on your door. On the one hand, you could reduce the amount of time you spend sick and miserable. You might also avoid dealing with the justice system, alienating your family, and losing the trust of just about everyone you know.

What follows are stories of people who saw the writing on the wall and faced their problems voluntarily, before it cost them their families, jobs, or freedom. In a way, it was harder for them, because they had to find the courage within to take that first step. But courage has its rewards as Linda reveals in the next story.

*Telling my husband about my addiction after being married only three months terrified me. I feared that he would leave me. When I finally got up the courage to tell him, he was very supportive and understanding. Together we went to see an addictionologist-therapist to help start my treatment. My husband and I went to counseling together and also individual therapy to work out our own issues on recovery.*

Another woman, Carol, wasn't able to be as open about her addiction with her spouse or family members. However, the strong healthy mental state she had before her addiction helped her solve her problem rationally and on her own. Carol had a long time addiction to opioids as a result of breaking her back and other injuries sustained in a horrible car accident. Actually, after the initial healing, a chiropractor was keeping her tolerably comfortable, but when the insurance would no longer pay for the chiropractic treatment, she went to a physician who gave her painkillers. She found them so pleasurable, she started taking extra doses. After 5 years of escalating tolerance to Fentanyl painkillers and Xanax to calm her, she threw in some other pills whenever the opportunity arose, sometimes not knowing what they were.

For many years, Carol's divorced mother had a constant companion, a kind man whom Carol thought of as her second father. His heavy drinking had not really been a problem in the relationship, but slowly his health and body were being destroyed by his habit. His final illness due to alcoholism was terrible to watch, and his death devastated Carol and her mother. As she explains the loss of her father figure became a turning point for Carol.

*"I thought, if daily doses of alcohol can do this to a strong, vibrant man, what are all the painkillers doing to my body? Then I began to think about what would happen if I was in another car accident and was injured or if I had to have another operation. The doctors would give me painkillers, but in doses much lower than I needed just to get up in the morning. My tolerance for opioids was so high, I'd need much more than the doctors would give me. I'd have to confess to my addiction. Or, even worse, maybe I would be unconscious and the doctors would operate on me thinking I was anesthetized when in reality I could feel every painful moment".*

These fears of pain and death haunted her, so she began to think of a way out.

*Instead of thinking,* **I have to have this pill***, I began thinking, a long time ago I was dealing with my pain without painkillers. My chiropractor was all I needed. If I could get along without pills way back then, I should be able to get along without them now.*

And so Carol began her recovery with these realistic, truthful thoughts instead of the blindness of denial.

Another woman, Susan, claimed to lead a picture perfect life with a husband, three kids, and devotion to her church. However, she also had a group of friends, wives, and mothers like herself, who traded prescription pills. Here's the story of what finally helped her break out of denial and see the truth.

*This past week I took a pill from a friend not even knowing what it was. I just knew it was some sort of narcotic and I had to take it! This made me realize just how desperate I am. I know that I am no different than the person buying drugs on the street. For years I've fooled myself into thinking it's okay because they are "prescriptions". Realizing all this made me seek help.*

Like Linda, Carol, and Susan, many people who take that first step on their own do so because of some major crises or turning points in their lives. The following two brief stories from recovering or soon-to-be recovering addicts relate jolting moments that inspired them to seek sobriety.

*My son asked me if he could have a new bike, but I didn't have the money because I had just spent it on Vicodin. That's when it hit me that I was putting my life and my family on hold for this drug. I knew then that I had to stop.*

*Little did I know what I was getting myself into! Two years later and many thousands of dollars wasted, I realized that I had to stop. I could not afford the medication without bankrupting my family's savings. So I went to my family doctor and told him about my problem. He was very understanding and referred me to a drug rehabilitation clinic. I am starting detox tonight – finally!*

*I conned so many pills from a friend with chronic pain that she was cut off by her doctor for supposedly using too many pills every month. Now she is up the creek without a paddle and really needs the OxyContin for terrible pain; she has never abused them. Also, I spent all of the "emergency" money in my bank account on OxyContin – three to four pills a day at sixty dollars a pill. It went real fast! I am now about to start a detox program, and I am petrified of going through the withdrawal symptoms, but I know this is for the best, I pray it is.*

The next story describes a more dramatic deliverance from denial and addiction than most of us can expect. Yet, it can happen, as Leslie explains.

*In five years I lost nine jobs, had four cars repossessed, lost friends, lost boyfriends, and overdosed in my bathroom with my little son in the house with me. It is only by the grace of God that I didn't die right there in front of him. Finally, I was ready to end it all after another breakup with the third emotionally abusive boyfriend in a row. I thought I was worthless. I hated myself and believed that I was a complete failure who couldn't change. I prayed and asked God to help me. When I got no answer, I figured He didn't hear me and didn't care. Though I didn't care about dying, I feared what would happen to my little boy, whom I loved greatly, if I took my own life. So I decided to give God one "last chance." Then, if He didn't answer me, I was going to kill myself or die of an overdose. My answer didn't come overnight but finally did less than three months later.*

*I experienced the best day of my life. A miraculous event took place one night that changed the course of my life forever. I went to a service at my sister's church. I was drawn there like a magnet. I never went to church—much less on a weekday. Anyway, the preacher said a special prayer for me. The moment he finished I fell to the floor, forced down by some unseen force. I felt hot and my whole body went numb. Everything faded around me. Then came the sound of the sweetest man's voice that I had ever heard. He said, "I had to take it from you—it was going to kill you." I felt certain it was God speaking to me. It was not a magic wand or anything—though it seemed like it at the time. I relapsed a few times, but I get stronger every day. I am not perfect—but I am a thousand times better than I was two years ago. The more I believe in myself and work through my traumatic history with my therapist the more I know I'll make it. A promise I make for myself and to God.*

In the next story Henry tells how letting go of denial set him on the path to recovery. He's not completely recovered yet, but he's well on his way.

*The turning point for me was last October. I had come home from work, and my long-time girlfriend (with whom I have a young son) had found evidence of my addiction while cleaning up the house and confronted me about it. I couldn't lie to her anymore. I told her the whole story of how I had started and stopped on and off several different times. At the time she caught me, I was not even actively taking the pills she found. She was very forgiving and said that she would do everything she could to help me through this. But soon afterwards, I started abusing pills again, and this time I could barely go a day without it. I came to her and told her I was back to using pills again and this time decided to tell my parents. They were disappointed, but they wanted to help me. I was able to go a few days without the drug, but I soon started my habit again. Finally, I went to a drug rehabilitation center for some professional help. I have done pretty good so far, but it is an ongoing battle every day.*

Todd, thirty-two, addicted to painkillers, found a miracle in the fellowships of Prescriptions Anonymous and Alcoholic Anonymous.

As most recovering addicts do, Todd has relapsed; however, he's not giving up.

*Once I realized that my "best" thinking got me into a huge mess, I began really listening to what the people at the meetings had to say. They all said the same things! They had done the terrible things I had done to get drugs…manipulating, stealing, lying, and the list goes on. They had denied their problem, they had tried to "fix" themselves, and they had repeatedly failed. They had lived through the same loneliness and fear as I was still experiencing. These peaceful, happy faces at the Narcotics, Alcoholics Anonymous, and Prescriptions Anonymous meetings had been where I was – and made it out. I realized I was not alone, and I didn't have to do it alone. I have stayed clean for nearly three years. They have been the best three years of my life!*

Love of children is an important motivator for those who voluntarily seek recovery. Beth, who only recently admitted to having a problem, cites her child as the biggest factor in her turn-around.

*In the past, I have spent as much as $200 or more on pills in a week. My daughter should be the center of our world, but she isn't. She deserves better. I am at a turning point. I realize that it is the simple things in life that will make me happy; having my child close to me and being clean and sober.*

The next inspirational story should be of help to Beth or anyone struggling with addiction. It demonstrates how wonderful it can feel to unburden yourself by sharing your secret with others and receiving much needed help and support.

*I think the turning point came when I ran out of my prescription again (this had happened a lot). This time I still had two weeks to wait for a pharmacy renewal and I went through a terrible withdrawal period, worse than any other time. I also remembered what the doctor had said about the amount I was already taking. It was on a Saturday when my dilemma finally became clear to me or at least as clear as you can be when you are addicted to narcotics. I started crying and didn't stop for days. I admitted everything to my husband that night and to the rest of my family the next day. First thing on Monday morning I called my doctor's office, crying uncontrollably, and said I had to come and see him. My husband and I went in that morning and I told my doctor everything as well. He informed me that he suspected this was happening and told me he was proud of me and respected me for telling him and my family. He assured me that he was going to help. He said he felt that he was partially to blame for what had happened; he had just wanted to help me with the headaches and honestly didn't know what else to do after we had tried so many things. My doctor gave me options for recovery including treatment facilities, counseling and Addiction Recovery Coaching offered by Prescriptions Anonymous.*

While voluntary treatment seems like a more committed way to seek recovery than being hauled off by the police, choosing to stop taking drugs on your own also means you can choose to return to drugs pretty easily. Ronda made her choice — or has she? At the very least, she has taken the first step of admitting she has a problem and asking for help.

*Today I told my husband. He is very supportive. I have twenty pills left which I gave to him so I can get off of them this time without going through withdrawal symptoms. My husband is going to give me one every eight hours. But I have three refills remaining on this prescription and I really do want this to be the end — but I know, if I want to, I can go get them refilled.*

If one bad thing occurring doesn't motivate you to stop living in denial, perhaps two bad things happening in one week will hit home, as the next story reveals.

*I never admitted to anyone or myself that I was an addict. Then a close friend broke down one day and cried for me to get help. I was shocked she knew what I was doing. Then, in that same week, I called a doctor at home trying to get pills, and he confronted me about my addiction. I was so ashamed that I ever let myself get so carried away.*

Whether the motivating moment to face addiction comes about because of concern for the well-being of a beloved child, fear of physical harm, or worry about finances or jail, every addict has his or her own priority.

One twenty-seven-year old woman named Amanda places physical appearance and beauty high atop her priority list. It was this vanity that both lead to her addiction and ultimately motivated her to stop abusing prescription drugs.

*My addiction started after I got breast implants. I took painkillers for a year and a half. A few weeks ago, I woke up and realized I had no more pills left. I looked at the complexion of my face and freaked out. I usually have a perfect complexion, but over the past six months it has gotten terrible. I believe it is because of the medication. I have quit cold turkey. So far, it's been okay; support from my addiction recovery coach, fiancé, and my mother has helped me a lot. It has also helped to see my complexion clear up and return to normal. Even more important than that, I have discovered peace of mind and regained my own self-respect.*

Joelle's tale seems to sum up all the reasons addicts discover for finally seeing the light.

*It is because of my guilt, the fear of what I am doing to my organs, the fear that I will get into trouble for getting these prescriptions refilled so many times, and my need to be free of this, that I am going to do whatever it takes to beat this once and for all.*

While there may be one point at which an addict gives up denial, usually there are several points. As you may have noticed, in several individuals' stories in this book, including mine, there is a statement along the lines of "that's when I knew I had a problem." Then later in the same story, a statement like, "That's when I *really* knew I had a problem" appears. Even further down there's often the claim, "That's when I knew I needed help." Just as the layers of denial are slowly peeled away, so is the dawn of truth something that usually comes in episodes. While some people experience a "miraculous" moment that immediately pushes them to seek help, most experience several small epiphanies, each leading one step closer to full admission of the problem and reaching out to those who can help.

Shawna (see Chapter 2), who had surgery as a very young girl and became addicted to pain medications, sought unnecessary surgeries by faking pain in order to get drugs and relieve stress in her life. Shawna's first moment of casting off denial was by no means her last moment of denial. It took many years and much suffering to admit the whole truth and get help. Still, the first step taken in seeking assistance lays the foundation necessary to build on. Here's more of Shawna's story:

*Before each surgery, I would sometimes wish that I would never wake up. I knew the risks involved each time, and I was completely ready to take them. What kind of life was this? Faking pain to get drugs. Undergoing invasive surgeries just to get psychological relief.*

*Even through all this, I would tell myself, "It's okay...the doctor's in charge." I still didn't know what an addict was. Meanwhile, I was being touted as a "spiritually strong young lady." I was being admired for enduring so much and with a smile.*

*Well, the next semester at college I signed up for courses again. This time I could go without drugs for only a couple of weeks before the need for relief was unbearably strong. Another abdominal attack. My roommates rushed me to the ER. I was admitted and on the operating table in no time at all. Something happened to me that day as I was being prepped for surgery...you could call it an awakening or a voice from God. But I could see exactly what I was doing for the first time. I started feeling cold and clammy, and I knew that if I went through with the surgery, I would die that day.*

*I told the doctor, "I'm sorry, but I can't have this surgery."*

*He looked perplexed, "What do you mean?"*

*"I'm sorry, I can't explain. Just please don't put me under."*

*"Okay," he replied, "but your parents won't be happy. They're going to be charged for it anyway."*

*My parents were livid and made me come home from college. Their insurance refused to cover any of the bill, which left them owing the hospital $5000. How could I blame them for being so angry? This caused me to go deeper and deeper into depression.*

Shawna at last knew what she was doing. Being sent home to angry parents with forty painkillers in her pocket, however, was not a prescription for recovery as we will see in later chapters.

Reading this book could be your first step away from denial or your seventeenth. However, when you have read these stories with tears of sympathy, fear of the same suffering the tellers of these candid accounts experienced, and longing for the happy endings some of them now have, hopefully you will decide it's time for you to let go of the last vestige of your own denial – and take the next step.

Perhaps you fear that your friends and co-workers will treat you differently if you admit to them that you're a prescription addict. I understand the fear. Some people may be surprised to hear you had a problem with pill addiction, mainly because they have never heard of this type of addiction before and they've never seen you pop a handful of pills. But once you begin to tell your story, if you choose to honestly tell *all* your story, they will respect you even more for coming forward and being candid with them. Others closest to you will be glad to see the difference in you and will support you in every way.

And what about your family? Your family may be shocked and disappointed to learn the truth or relieved to put a name on the problems they have been observing in you for quite a while. Then, in all likelihood, they will be proud of you for coming forth and admitting to them that you need help. They will support you and try to understand your illness. Be patient with those that don't understand; remember this is new for them. It may take time for them to fully grasp what prescription and over-the-counter addiction is all about. Some things take time to mend. Together you all can heal and learn together.

As you want them to forgive you, forgive yourself. Most of us don't always see problems coming until something goes completely wrong. Sometimes we don't see an oncoming car until it's already too late to avoid a collision. We don't foresee other misfortunes that we wish we could have prevented but had no way of stopping. Why should an unexpected disease be any different? Prescription addiction is a disease, not a character flaw. Some people are more sensitive than others to the effects of addictive medications, including over-the-counter medicines, and may feel euphoric states more intensely. There is also a genetic factor in drug dependence. For a person who is psychologically or physiologically addicted, the body's chemical processes are altered so that the drug becomes essential for some of the normal metabolic functions. Prescription addiction is the resulting uncontrollable craving for our drug of choice. This is the tragic truth. Quit beating yourself up about it and start working to change it by reading on. In the next chapter you will find out who and where to ask for help.

> > > 5

# Getting Help

*"Where can I find someone who understands?"*

Now that you have said it out loud—"I am addicted and I can't solve my problem by myself"—it's time to seek assistance from people who have the expertise to get you the treatment you need.

## The Five Essential Options

The five essential options to successfully recovering from your controlled substance and over-the-counter drug addiction are:

> Finding a **treatment center** or other healing environment where you can safely detox;
> Obtaining an addiction **psychiatrist, addictionologist, psychologist;**
> Obtaining a trained and certified **Addiction Recovery Coach** for aftercare at home after release from an inpatient or outpatient facility so that you can continue focusing on your recovery and prevent relapse;
> Joining a **support group;**
> Getting a **sponsor or mentor** that has more than one year of sobriety from pill addiction.

Maybe a few people have succeeded without all five, but they are special cases. You have made a brave decision to recover from your addiction. Now give yourself a chance for success: Find all five elements as soon as possible and commit yourself to each of them. Make this the most important life changing decision you've made in weeks, months or perhaps in years.

## 1. Find a Treatment Rehabilitation Facility

If you have been caught, that is, you were found disabled or unconscious and an ambulance was called or you were apprehended doing something illegal, you may have been whisked off to a treatment facility without having any choice in the matter. If you came to the conclusion that you needed help on your own or were persuaded to seek help in a rational moment, then you will have a part in choosing the type of facility in which you will detoxify or "detox." You can obtain a recommendation of a particular drug treatment center by searching on www.prescriptionsanonymous.com or by calling your local hospital, asking your primary physician or one of his nursing staff members, by personal recommendation or, if you have the opportunity, by going to several facilities to look them over and ask questions. If you truly have no one you can ask, search online; type in your browser "Drug Treatment Rehabilitation" for a list of treatment centers near your location or state. Alternatively, you may choose to detox at home. If you do so, I urge you to seek out a licensed therapist or Addiction Recovery Coach **first,** one who will guide you in making the decision about how and where to detox. Unfortunately, most addicts who seek help do so in a crisis situation in which they must make quick decisions with little information. If you are in such a situation, try to contact an informed person—doctor, therapist, addiction recovery coach—for assistance first.

In my own case, I had been lost on a highway and finally got home with my face numb from overdose. I felt as if I was having a stroke. Frightened, as soon as I got home I called the toll-free telephone number printed on the back of my insurance company card labeled "Mental Health/Substance Abuse referral information." I told the person who answered that I was addicted to prescription drugs and in bad shape. I asked for the names of professionals in my area whose services would be covered by this insurance. The insurance representative gave me three drug treatment facilities within my location along with their contact numbers. The representative realized I needed to be seen that same day and offered to make an appointment for me. Given the need for immediate help without calling 911, the insurance representative made an appointment with the only psychiatrist who could see me that day. This doctor happened to specialize in child psychiatry, but he did what was best for me. When I showed up in his office, he took my car keys away from me and gave me a choice of being taken to an inpatient treatment by ambulance, the police, my husband, or a friend. I chose a friend, because I was too ashamed to face my husband, who had never suspected I was addicted to pills. The psychiatrist himself telephoned my friend and saw to it that I was on my way to a treatment facility where he was affiliated. Because he specialized in children, the psychiatrist did not end up being my long-term therapist, but he was a godsend at that turning point in my life.

For those of you who think you want to see a therapist but do not want to go to a treatment facility, you should be aware that if you are in danger of harming yourself and others when you arrive at the therapist's office, the therapist has the legal right to call authorities and involuntarily send you to a treatment facility for seventy-two hours in most states, regardless of your wishes, and rightly so. If you are driving under the influence of drugs, you are in danger of harming yourself or others. If you go to a therapist in a relatively sober condition, however, you and the therapist together can decide in a more leisurely fashion what kind of treatment options are best for you.

You have the choice of detoxing in a treatment facility or at home under the supervision of a psychiatrist and/or addiction recovery coach. This decision is best made with your physician or therapist, taking into account not only your addictive behavior but your home situation and resources. Those who do not go to a treatment facility must undergo the process of withdrawal with strict supervision by a therapist, addiction recovery coach or physician. The therapist or physician gradually tapers down the dosage of pills to minimize the discomforts of physical withdrawal while requiring frequent follow-up visits. Addiction Recovery Coaches cannot make adjustments with your medications or prescribe, only a licensed healthcare professionals can adjust your medications safely. Inpatient treatment is a surer and safer way of detoxing because you will get more intense medical attention in the treatment facility than you'd get choosing the other options, followed by recovery coaching at home, and, usually, by earlier introduction to support groups.

It spares your family the stressful experience of your withdrawal. The following lists show the advantages of receiving care at a treatment facility and the disadvantages of going through withdrawal on your own.

## Advantages of Going Through Withdrawal at a Treatment Facility

- *Medication management*
- *Support groups*
- *Safe environment*
- *Detoxification supervised*
- *Suicide watch*
- *Non-judgmental environment*
- *Vital signs monitored daily*
- *Depression supervised*
- *Not feeling isolated or alone*
- *Changed behaviors learned*
- *Inpatient counseling*

## Disadvantages of Going Through Withdrawal at Home

- *No supervision of withdrawal symptoms*
- *Health risks*
- *Depression*
- *Isolation*
- *No guidance or support link*
- *Anxiety*
- *Dangerous environment (craving triggers)*
- *Confusion and fear*
- *Lack of self-esteem*

Those of you who feel you might be the kind of individual who can successfully kick your drug habit at home or by yourself, remember that while a few addicts have done it, it's hard work and recovery is less certain. Carol, whose comments were shared in Chapter 4, is one fortunate individual who succeeded in this difficult endeavor.

## Carol's Story

*During my forty-one years of life I have learned that a human being has many faults and many strengths. There have been many trials and tribulations in my life that have tested my inner strength. This will be the first time I tell my story to anyone. I never told my husband or my family about my pill addiction in fear of judgment and criticism.*

*I was driving home one bitter, cold December morning with a girlfriend in my small compact car going fifty miles per hour when my left front tire blew out. I lost all control of my car. The car began turning in circles on the highway and then rolled over and over, tumbling out of control. During the first roll, my girlfriend Susan, who was sleeping, was thrown out of the passenger door. The door had been locked at the time, but the force of the tumble and of her body broke the door lock and window. She lay prone at the top of the hill and in disbelief watched my car continue to tumble with me still inside. Susan was horrified watching me, her friend, trapped in a vehicle that was being torn apart. It felt like an eternity to me praying for the vehicle to come to a stop. Then, in an instant, I was thrown out the windshield and trapped under the car.*

*Susan managed to pull herself to the highway with a broken neck and shoulder to flag down an eighteen-wheeler traveling through town. He radioed for an ambulance and police while trying to help Susan. He then made his way down the hill to try to help and comfort me. He asked if he could call someone for me, like my mother. (I was only nineteen and unmarried at the time.) Emergency crews were unable to free me from the wreckage for about ninety minutes. When I was finally freed, paramedics placed me on a gurney and backboard. Susan and I were able to ride together in the ambulance. It was comforting and reassuring that we were both alive.*

*Minutes after arrival at the hospital, I was confronted by a very insensitive ER doctor who told me I would never walk again. My mother had arrived at the hospital before us, thanks to the truck driver who had called her while we were en route to the hospital. She cried, afraid of my prognosis but grateful I was alive. I have my mother's fighting spirit and will to overcome just about anything. I kept this spirit and strength throughout my recovery from a back that was broken in four places and a neck that was broken in two places. My pain was unimaginable and only after many, many hours of X-rays and examinations, the doctors finally gave me several types of pain medications. I stayed in the hospital under heavy doses of Morphine and OxyContin for nine days. I then asked to be tapered off these medications so that I could focus, feel, and pull my thoughts together to see what I really could do and not do physically, on my own. I underwent painful physical therapy several times a day, wondering what my real chances would be to walk again or even tie my shoes.*

*It felt as if every time a doctor came into my room it was with a voice of doom filled with bad news. I chose to tune them out with their negative attitudes and opinions. I told them that I was entirely too young to be paralyzed and, no matter what they said, I would walk again. Susan was discharged from the hospital to continue her recuperation at home with physical therapy. After two weeks in the hospital, I was discharged with the personal determination that I would walk again. During months of physical therapy and living in pain twenty-fours a day, I made progress. After nearly two years, I was able to walk normally and return to work. I reduced my medications to only a few painkillers a day, but I still felt depressed and anxious.*

*Two years later, I was told I needed a hysterectomy because of complications from the accident. I was prescribed more painkillers, including OxyContin and Xanax for anxiety. I became very depressed knowing I could never give birth. I had no one to talk to about my feelings of emptiness and sadness. I was married now, but I could not even talk to my husband about my feelings. My entire life was about helping others in their struggles of pain and emptiness. I learned as a child from an abusive father to keep all emotions bottled inside, not ever asking for help. I was told to fix my own problems and not bother anyone else with them. My best defense was acting the part of a "perfect" child.*

*Several years went by. I was now manipulating the healthcare system, increasing my dosages as I pleased and changing doctors to keep refills promptly supplied. I even convinced myself that if I decreased my pill intake for a few days periodically, this would mean I wasn't an addict. Then I increased again soon after with a larger dose. I convinced myself I was always in control, not realizing my pills were controlling me.*

*The reality of addiction struck me one day when another friend and I were watching a movie at the theater; we swapped pills like people sharing popcorn or candy. We both laughed as we swallowed pills not even knowing what the pill was, and we didn't care about the consequences we could have faced. It didn't even matter what movie was being shown, only getting high mattered. Suddenly it turned sour. I drove home in tears thinking it really wasn't funny or fun anymore. I had become no better than any other addict needing a fix to feel better about myself. If I wanted to be a better person, I had to do the work...alone. I wasn't ready to share my misery with anyone!*

*I called my medical insurance first, but they wouldn't cover inpatient treatment or counseling. My second call was to my neurologist, who had written my recent prescriptions for pain medications, to inform him that I wanted to get off all medications, that I had become dependent on them, and that I needed his help to gradually decrease the dosages. I was honest with him about all the substances I was abusing, including over-the-counter sleep aids.* He reassured me that he'd heard stories of prescription addiction every day and that the number of patients complaining of their misuse increases every year. Without hesitation, he worked out a treatment plan with me and also gave me information to call an addiction recovery coach to monitor my progress and give me ongoing recovery coaching to be aware of signs for possible relapse. He prepared me for possible side effects of decreasing my doses after my body had become accustomed to much higher amounts. He tried to convince me to talk to my husband or mother about my problem, but I couldn't. I replied I was too ashamed, embarrassed, and angry to reveal my weakness.

Emotionally, I always felt pills were my survival link to living a normal life. Pills kept me feeling balanced and normal (I thought); without them, I would crumble and lose control of everything I'd worked so hard to get back since my accident. Once again, I turned to my inner strength, praying for guidance to pull me through this, as I had to do this for myself and for no one else.

Even with excellent guidance from my doctor in tapering my doses, I began to feel the effects of withdrawal within two days. I felt edgy and irritable and had difficulty with concentration. After one week, I was getting up in the middle of the night with sweats and throwing up, classic withdrawal symptoms. My husband and I were arguing over the littlest things. He was unhappy that I didn't want to join in activities I used to enjoy when I was on pills. He would go out on the boat for a ten-hour day. I just knew I couldn't sit on a boat with him and a dog for ten hours without going nuts. My husband noticed, of course, and while he was still unaware of my condition, he was showing concern about what might be wrong. I isolated myself from family and friends, fearing they might guess what was wrong. By the second week, my withdrawal symptoms were lessening, but I was severely depressed, still not able to confide in anyone or even wanting to.

After three weeks, I returned to work, which helped me focus on something else and forget my own troubles. I began a regimen of exercises at home and joined a gym to alleviate stress. I was told exercise can help sweat out the toxins in my system faster. Even though my withdrawal symptoms lasted on and off for about six months, after four weeks I could function daily without disruptions in my day.

My withdrawal symptoms finally ceased, but I knew I needed to talk to someone about the emotional distress I had buried for years. More importantly, I needed support. I needed someone to whom I could unburden myself of my fears, confusion, and shame. I couldn't carry this on my shoulders alone any longer. I went to see my best friend, the one I'd shared pills with in the theater.

She had recently overdosed and nearly died from the same disease that I now live with. She was admitted into a treatment facility and recovered. As I was also recovering, I watched her transform from someone who didn't give a damn whether she lived or died to someone "making a difference", supporting those who feel they also are suffering alone. Her name is Cindy Mogil-Cooley, Certified Addiction Recovery Coach for individuals seeking aftercare from addiction treatment and family coaching to help families reconnect after their loved one returns home from treatment.

My husband still knows nothing about this. I do not regret not telling him. I honestly think he could not have dealt with it and that would have created added strain, perhaps even divorce. As it is, he notices I am a happier person with a good attitude. He just knows he likes the new me better than the old me. That's the way I want to keep it.

Carol's story is a remarkable one, and 10 years later she is still in recovery. I should add that most of us, including myself, could never have done "the program" at home or without telling a spouse and those closest to us. Also, I must note that, as hard as it is to tell your spouse or other loved ones, getting your addiction out in the open creates a hugely refreshing freedom. You don't walk on eggshells anymore. Your spouse knows the worst, so there is no more fear of the truth from then on. This atmosphere of honesty allows us to build stronger relationships based on trust. I respect Carol's decision; her marriage indeed might not have survived the trauma of her ordeal had her addiction been out in the open. Still, I don't envy her forever carrying this secret at home.

Susan also tells of her abuse of prescription drugs and her desire to recover. She struggled with her addiction to opioid prescription medication for more than twenty-three years.

## Susan's Story

*I went on vacation in July and, as I stood in my hotel room counting my pills, I looked up and saw myself in the mirror. I knew I had long since passed the recreational drug use stage. When my husband went to work the next day, I began to call treatment centers. They told me that with the amount of pills I had been taking, it was dangerous for me to quit cold turkey.*

*Since I was afraid I'd lose my job if I took any more time off, I went to my doctor and asked if I could speak to him off the record. He said, "Yes," and I told him the WHOLE truth about my abusing prescription drugs and that I was desperate to quit. He told me I would need to cut back a pill per day. He also told me I would feel awful. I was up to ten Vicodin painkillers and twenty Soma sleeping pills a day, and I really didn't want to spend thirty days detoxing. Without my doctor's consent, I stopped in five days at home. It was really rough for me in the first three days of detoxing and for the next few months. I felt as though I was a child again; I was afraid of everything. I started going to Prescriptions Anonymous and Narcotics Anonymous. I got a sponsor and addiction recovery coach, whenever I feel like I am losing my sanity and someone to help guide me through the recovery aftercare process. I was also fortunate that, my addiction recovery coach gave me a list of detox side effects literature and goal planning activities to work on everyday to prevent relapse.*

*Whatever road you choose, I am living proof that it can be done. No matter how rotten you feel as you detox, you never have to feel that way again if you don't pick up another drug. Life really does get better! I now have five years in recovery and sponsor others to find what I did...peace and happiness.*

In a way, I am reluctant to tell you about these people who seem to have kicked their addictions to prescription drugs at home with only moderate support from doctors and support groups because many, even most, people cannot succeed this way and detoxing alone could be potentially dangerous. I don't want to give unrealistic hope to addicts, leading them to believe that they can recover from drugs without the consequences of anyone knowing. To some extent, opening up to people, letting them know what you are going through, and experiencing a healing process with them is the essence of recovery. In the chapter on denial I have even described the excuse, "treatment in a treatment center is not an option," as a form of denial. It is rare that an excuse for not entering a treatment center is reasonable or rational.

However, the next chilling story shows that getting treatment may not be so easy. Don't give up! Try and try again!

*I just decided to get off pills two day ago. Although I was only on three Fentanyl pain pills a day from shoulder surgery, withdrawal still hurts badly. I went to a clinic to get help and they turned me away. They said I had to be on a minimum of at least twenty pills a day for the past six months before they would treat me. I couldn't believe it. My body feels like I had been taking thirty pills a day for three years. Even at three pills a day, I feel withdrawal symptoms that are just killing me. I am hoping that this is the worst of it.*

In support group meetings and online chatroom discussions, caring people urge others to seek outside help with statements like, "You can't quit at home. I know. I've tried it numerous times." And even of those who have quit on their own at home, many aren't successful at maintaining long-term sobriety without the education that working with an Addiction Recovery Coach and/or total care a treatment center provides. After all, *quitting* is not the same as *recovery*. As one recovering addict put it, "Quitting is not the real problem. The real problem is finding a way to get off and stay off your drug of choice."

If you have made the big step to get help at a treatment center, either by yourself or with a therapist's recommendation, you will be "assessed" there by a staff psychiatrist or other addiction staff counselor to plan the best treatment plan for you. If you have a therapist, his or her recommendations will be included in your treatment plan as well because he or she knows your history and you have already established a relationship with someone you trust.

A complete assessment involves being asked a lot of questions. It is to your advantage to answer these honestly and completely. Therapists and rehab staff will never judge or criticize you but only assist you in getting you the best treatment plan possible. You will be asked:

> To provide medical history.
> To provide your history of prescription pill abuse, including over-the-counter medicines and any other mood-altering substances.
> To provide your patterns of abuse (use every day, night, morning, afternoons?).
> How much and how many pills you take every day.
> What your drug of choice is.
> What other types of drugs and intoxicants (e.g. mixing with other medications or alcohol) you use.
> How you are functioning psychologically, educationally, occupationally, spiritually, socially, interpersonally, and recreationally.
> How you are obtaining your pills (e.g. from your family physician or dentist, through forgeries, by calling in your own refills or someone else's, by multiple unnecessary surgeries, from the Internet, or stealing from emergency rooms, friends, or family members.)
> How much money you spend on prescriptions and over-the-counter medicines per month.
> If you have any blackouts, memory loss or withdrawal symptoms.

As the assessment progresses, the "interviewer" will be observing you for any mood, anxiety, personality or other disorders you may be unconsciously exhibiting. He will be observing your physical appearance, behaviors and how you interact with others who may be with you during your assessment meeting.

The interviewer will ask about family members who also may have a substance abuse dependency or psychiatric illnesses, since many mental disorders tend to run in families like any other disease.

The treatment facility, in my experience, is the best place, maybe the only place, to detoxify your body and go through withdrawal from drugs while under supervised trained staff. This process is discussed again in great detail in Chapter 7.

## 2. Obtain a Therapist (psychiatrist, addictionologist, psychologist, counseling social worker)

You may have chosen a therapist before coming to the treatment center. Do you still trust and have confidence in this therapist? Do you feel he or she understands addiction and has the necessary knowledge and experience? If so, you are set. If not, you can change to someone more experienced in prescription addictions.

Or perhaps the treatment center has assigned a therapist to you. Certainly you can accept or veto this choice, or you can try the recommended therapist for a while. If it doesn't work out, you can always change; believe me, I did.

In my case, the treatment center assigned me a psychiatrist. He may have provided excellent care for others, but he didn't help or understand me at all. When he asked me if I was sleeping well and I said "not at all," he prescribed Ativan without reviewing my addiction history in my chart. Ativan is very addictive, which I well knew, but I was an unstable sick person, so I said, "Fine." He said he was going to give me ten pills to help me sleep for ten nights, then he told me to come back in two weeks. When he actually wrote the prescription, however, out of habit he wrote it for thirty days. My relapse was sealed right there. This doctor, to give him the kindest judgment, did not understand pill addiction or take the time to review my chart. Unfortunately, many healthcare providers are quick to make an assessment based on little interaction with their patients and end up writing a prescription to "fix" your problems.

When I voluntarily returned to the treatment facility in relapse and had detoxed again, I was in an "after-care" group. This is a group which meets at the treatment facility under the guidance of a trained counselor. It was Dr. Angela Cornell, who proved to be excellent for my emotional needs and who was experienced working with pill addiction and multiple post-traumatic stress syndromes. She has also written the foreword to this book.

You need a therapist with training and experience with addiction and/or an Addiction Recovery Coach, but more important than credentials, in my opinion, is a recommendation by someone in recovery who has successfully been seen by the therapist or Addiction Recovery Coach. Good places to find such a recommendation are support groups or internet listings of treatment facilities, Addiction Recovery Coaches, and intervention centers.

## 3. Hire a Certified Addiction Recovery Coach for active addiction options and aftercare treatment coaching

In Addiction Recovery Coaching, clients are held accountable for their decisions and actions, improve their performance, become educated on drug and alcohol addictions, and improve their quality of life. An Addiction Recovery Coach sets parameters for the conversation, listens, contributes observations and questions, provides a road map for success, and assists clients in achieving their desired goals. An action-based Addiction Recovery Coach accelerates the client's progress by providing greater focus and awareness of choices, actions, and responsibility. Addiction Recovery Coaching develops a coach-client team. A coach meets clients where they are now, determines where they want to be, and holds them accountable to the steps they have chosen to get there.

More and more treatment centers want their clients to have a professional Addiction Recovery Coach before they leave treatment to help them stay in recovery. Pilot studies being done at well-known treatment centers on the efficacy of professional Addiction Recovery Coaching have found that of 100 clients who received recovery coaching for aftercare treatment only 26 relapsed, and, of those who did relapse, 90% got back on track in recovery.

Therapists often work with clients on past childhood, adult, and family issues and try to discover why a person is stuck. Addiction Recovery Coaches **don't** work with clients on their past issues, that is left to the therapists and treatment facilities. An Addiction Recovery Coach is not a sponsor, therapist, or friend. Addiction Recovery Coaches **do** work with clients on how their life is now and how they would like their life to be in terms of health, work, relationships, finances, etc. They ask "what" and "how" questions to create obtainable goals and plans. They help clients stick to their plans for relapse prevention and a healthy lifestyle. By the way, coaches and therapists work well together; some people love having both.

"How is a sponsor different from an Addiction Recovery Coach?" I am often asked. Sponsors are volunteers who help others work the Twelve Steps in order to stay clean and sober. Certified Addiction Recovery Coaches are paid and highly trained professionals. Sponsors stick to the Twelve Steps, fellowship, and traditions and tell the sponsee what to do in order to recover from addiction. Some people seeking recovery may prefer support groups other than those that focus on the Twelve Steps or just want to become sober on their own. Professional Addiction Recovery Coaches will support them in their choice. Some Addiction Recovery Coaches charge $100- $300 per hour depending on location and some will work with you on a sliding scale based on income. The number of visits is determined based on a client's needs, urgency, and financial abilities. Professional Certified Addiction Recovery Coaches will have a written agreement outlining goal settings, expectations between recovery coach and client, cost per hour visit, day, week, month or 24-hour coaching for a limited number of days. As of the writing, most recovery coaching isn't yet covered by insurance, but check with your policy provider. Either way, hiring a coach is a lot cheaper than relapsing or going back to treatment or even not being able to work. People who use coaches make better decisions, exhibit stronger determination to stay in recovery, and spend less time struggling alone. Ultimately only you can decide if Addiction Recovery Coaching is a reasonable way to protect your investment to stay in recovery. Having the tools, support, and wisdom you need in order to overcome the obstacles of recovery are critical. Resources for finding an Addiction Recovery Coach can be found at www.prescriptionsanonymous.com including referrals for Addiction Recovery Coaches and treatment facilities at different locations and states.

### 4. Join a Support Group

If you have been in a treatment facility or consulted a therapist, you will probably have been introduced to support group meetings almost immediately, although you may not have participated. You may be required to go and, even if you go reluctantly, you will soon see how valuable they are. You will discover what being truly honest really means. You will discover others have the very same feelings you have. Later, you may also be in an "after-care" group, which is another part of your treatment even though it will be on an outpatient basis.

When you are released from the treatment center or ongoing outpatient treatment care with a counselor, you will be given the names, places and times for support group meetings in your area. These may include chapters of Narcotics Anonymous (NA), Alcoholics Anonymous (AA), Al-Anon Family Support, and Prescriptions Anonymous. The last organization was not in existence when I was released from my treatment facility and, while I found AA and NA helpful and even critical, something was missing—people who had similar experiences to mine. There was no group that could share with me the special circumstances of prescription addiction. That is absolutely why I founded Prescriptions Anonymous in 1998 and became a nationally Certified Addiction Recovery Coach to work with individuals and families in recovery in all states whether in person, phone or Skype. In any case, there are many reasons to utilize all of the relevant groups within your reach. First, you will need frequent meetings in the early weeks and months after your treatment. Second, since every group has a different perspective, different people and a different "feel," it takes time to find a group you are comfortable with. After you've visited several different group meetings, you can decide with your therapist which groups you do not need or like and choose the one that best fits your needs as you embark upon the road to recovery. If 12-step support groups don't feel like the right choice for you, then you might consider hiring a professional Addiction Recovery Coach to work directly with you one-on-one to set recovery goals and work on relapse prevention. If you decide to go to meetings and they become too repetitive or unhelpful, simply go to other meetings. These groups are flexible and forgiving. You will not be criticized if you suddenly decide a particular group isn't working for you. You will also be welcomed without judgment when you attend a meeting for the first time, yet you won't be forced to participate any more than you'd like to.

It is for these reasons that I strongly urge recovering addicts not only to attend support group meetings or hire an Addiction Recovery Coach in the beginning, but to continue attending meetings long after recovery begins. As a lifelong activity, it will foster lifelong recovery.

### 5. Get a Sponsor or Mentor (if you are in a 12-step based program)

Sponsorship is a mutual and confidential relationship between two people, sponsor and sponsee, who are in recovery for similar addictions, and, in the case of Al-Anon, for family members of a person in active addiction or recovery. The sponsor is a person who has been in recovery for at least a year or two and has the proven skills to maintain sobriety through experience. The sponsor is a special person with whom a new member can discuss personal recovery problems, confusion, anxious moments, trigger cravings, and uncertainty. The sponsor willingly shares experiences, strength, and hope while creating a sense of security. This person contributes the wisdom of his or her experiences in recovery while standing fast and providing stability and seasoned advice as you go through your own recovery. Because a newly sober addict is emotionally vulnerable to filling the void and treating the pain in his/her life with a new romantic or sexual interest, the sponsor must not be of the gender to which the person in recovery is sexually attracted.

Sponsors are usually found through support groups. If the issue of sponsorship is not mentioned within a group, a new member should feel free to announce that he is looking for a sponsor and ask for recommendations. Sometimes a person willing to be a sponsor may be a regular member of the group. Often, however, the person is not currently an active member or your group but is a sponsor to someone else in the group and may also sponsor you if she is willing to take on more than one person at a time. My long-term sponsor had five people under her wing. People willing to be sponsors usually make themselves known to professionals and support groups. If you cannot find a sponsor through your group, ask your therapist and the staff at a treatment center for recommendations.

Once you have found potential sponsors, you should do an informal interview with several to find a person that "clicks" with you. You must be comfortable and able to be honest and open with this person or you won't call him or her when you should or allow the person to be the best help he or she can be. If the first sponsor you meet doesn't feel right to you, seek another one. Don't worry about offending your sponsor if you decide to find someone new. Your sponsor should want what's best for you and be able to part on amicable terms. Chances are your sponsor went through the same process as you when looking for the right sponsor in the beginning. Don't hesitate to do what's in your own best interests. The recovery process is too fragile and important for you to depend on the help of an individual with whom you don't share a bond.

As you can see there are differences between an Addiction Recovery Coach and sponsorship. The sponsor sets rules that will be most helpful for you and will make the relationship possible for him or her. It starts somewhat like a business arrangement. The relationship, however, is highly personal.

For example, I require those whom I sponsor to call me every day for the first two weeks because their judgment about when to call is not yet highly developed or routine.

**Intervention: If you are not the addict but the addict is your loved one, what can you do?**

Addicts in strong denial are the most typical candidates for an intervention. According to Healthy People, a program of the U.S. Department of Health and Human Services, nearly 95 percent of all substance abusers don't even recognize that they have a problem. Others aren't in denial at all, but they are fearful of undergoing treatment because they know they'll have to endure withdrawal. Most addicts have heard horror stories from others, or they have experienced withdrawal once or twice on their own, and the last thing they want is to experience it again.

Those who struggle with co-occurring addiction and mental illness often battle more inner conflict over whether or not to seek help. Some 53 percent of drug addicts and 37 percent of alcoholics are living with a severe mental health disorder, according to NAMH (National Alliance on Mental Health). They may not always have the luxury of thinking clearly, and when they do, it can be difficult to trust their own thoughts.

A professional interventionist can best determine the type of intervention an addict needs. The process of getting the addicted individual to the treatment facility should be carefully thought out ahead of time. Every moment that goes by is an opportunity for the patient to get cold feet and refuse to go.

Generally, it is best if the interventionist is the person in charge of transporting the patient. A long car ride or flight to a treatment facility with a family member or loved one only gives the patient time to play on emotional weaknesses and allows the addict to divert from the treatment plan ahead.

## Different Types of Interventions

If you have a close friend or family member who has a drug or alcohol addiction, you may find yourself searching for ways to help that individual. In most cases, people who are addicted to controlled substances, illegal drugs or alcohol do not readily admit to anyone (including themselves) that they have any type of problem. If this is the case with your loved one, then an intervention may be your best course of action. The first thing you should know is that interventions always need to be conducted by trained, licensed professionals. Before choosing an intervention specialist, you need to make sure that the person is fully qualified to conduct interventions. Once you have made your selection, the intervention specialist will be able to determine which type of intervention is most appropriate for your loved one.

Some of the most used types of intervention are:
> Workplace
> Emergency/Crisis
> Family
> Teen/Student
> Johnson's Approach

**Workplace intervention** takes place, of course, when a coworker that you are close to has a drug or alcohol problem. In some cases, you may not necessarily be good friends with a coworker, but you may be around that person for a lot of time every day. Being in close contact with someone on a regular basis will frequently alert you to any drug or alcohol problems that individual may have. If you notice such problems, it is your responsibility to try to obtain help for that individual without trying to get that person in any kind of trouble.

**Emergency or crisis intervention** should take place in situations where a person you care about has become a danger to himself or others. In these cases, an intervention needs to be implemented right away.

**Family intervention** occurs when one member of the family develops an addiction to drugs or alcohol, and the other family members decide to intervene to obtain help for that individual.

**Teen/student intervention** is much like family intervention except that it takes the special needs of young people in mind in the designing of the process. It is imperative that if you are seeking an intervention specialist to deal with a teenager that you choose someone who has been specifically trained to deal with people of this age group. Treating teenagers is a much more delicate matter than treating adults, so they must be handled differently.

**Johnson's approach** utilizes a forceful mode of confronting addicted persons. Whereas most intervention processes utilize a more tactful, delicate methodology, Johnson's approach promotes the idea that using force is the only way to get through to people with addictions.

Whatever method you and your intervention specialist choose, you must realize that interventions are very emotional and intensive and require dedication to the task at hand.

**Financing Recovery**

I wish money was not an issue when planning addiction recovery, but for many, the first question they worriedly ask themselves is, *Where's the money going to come from?* Your family may be wondering the same thing. Money is an important consideration for almost everyone, so it's necessary to address that matter here.

Hospitalization in some treatment centers can cost $1200 a day, costing $20,000 to $36,000 a month or more if you don't have substance abuse health insurance coverage. Treatment by a psychiatrist as an outpatient usually costs between $175 and $300 per fifty-minute session. Clinical psychologists cost somewhat less, as do other kinds of counseling specialists based on your state and location. Health insurance may cover all or large part of treatment in all of these categories. In that case, the more expensive professional treatment covered by insurance may actually cost the individual less money than a cheaper treatment option not covered by health insurance.

Do you have health insurance? If you do, your insurance company can offer a list of treatment facilities that will be covered under your specific policy plan. Many companies will offer assistance to their employees. Check with your human resources department for mental health referrals under your company insurance policy. Calling your insurance provider will tell you exactly how many days of treatment they will pay for, based on inpatient or outpatient rehabilitation. Your insurance will also inform you of your choices of therapists to help you with physical and psychological problems.

If you **do not** have insurance coverage that covers mental healthcare and substance abuse treatment, find out if your community, county, or city has a rehabilitation program that is billed on a sliding scale. Look up the name of your county or city on the internet. It's sometime hard to know what heading is the right one for finding help with addiction recovery because every state, city, and municipality seems to use different names for their various services. Look through the listings until you find the Health Department. Under that or separately, look for listings like Alcohol and Drug Treatment, Drug Rehabilitation, Family and Children's Services, individual Health Centers, Mental Health, Social Services, Substance Abuse, or Suicide hot-line. Look at every heading and call the one most closely related to substance abuse or ask someone at that number to refer you to a public program. Often free healthcare is provided for those whose income and assets are below a certain standard; others charge on a sliding scale according to income, for example, an Addiction Recovery Coach listed on *www.prescriptionsanonymous.com*. Call and ask what options are available for your recovery needs and income level.

Another option is to call a private treatment center of your choice and ask if someone on the staff can talk to you about financial assistance programs that apply. Or you can contact a large hospital in your area. Ask to talk to the social worker. Most public hospitals have social workers on staff who will talk to you, whether or not you are currently admitted to that hospital. Sometimes you can walk in and find a social worker in her/his office. However, it's better to make an appointment than to show up unannounced and discover the social worker is unavailable to meet with you. Nonprofit organizations like United Way often provide mental health and other services that are billed on a sliding scale.

It may well be that you do not qualify for financial assistance because your income is too high, but you still think you cannot afford to pay for extensive medical care for your problem. If it takes you and your family the rest of your lives to pay off the resulting bills, it will be worth it because it will give you back the rest of our life. Your life is worth it. Your family is worth it. Debt is better than addiction or the loss of a loved one due to pill overdose. I know from experience.

## Go to Your Primary Care Physician

Now that you have the five essentials in place to help you with recovery, you may wonder about your other "ordinary" healthcare needs. What if you get a sinus infection, pain in your abdomen, a strange rash, or any of the many ailments that used to send you to your family doctor? Your psychiatrist isn't going to treat them. Is she? You'll continue to go to a primary care physician, also called a family practice physician, an internist, or general practitioner. It is important that your primary care physician, who perhaps was your doctor when you became addicted to medication, is made aware of your condition. Even with several years in recovery, I will inform new healthcare providers and remind old ones that I have an addictive personality and am in recovery from controlled substance abuse. Healthcare providers don't need to know all the details of your addiction only that you have had addiction in your past and prefer not being prescribed anything that could jeopardize your recovery. Maintain open and honest communication with all your healthcare providers to prevent relapse and manage triggers and cravings.

For each of your original or current primary care physician and other doctors and dentists you have seen in the past, ask yourself, was this the doctor under whose care you became addicted? Did he over-prescribe medications? Was she a part of your addiction problem or did you do this on your own? Did he ignore the addiction or foster it? Or did you deceive him, hiding your abuse of prescriptions too well? And if she did not foster your addiction, is she knowledgeable about addiction and the latest information about the addictiveness of drugs?

The physician-patient relationship is seriously distorted when either party fails to abide by his or her responsibilities. The American Medical Association (AMA) has developed a categorization for physicians who mis-prescribe drugs know as "The Four-D Classifications": Duped, Dated, Disabled, and Dishonest.

**The Duped Physician:** A duped physician is one who inadvertently supplies drugs to a prescription addict because the medication abuser posing as a patient has deceived the physician. In this case, it is primarily the patient who has failed to meet his or her responsibility.

Prescription abusers who do not want their drug dependence treated, but rather want access to the medications for which a physician is the gatekeeper may create the illusion that they are seeking medical attention for a disease or illness for which the desired drug would be appropriate. Manipulations or scams for medications can be quite sophisticated, innovative, and impossible to unravel in the time available for the physician-patient interaction.

When patients have used deception to obtain medications or use them in ways other than those prescribed by their physicians, they have violated their responsibility in the physician-patient relationship.

**The Dated Physician:** Some physicians mis-prescribe medications because the information on which they base their therapeutic choices is obsolete, incomplete, or just plain wrong. Prescribing practices change over time as new medications become available or as new clinical information and scientific study result in new guidelines. By not keeping abreast of current prescribing practices and of abuse patterns of the prescription addict, out-of-date physicians cannot meet their responsibilities to practice medicine at the same standard as other practitioners in the community. The dated physician is simply ignorant and has failed to uphold his responsibilities to his patients.

**The Disabled Physician:** The American Journal of Psychiatry showed that rates of chemical dependence in physicians are roughly equivalent to those of the rest of the population; estimates range from

3 percent to 5 percent. Physicians whose judgments are impaired by mental illness, alcoholism, or by their own use of psychoactive drugs may prescribe medications irresponsibly to their patients. Moreover, such physicians may withhold from patients medications that are necessary because these physicians fear that their overall prescribing patterns may draw attention to their own misuse. Disabled physicians breach their responsibilities to their patients because they do not bring to the physician-patient relationship their best judgment, attention, and skill.

**The Dishonest Physician:** Dishonest physicians are those (less than 1 percent) who use their medical licenses to deal drugs. When a prescription addict consults with a dishonest physician, the physician does not have the patient's well-being in mind as the primary concern. Such physicians are not treating illnesses; they are perpetuating addictions under the guise of legitimate medical practices to avoid prosecution. Dishonest physicians fail to meet their responsibilities to their patients in every possible way.

Physicians who fail in their responsibilities to patients should be censured. The American Medical Association (AMA) in recent years has helped state medical licensing boards and enforcement agencies develop ways of intervening with mis-prescribing physicians sooner than they used to and with a broader range of options. However, the AMA emphasizes, the current tendencies to assign fault to physicians when patients have violated their responsibilities is unreasonable and unfair to physicians. When patients deceive their physicians or use their medications other than as prescribed, society should hold the patients, not the physicians, accountable for the inevitable adverse consequences.

My uncle Tom had been diagnosed as suffering from extreme emotional instability, known as bipolar disorder, for more than forty-five years. His family physician for forty years had prescribed an expensive medication not covered under his insurance policy, a potentially dangerous drug called lithium, to stabilize his drastic mood swings. Uncle Tom had been in and out of treatment facilities for mental illness most of his adult life with his dear wife of thirty-eight years by his side. Because money was scarce and insurance coverage paid very little, they weren't able to buy all the medicines Tom needed, especially the lithium, which was supposed to be taken on a regular basis. Knowing this, Tom's doctor often came by their house in a little Vermont town to drop off samples of lithium and other medicines, so they rarely needed to purchase prescriptions at the drug store.

Uncle Tom died from heart and kidney failure, not ever understanding "why." Two weeks prior to Tom's death, his doctor and friend died. Tom had to find a new doctor to continue his healthcare. One week after the death of his doctor, Tom found a new family physician. After giving Tom a thorough physical examination, the new physician asked Tom and his wife about his past medical history and inquired about the last time Tom had any blood work done or an overall physical. Tom replied that he had never had a complete blood work or gotten a physical from either his previous doctor in the forty years that he had been treated by him or from any doctor in the many hospitals where he was treated. His care had primarily been through verbal complaints about the pain he was feeling on any given day. He said doctors listened to his heart and took his blood-pressure but no blood-work was ever ordered. Tom's new physician was shocked by what he was told and ordered a complete blood workup on Tom. Tom's doctor was not surprised when the blood-work results were abnormal, indicating life-threatening health problems. The doctor told Tom that his kidneys were so badly damaged by the ongoing use of lithium and other medications that he couldn't even put Tom on kidney dialysis. The damage was irreversible. Tom passed away at the young age of sixty-four, two weeks after his original doctor died. Uncle Tom died from heart and kidney failure.

The causes of the doctor's death make me wonder if the doctor himself was addicted to something. Whether he was *Disabled* or not, he was most certainly *Dated,* practicing outside his area of expertise or grossly negligent. Lithium is known to be a valuable but problematic psychiatric drug. The use of lithium by every standard requires frequent monitoring of kidney function through blood tests. Any sign of a problem indicates the need for an immediate change of treatment. This physician should have been reported to his state board for inappropriate distribution of a controlled substance. Even if no action was taken against him, the inquiry might have made him remember the Hippocratic Oath "First, **do no** harm."

So the question remains: What about your primary care doctor?

If you've been seeing any healthcare professional for a long period of time, you may feel a sense of loyalty to that provider such that the thought of switching to a new doctor seems like an act of disloyalty. Even so, you must pay attention to any subtle or gross signs of negligence that may indicate it's time to fire your doctor. This is your right as a patient; your life and preventive relapse may depend on it. Ask yourself: *Is my doctor hazardous or a healthy choice for me?*

## Bad Healthcare Providers

• She always acts rushed.

If a doctor spends less than three to five minutes with you, it may be because the bottom line or corporate regulation is on her mind, according to Jamie Court, co-author of *Making a Killing:*

HMO's and the *Threat to Your Health*. "Doctors have a fixed budget for each patient...The result of this reimbursement system, known as capitation, is that the less they do for you, the more money they make." Doctors have an incentive to take on more patients while spending less time with each of them. "Unfortunately, when you speed up the conveyor belt," says Court, "there are bound to be more errors."

- He displays inappropriate behavior.

Inappropriate touching can range from lingering too long over the breasts or genitals during an examination to an unnecessary rectal exam. The question here is how comfortable you feel with what your doctor is doing. Is there a second person in the room with you, such as a nurse or assistant, while the examination is being conducted? You can insist on it. Unacceptable behavior can also include verbal comments such as: "You're my last patient of the day so I'm free after this," or "You're cute." Innuendo or suggestive jokes should not be made at any time during the examination. Sometimes behavior that seems inappropriate to a younger adult will not bother an older adult because he or she and the doctor are from a generation where such behavior may have been commonplace. However, don't chalk up a doctor's inappropriate behavior or comments to generational differences. If your doctor makes you feel uncomfortable or uneasy, even if you can't put your finger on why, it may be time to find someone new.

- She talks down to me.

Even though you may not have a medical degree, you shouldn't be made to feel as if you're too inadequate to understand your diagnosis. The doctor shouldn't withhold information because "You won't be able to understand it." Usually, it is a good idea to ask for clarification in simple language when you don't understand and to jot down technical names and medical terms used in diagnoses. This way, should you decide to go to the library or an online site of a reputable medical center or journal to research your illness or should you change doctors, you'll be able to report your diagnosis accurately to your new physician.

- He is not open to alternative health solutions.

Some doctors have extreme difficulty believing in alternative health solutions such as chiropractic or herbal medicine or newer medical measures he's not familiar with. Debates with your physician on these topics can lead to bad feelings and serious complications in your relationship. If you can't accept or believe in your physician's approach to your healthcare needs, it is probably time to shop around for someone new.

- He "tells me" what I'm going to do.

Some doctors leave you with an impression of: "We do things my way, or I won't see you again." Such doctors get irritated when patients voice an opinion about health decisions, considering this a sign of disrespect. Patient and doctor should have a mutual respect for one another. Any healthcare provider who does not appreciate that it's your life and your quality of life at stake should be replaced. Your healthcare should constitute a partnership involving communication, decision-making, and follow-up that will lead to a better prognosis for you and a healthy physician-patient relationship.

The idea of dropping your current doctor and looking for someone new may seem like an overwhelming task. But it doesn't have to be. Don't let changing doctors become a stressful affair. Following are some tips on how to change healthcare providers without anxiety.

First, choosing a new doctor or therapist will take some research on your part. A recommendation from a friend or a patient who has varied experience with a doctor is a good start. Also, if you know some unbiased healthcare workers who have worked a variety of doctors, ask them. Their recommendations could be valuable. Sometimes local publications run lists of doctors most recommended by other healthcare workers in their fields. Also, it is especially important that you find a physician knowledgeable about addictive medications, for this will be a key step in safeguarding both your health and sobriety. Such a physician can help a recovering addict weigh possible alternatives to popping pills for minor pain, anxiety, or sleeplessness. Recovered members of your support group or recovery coach may give you information about who to choose and who to avoid based on this special criterion. Make a list of doctors based on the recommendations you've received and check to see which physicians are members of your healthcare insurance plan. Be sure to remove from your list all the names of those doctors whose services will not be covered by your health insurance.

Once you have narrowed your list of recommended physicians, interview at least two or three before you leave before you leave the old one. Doctors who won't agree to an introductory interview are ones you probable shouldn't consider. Some professionals will charge a nominal fee for a fifteen-minute visit, but most doctors will not charge anything. Doctors that are currently accepting new patients will invite you to a "meet and greet appointment" with the physician of your choice. The purpose of this meeting is to get acquainted with your physician and only intended to discuss and review your medical history.

After you have chosen your new doctor, his/her office staff will help you arrange to have records and lab reports forwarded from your former doctor. Your new doctor will need your signature giving authority to request copies of your medical records from your former healthcare provider. Also, check with your managed care plan about changing doctors as some have rules about how often you can switch doctors.

You don't need to make excuses to your original doctor or staff, especially if you think you may return to him or her. However, if your previous doctor's behavior was disrespectful or inappropriate, consider writing to tell him or the office manager why you're leaving. HMO and PPO plans are also interested in your grievance about any doctor they represent or refer customers to. Medical State Board investigators are increasingly pursuing disciplinary investigations of doctors who behave inappropriately, so serious misconduct should be reported to your state regulatory agency.

When you make your first visit after selecting your new physician, honestly and openly explain your addiction disease and your concerns about relapse with prescribed and non-prescribed medicines.

Always ask the doctor what your diagnosis is before a new prescription is written. Do not ask for or accept a prescription written for tolerable, short term symptoms.

When a prescription is written, ask why the medication is being prescribed, how to use it correctly, and what side effects may be experienced. Many doctors will write a prescription for 90 pills instead of 30, thinking it's more convenient for the patient and less refill calls to the office and pharmacy. Request that your prescriptions be written for a 30-day supply with refills if warranted. The pharmacist will inform your healthcare provider that you tried to refill too soon or if he or she suspects prescription abuse or addiction. Make and keep a follow-up appointment with the doctor when the medication is finished.

Though it sounds relatively simple on paper, finding a new doctor will take some work and some time. Again, it does not need to be a stressful or anxiety-inducing task. Do not let fear of dealing with this problem prevent you from seeking a new primary care physician; this task is essential if your current doctor aided—knowingly or unknowingly—our addiction to prescription medication.

Remember the first five steps so necessary for an addict to battle addiction: finding a treatment center, obtaining a therapist, hiring a certified addiction and family recovery coach, joining a support group, and getting a 12-step sponsor or mentor. If you are not the addict but are concerned or responsible for one in denial, consider contacting an interventionist if needed. Don't hesitate to rely on the aid of one or all of these resources if you need support, guidance, or assistance when seeking help.

## >>> 6

# DIAGNOSIS

*"When I finally got clean and sober,
I discovered I was still suffering with
co-occurring disorders."*

When you arrive—high, woozy, and disoriented—at a hospital, treatment center, or physician's office, diagnosis may seem like a no-brainer: You are an addict. The arsenal of ills in your purse or pocket and the drugs in your bloodstream will tell the doctors and clinical staff to what you are addicted. The initial treatment is fairly clear: Get you off drugs and alcohol; detox your system.

After that, the picture gets muddled because addiction is not only a physical and biological affliction, but also a complex behavior pattern with varying causes and manifestations. Addiction is rarely simple. You have to alleviate the symptoms and at the same time address the causes. Addiction plus a related mental health disorder is commonly known as dual diagnosis. According to a 2014 National Survey on Drug Use and Health, 7.9 million people in the United States experience both a mental health disorder and substance use disorder simultaneously. More than half of those people—about 4.1 million—are men.

We who are addicted don't come into treatment saying, "I am addicted to several substances and behaviors," nor do we say, "I am an addict, but I have a dual diagnosis, so let's explore my other mental problems, too." We don't blurt out all our behaviors and problems because we are either afraid to reveal too much or we are ignorant ourselves of all that is troubling us.

Therefore, the diagnosing physician or team must know how to discover all the addict's significant disorders with or without that person's cooperation. At the same time, the recovering addict must learn how to live and cope with the complexities of his or her layered illnesses.

**Cross-Addiction**

*Cross addiction* means an individual's struggle with two or more addictive behaviors especially when that person adopts a second addiction while in recovery from the first. According to *Detox to Rehab Resource Network,* a new addiction may mistakenly seem justified by being somehow less severe, keeping the individual away from the original addiction or by simply being different. Many people have the mindset that a specific substance or behavior is their problem, and that other addictive substances or behaviors won't be an issue. This is often not the case.

Some may excuse their new addictions because they are based on prescription instead of being illicit drugs or because they are activities instead of substances, but any of these can have negative consequences on their lives. They may have repercussions such as declining health or destroying relationships and work life. Whether a new addiction involves a substance or a non-substance, engaging in the new behavior is not healthy itself and could also be a back door to relapse into the original addiction. Addicts on their way to recovery for one addiction may enter triggering environments or situations due to a new addiction or open their minds to the patterns of thought linked to unhealthy behaviors.

For example, if a person is in recovery for opioid pain killer abuse and becomes addicted to benzodiazepines (also called "benzos" tranquilizers in the addiction world), he or she may end up doctor shopping for benzodiazepines as previously done for pain killers. This could reopen the temptation to get pain killers and start taking them again.

A person recovering from alcohol use disorder who then becomes addicted to gambling may feel more compelled to drink again when in a casino surrounded by partying. The bottom line is: If the new substance use or behavior results in negative consequences like the ones caused by the original addiction, then it is probably a new addiction, and it is certainly a problem.

If an individual avoids duties and responsibilities due to the new behavior, withdraws from activities that used to be valued, starts lying about the new activity or substance use, or experiences a decline in health, then a new addiction has likely developed.

In 1989, during her husband's unsuccessful presidential campaign, Kitty Dukakis checked into a private clinic in Newport, Rhode Island, for treatment for dependence on alcohol. The Massachusetts First Lady confessed much later in the campaign to a twenty-six-year addiction to amphetamine diet pills, a reliance she had overcome in 1982. Or thought she overcame. In reality, it appears that she gave up the amphetamine dependence for alcoholism.

Says counselor Fred Holmquist of the Hazelden Betty Ford Foundation in Center City, Minnesota, where Dukakis was treated for amphetamine abuse, cross-addiction is "like switching staterooms on the Titanic."

While Dukakis and millions of others have gone from taking one legal drug to another, many people are dependent on several mood-altering substances at the same time. In another famous case of cross-addiction, former First Lady Betty Ford mixed liquor and tranquilizers. Her experience with addiction and recovery led her to found the famous Betty Ford Clinic in 1982 in Rancho Mirage, California. When you read about celebrities going into treatment, you often hear they have been abusing several substances.

However, it can be dangerous to cite celebrity examples of drug addiction because it may lead people to believe that the pressures of fame, the wild life of Hollywood, and the medical gurus of exotic drugs in Tinseltown create a special situation where addiction is able to happen. The next logical step is to assume addiction can't happen to "ordinary" people like you and me.

As an "ordinary" person, I can tell you that you may quickly become addicted to one or several drugs as soon as you are addicted to the first one. After becoming hooked on one drug, for the addict seeking mood alteration, almost any other drug or adrenaline-pumping activity will do in a pinch. When I went into treatment, I had thirty-seven pills in my purse of probably a dozen different kinds. Almost any pill would do for me because, if I took enough, almost any medication, even over-the-counter medicine, would give me a buzz or euphoria, thus saving me from the necessity of dealing with the real world or the underlining problems.

I've heard many stories from recovering addicts citing the use of several drugs together or switching from one to another. They didn't realize their behavior would lead to addiction, let alone abuse of a variety of drugs. This lack of initial intention is one thing that distinguishes prescription addiction from addiction to illegal drugs.

One recovering prescription addict remembers that, when she was first admitted into treatment, she told her therapist she was addicted to her painkillers.

*I'd had back surgery and was given painkillers for pain. The doctor told me to take them "as needed" (written on the prescription as prn), so I did, without question or hesitation. I quickly got addicted and needed help. I went into a treatment program for two weeks until I felt well enough to go home. When I got home, I felt good, but I couldn't sleep through the night. The next day I went to the store and bought over-the-counter sleeping aids, never realizing that I couldn't or shouldn't have them. I didn't know I could relapse with them. I took them every night, sometimes one, two, three pills not realizing at first that I was addicted. All I know was they were helping me sleep. After a month I decided to not take anymore, and I discovered I couldn't get to sleep. So I continued my new habit, telling myself that the sleeping pills were over-the-counter and not addictive drugs.*

*My therapist noticed a mood change in me and asked about the prescriptions that I'd been on lately. I proudly told her I was only taking the over-the-counter sleep aids because I thought they were safe. I was wrong. I had to be readmitted into the treatment center for addiction and knew I couldn't quit on my own at home. No one ever told me about the dangers of cross-addictions before.*

Cross-addiction includes abuse not only of multiple substances, but of activities as well. For example, Gary, a recovering controlled substance addict, told his support group that when he became drug free, he felt as if something had died inside of him.

*I honestly thought that, if I gambled a little, I would put excitement back in my life. I never put it together that pill addiction and gambling were the same. I started out playing dollar numbers on the Lottery,* which eventually lead to one-hundred-a-day lottery numbers. My checks began to bounce, my credit cards were maxed, and I borrowed from family and friends. When my wife found out, she was furious. My sister rescued me and helped me locate Gamblers Anonymous.

Gary's story illustrates the fact that kicking one addiction leaves a void, which must be filled. According to Dr. Robert Lefever, director of PROMIS Recovery Centre in London, "Cross-addiction is the inevitable outcome of treating individual addictions without tackling the root cause—inner loneliness."

If the root cause is not eliminated through therapy, other addictive behaviors may replace or accompany substance abuse. Common addictions are gambling and eating disorders, but doing anything to excess or to the point that it is detrimental to you or your family is considered addictive behavior. This might include excessive television watching, computer game playing. or on-line chatting—activities that are not harmful in appropriate amounts. Addictive behavior might also include excessive participation in sexual activity, exercise, and work—normally healthy activities in the appropriate contexts, but unhealthy when used inappropriately or in excess to avoid dealing with boredom, tension, stress, fatigue, pressure, and loneliness.

My cross-addiction was shopping. I bought things I didn't need. I bought things I didn't remember buying. I bought things I couldn't afford. I started out doing it unconsciously; I just thought I deserved something new for myself. The euphoria I felt when I bought something, no matter how short a time it lasted, gave me a sense of inner peace and pleasure. What I didn't realize was that I had a cross-addiction, and it was excessive shopping to fill a void I was feeling from being in recovery.

Here's how it happened. Shortly after coming home from my treatment center, no longer filled with pills and alcohol, I was so proud of myself that I thought I deserved a reward (and my husband agreed). I chose the reward carefully, deciding to buy myself a new sweater. I couldn't wait to get up, dress, and go out to the car, all the while thinking about where to shop, which mall to visit first. I was excited; I felt as if I was high again on pills. My legs couldn't walk fast enough in and out of all the stores filled with pretty clothes and shoes. By the end of the day, I not only found my perfect sweater, but also picked out slacks, shoes, a purse, a blouse and jewelry to match. My husband never saw the bill because I hid it from him just as I once had hidden my pills. I only showed him my sweater because that's what I had told him I was buying. Months later, when my husband got a call from the credit card company for being late on payments, he exploded with anger. I had been spending in excess of $2000 a month on clothes. Soon, my euphoric feelings were quickly replaced by shame, disappointment with myself and embarrassment. I was amazed I could lie so easily to my husband and friends. The habit of deceit I had developed over the years to hide my drug addiction had taken over once again. I somehow justified my behavior by telling myself that at least I wasn't still abusing prescription pills, never recognizing my compulsive shopping as a new addiction. I continued my second bad habit for almost a year before my hefty credit card bills and bounced checks caught up with me. I promised my husband I would talk to my counselor and sponsor about this new abuse, and my husband took my credit cards and checkbook away until we could get the credit card accounts lowered.

It was only in therapy that I recognized my shopping "problem" also was an addiction. It was not a new addiction, but the same old addiction in a new guise. Another inanimate object had replaced my pills and had become my new best friend. I had found something else to preoccupy my mind. I found it easier to cover up my emotional pain by spending money rather than talking about the underlying pain and working through it. I still had not come to grips with my feelings or the necessities of living in the "real world." I thought I could work on my treatment and still have an escape from life without paying the consequences.

For prescription addicts, the most common cross-addiction is abuse of alcohol, but there are other significant areas of abuse as well.

**Alcohol Abuse:** A healthy person knows when to stop drinking alcohol and sets limits prior to drinking. When he or she reaches that limit—whether it's a certain number of drinks or a certain feeling, the in-control person stops. The addict does not. Those who are alcoholics convince themselves that they need alcohol because they're shy, sad, lonely or because it calms their anxiety or anger. If they have used alcohol before, it seems natural to do it again, even while taking prescription drugs.

Statistics show that women are more likely than men to use alcohol in conjunction with pills. Some women don't listen to their doctors' warnings about drinking while taking prescribed drugs, or their doctors don't warn them of the dangers of mixing the two substances. Statistics show that 90 percent of drug overdoses involve women who are abusing legal substances such as alcohol or prescription drugs. Alcohol is the most common second drug chosen by the prescription addict.

**Gambling:** All types of gambling can become addictive, regardless of whether a person gambles on races, games, or numbers or whether he plays with tickets, machines, or cards. Gambling is defined as the wagering of something of value, usually money, on the outcome of an event or game. As an activity heavily criticized by some, gambling still faces many legal restrictions in the United States. Even so, according to the National Gambling Impact Study

Commission and The Statistics Portal, the gambling industry makes a total contribution of around $137.5 billion in U.S. dollars to our economy annually and directly employs more than 730 thousand people. Worldwide, the gambling industry was predicted to grow annually to reach $495 billion U.S. dollars by 2019.

Visiting casinos is not the only way to gamble. Another growing segment of the gambling industry is online. The global market size on online gambling was expected to reach over $59 billion U.S. dollars by 2020, increasing by around $20 billion U.S. dollars in just five years. The largest share of this industry segment is made up of casino gambling and sports betting.

Sooner or later, virtually all compulsive gamblers resort to illegal activities to support their gambling addiction. After all, money is the substance of their addiction. German researcher Gerhard Meyer noted that "Physiological responses to gambling enhance mood and… winning has the ability to produce a euphoric state." In Meyer's study, ten men played blackjack at a casino. When playing for money, the men's heart rates and hormonal secretions rose considerably more than when they didn't play for money.

The release of hormones when betting produces a rush similar to that of certain drugs and may be just as addictive. The risk itself is exciting, and the lure of the big prize on the next ticket or roll of the dice is reinforced by occasional pay-offs. Almost all gambling opportunities, including state-run lotteries, are advertised with a heavy emphasis on the big win; none mention, at least not loudly or in large print, the constant risk and the unrelenting losses of players. Those on the borderline between rational judgment and the desire for an emotional life may be pulled over the edge into gambling.

**Sex:** According to Patrick Cannes at Gentle Path at The Meadows in Wickenburg, Arizona, several signs of sex addiction can help identify if a patient has crossed the line from a healthy enjoyment of sex to addiction that needs professional assistance.

Indications of problematic sexual behavior include:
- Loss of control of behaviors
- Preoccupation with sexual acting out behaviors
- Significant adverse consequences
- Continuation despite consequences

Sex addicts will continue to engage in the sexual behavior despite financial problems, potential arrest, health risks, or broken relationships. The condition can destroy relationships and cause an individual to feel enslaved by their addiction to sexual thoughts and acts. Sex is part of a normal, healthy life; however, when sexual activities or thoughts become consuming or habit-forming, it crosses the line into addiction. Sex addicts go down the same path as those with other addictions. There is a repetitive struggle to control behavior, which is followed by a deep sense of despair for continuously failing to do so. Self-esteem gradually decreases, increasing the need to escape into addictive behavior. Powerlessness is a key element of addiction.

Karen, a recovering prescription addict, is a case in point.

*"I never thought my sexual behavior was a problem. I was competing in a mostly male corporate office. I thought about sex all the time, fantasizing about my co-workers. Then I cruised the bars and picked up men, paid men for sex, everywhere, three or four times a week. I thought it validated me as a desirable woman. I came close to totally self-destructing. I never considered myself a sex addict until I entered treatment for prescription addiction, but sex really is another kind of drug".*

***Eating disorders:*** Clinical Director David Hahn, MD, of the Renfrew Center, a Philadelphia treatment center for eating disorders, found that many of the same factors that make people susceptible to addictions also make them prone to eating disorders.

A compulsive overeater centers her life around food the same way an alcoholic does with alcohol. Food acts as a tranquilizer. These people will eat a box of cookies or an entire cake to make themselves feel good or as a way to relieve stress. Cravings for sweets may also be linked to the same physiological mechanism that sets up an addiction to drugs. Recovering alcoholics have often noted a craving for sweets.

The opposite behavior, but the same addictive process, is apparent in anorexia. Charlotte explains what happened to her when she was in recovery from substance abuse.

*"I have always had a need to be in control of everything in my life. After undergoing treatment to understand all there was to understand about addiction, I still felt out of control for some reason. I thought everyone was controlling me—colleagues, friends, and family. Then I got the bright idea that the one thing no one but me could control was how I ate. So I ate one meal a day or none at all, just snacks. I lost twenty pounds in six weeks. Eventually I realized this was another cross-addiction I needed to learn about and learn to live with."*

For some, the addiction starts with dieting. When stress and guilt over her troubled marriage came to the forefront, Carolyn began to lose weight. She went down to a size two. At that time, she never considered herself an addict. After all, Carolyn didn't take pills, and she wasn't much of a drinker. However, she now realizes she was addicted to starving herself.

*It took all my concentration to avoid eating. You wouldn't think so, but it did. It kept my mind off what was really bothering me—a problem I couldn't cope with in my marriage.*

Carolyn's mother and sister worried about her weight and her tiny appetite. They took her on vacation. When she got up in the middle of the night to go for her third jog in twenty-four hours, they'd seen enough. In the morning they insisted she go to a doctor, who diagnosed her illness as anorexia. Luckily, Carolyn allowed herself to be cared for by the doctor, a nutritionist, and a therapist who specialized in eating disorders. As she began to understand her disease, she slowly increased her eating, limited her running to reasonable hours, began to change her image of herself—and began drinking to excess. If she couldn't starve herself, she had to do something to ease the pain of things going wrong in her marriage. Now, still in the care of a therapist, she has turned to a healthier approach to dealing with her life—facing her problems using new insight and new skills. She has a long way to go because the pressures are great, but at least Carolyn is not adding illness to illness and crisis to crisis by altering her moods chemically or starving herself.

Other prescription addicts report gaining weight. One prescription addict confessed to a weight gain of eighty pounds along with lack of interest in personal appearance.

Compulsive overeating often accompanies or follows addiction from most controlled substances and alcoholism. Food brings comfort to those who feel guilty about their addiction or are just plain lost and lonely.

The habits just described—alcohol abuse, gambling, sex addiction, and eating disorders—are some of the most problematic cross-addictions, but they do not comprise an all-inclusive list. Any substance or activity improperly used can become a dangerous addiction. Nicotine is an obviously addictive substance, as are coffee and other caffeinated products. People who drink coffee and smoke at the same time are using mild uppers and downers; likewise, people who smoke while drinking alcohol are using two kinds of mood-altering substances. Some habits are more problematic than others.

Even "virtuous" activities such as exercise and work can be addictions or cross-addictions. Ron was a runner. Like Carolyn, he ran miles and miles in all kinds of weather, becoming very skinny, because he didn't consume enough calories to compensate for those he lost running. His muscles looked great; his body fat composition was the envy of his friends, but he was not well. Ron ran to avoid thinking of a number of severe disappointments in his life. The admiration of his friends made up somewhat for his other seeming failures.

Then there's the workaholic. Jack worked seven days a week, fourteen hours a day. He enjoyed the amazement and admiration of his colleagues, but most of all he was working to the point of exhaustion so he wouldn't have to deal with discord with his wife or a lack of connectedness with his children. During Jack's brief waking periods at home, whenever his wife said anything that sounded like a complaint or a conflict in the making, his hand automatically reached for his car keys. He would go to work day or night, remembering something he needed to do at the office. No one could ever call his behavior anything but a virtue, Jack told himself. He was doing it all for his wife and children.

Work and exercise addictions often accompany substance abuse. One prescription addict tells how he always took a lot of pride and joy in providing a good lifestyle for his family.

*Making my family proud and happy has always been a priority for me. After all, I was the "breadwinner," and I felt that was my role in life. I continually brought home a steady paycheck by working forty to fifty hours a week. When I was popping pills, I probably took off an average of ten to fifteen hours a week between doctor shopping and going to different pharmacies so I wouldn't be labeled a "regular customer" at any one place.*

*After working with my addictionologist and psychiatrist to taper down my pills and eventually get off all unnecessary prescriptions and over-the-counter medicines, I vowed to take better care of myself and appreciate my family and their needs. One way to do this I thought was to make more money and give them more things to make them proud of me. My work always gave me pleasure, so I chose to increase my time at work to sixty to seventy hours a week.*

*What I called fun my family called being a workaholic. I thought that, if they saw me working hard, buying them new things and taking fewer vacations, I was doing good. My illness had transformed but not disappeared. Now I was getting high from working long hours and making lots of money. I admit it got me excited to see the extra money in our account, but my family questioned my motives. Was I helping them or was this just another way to avoid working on the underlying issues that had caused my prescription addiction? I discovered in therapy that I was covering up childhood and family issues. My father rarely was home. His work behavior told his kids that it was more important to provide a living than to provide a loving home. I remember being angry that I didn't have a father growing up because we rarely saw him. I had to learn to balance my adult life so my wife, my children, and I could all come out winners.*

Addiction drives us to do things that are against our better judgment and are ultimately destructive because of their consequences. The addict denies the addiction. The addict finds that the activity, situation, or substance craved alters his mood in a desirable direction—in a way no other alternative can. Thus, the habit grows into an addiction and becomes a "trusted friend" and, when the addiction ceases, the person feels he has lost his best friend. He's understandably anxious to find a replacement. The result: cross-addiction.

## Dual Diagnosis

The National Survey on Drug Use and Health (NSDUH) 2018, reported **45** percent of people in the United States struggle with a dual diagnosis. People diagnosed with a mental health condition are about twice as likely as the general population to suffer from a substance use disorder. According to the Substance Abuse and Mental Health Services Administration (SAMHSA) 2014 National Survey on Drug Use and Health, an estimated 43.6 million (18.1%) American ages 18 and up have experienced some form of mental illness. For 2017 it was reported, 20.2 million adults (8.4%) had a substance use disorder. Of these, 7.9 million people had both a mental disorder and a substance use disorder, also known as co-occurring mental and substance use disorders.

People who have one disorder are obviously at higher risk for developing related disorders. For example, an individual may have two disorders, each of which represents an alternative response to a similar set of problems, or one disorder leads to the development of another.

The American Psychiatric Association in Washington, D.C. has published a list of the mental illnesses most commonly linked with substance abuse in a Fifth Edition of the Diagnostic and Statistical Manual of Mental Disorders. They are:

- Antisocial personality disorder: A pervasive pattern of disregard for, and violation of, the rights of others. The disorder is characterized in part by risk-taking, criminality, and pathological lying.
- Anxiety disorders: A group of disorders characterized by unrealistic fear, panic, or avoidance behavior. These disorders include (among others) panic attacks, phobias, obsessive-compulsive disorder, and generalized anxiety disorder.
- Bipolar disorder: A disorder characterized by alternating manic and depressive episodes.
- Depressive disorders: A group of disorders including various forms of depression and manic-depression.
- Generalized anxiety disorder: A disorder characterized by a least six months of persistent and excessive anxiety and worry not resulting from exposure to a drug or medication.
- Major depressive episode: A period of at least two weeks during which there is either depressed mood or the loss of interest or pleasure in nearly all activities.
- Mania: A period of abnormally and persistently elevated, expansive, or irritable mood.

- Mood disorders: depressive and manic disorders.

- Panic disorders: A disorder characterized sudden, by unexpected, and persistent episodes of intense fear, accompanied by a sense of imminent danger and an urge to escape.

- Phobia: A marked and persistent fear of a specific object or situation not normally feared.

- Social anxiety disorder: Also called social phobia, is intense anxiety or fear of being judged, negatively evaluated, or rejected in a social or performance situation.

- Post-Traumatic Stress Disorder: A disorder often brought on by major emotional trauma such as sexual or physical assault. It is characterized by the re-experiencing of the traumatic event (in dreams, illusions or hallucinations) and by avoidance of stimuli associated with the trauma.

- Schizophrenia: A chronic disorder characterized by illusions, hallucinations, and disorganized thoughts and behaviors.

The American Board of Psychiatry and the American Society of Addiction Medicine states, "It is critical to identify the coexistence of a major psychiatric disorder or personality disorder because, if it is not appropriately treated, it often results in relapse to substance abuse. To complicate matters, individuals may present with various types of psychiatric symptoms as a result of their response and reaction to involvement with addiction treatment.

The combination of depression and addiction often causes diagnostic difficulty for healthcare providers trying to determine appropriate treatment. According to Steven Lynn, M.D., psychiatrist in Smyrna, Georgia, depression and addiction have much in common.

The medical community considers both depression and addictive disorders to be biological, psychological, and social illnesses. Prescription addiction can masquerade as depression or manic depression, so the distinction must be made between depressive symptoms that are a part of addiction or withdrawal and depressive illness itself. This is made difficult by the similarities: impulsiveness, difficulty concentrating, and feelings of hopelessness, inferiority, and grandiosity. And, of course, denial.

When a dual diagnosis is made correctly, treatment can be individualized more effectively. Unfortunately, many people don't know they have dual disorders until treatment has already begun. Their healthcare providers may make a belated dual diagnosis, or the patients may discover a second disorder on their own through another mishap in their life, such as ongoing depression or compulsion to abuse another addiction.

*"I felt I didn't fall into any category for treatment until I began to read books on dual diagnosis,"* says Erin, another recovered addict. *"Then I found a therapist who understood prescription addiction and depression occurring together, so that I didn't need to find two different doctors to treat each illness."*

The prognosis is much poorer when a misdiagnosis is made and carried forward. This is what happened to Tony, now a recovered pill addict.

*When I first began treatment with my therapist, I thought I was being treated for prescription addiction only. I didn't feel depressed, but my moods were like a roller coaster out of control. I thought I was just hyperactive, because that was what doctors told my parents years ago. They prescribed Ritalin. I quickly got addicted to it, even sold it to other kids as speed. After two or three visits with my current therapist, she told me I had been misdiagnosed and that I wasn't hyperactive but rather bipolar, meaning I had extreme mood swings (highs and lows). I felt angry about the earlier misdiagnosis but was glad that I now have the answers to my nightmare.*

The difference between addiction alone and dual diagnosis is illustrated by Carol and Shawna, whose stories have been related in previous chapters. Carol was afraid to tell her husband she had been addicted to painkillers throughout their entire marriage. She wanted desperately to quit, but she was sure he would be very judgmental and perhaps even divorce her. So she worked it out with her doctor to supervise her withdrawal and recovery at home without her husband ever knowing. She has been sober now for 15 years. To this day, her husband is unaware of her past addiction. Carol characterized herself before addiction as strong and clearheaded. It appears she became addicted to painkillers after surgery without suffering from depression or any other mental disorder throughout. Her recovery wasn't easy, but it was possible without inpatient treatment, frequent relapses, or emotional breakdown. In contrast to this, Shawna, who during her youth had twenty-some unnecessary surgeries just to obtain legally prescribed painkillers, suffered depression and even suicidal thoughts for decades. Now recovered, she works with a recovery coach regularly who helps her stay focused and strong throughout her recovery and eliminate any possible relapse behavior patterns. When asked if it's possible to recover from home, Shawna replies: only if you're working with a Certified Addiction Recovery Coach at home or addiction therapist who understands pill addiction and will monitor your progress daily in the beginning, then continue monitoring aftercare when needed or as instructed. Recovery at home is extremely difficult for any addict and even more so for those with other mental disorders—dual diagnoses not yet diagnosed.

**Why do some people have dual diagnoses?**

- Some individuals may have a mental illness that creates feelings of sadness, anxiety, or fear and then turn to prescription drugs or alcohol for relief, creating a whole new set of problems.

- Some may start with addiction to prescription medication or other substances that alter brain chemistry and other organs. As the drug assaults normal brain function, mental illness may develop as a result.

- Others may have both disorders at the same time and independently; one illness does not cause the other, but it can affect the other.

Many addiction counselors who work with dual-disorder clients are often distracted by the "chicken or the egg" question. That is, did the prescription medication addiction come first or did the psychiatric disorder? It doesn't matter! In either case, the risk of relapse is high if therapy doesn't recognize and address both conditions effectively. Treatment is hampered when the medical professionals who treat the mental illness and those who treat the addiction are not working in concert.

## Treatment

Whatever its origin, the pain and suffering caused by mental illness is just as real as that caused by a physical illness. Mental health practitioners work with patients to first alleviate the pain, then treat the underlying causes of the problem. Treatment may consist of medication, individual coaching/counseling/therapy and family counseling/therapy. It may involve an inpatient hospitalization (treatment facility), partial hospitalization, or intensive or regular outpatient treatment with a therapist and aftercare recovery coach. In any case, there are several serious issues unique to dual diagnosis that must be dealt with at each stage of treatment.

According to the Department of Health and Human Services' Center for Substance Abuse Prevention, there are three approaches to treating dual disorders:

- **Sequential treatment**: The person goes first to one kind of therapy and then to the other, alternating procedures.

- **Parallel treatment**: A person participates in two different kinds of treatment at the same time.

- **Integrated treatment**: Generally, the most effective. In this plan the individual gets help for both disorders in one treatment program.

In integrated treatment, an addicted individual with a co-occurring disorder stands a better chance of being in the care of a professional who understands both problems and who is willing to address the special challenges of a dual diagnosis. Integrated treatment strives to provide clients with the necessary tools to cope with stressful situations, to improve their ability to get along in daily life, and to help them make positive changes toward a healthy lifestyle. Recovery coaches and therapists work very well together for ongoing care during and after treatment.

The American Psychiatric Association says that, ideally, dual diagnosis requires special training of the treatment team members in both chemical dependency programs and psychiatric programs. This is especially important because the typical treatments for each have some major differences with which the treatment team must be familiar;

**Typical Treatments for Addiction and Psychiatric Disorders**

**Psychiatric Treatment**

- Goal: Resolution of mental disorder or symptom relief.

- Use medication as needed or directed.

- Psychiatrist writes orders and informs staff.

- Program flexible: Emphasis on communication, relationships and decision-making skills.

- Discharge when symptoms are under control with psychotherapy and/or psychotropic drug therapy.

**Addiction Treatment**

- Goal: Recovery. Stabilize sobriety

- Abstinence: Avoid mood altering medications except for those closely supervised by healthcare professionals.

- Treatment decisions made by a team. No quick changes and attention paid to enabling and splitting behaviors.

- Program structured: Emphasis on active learning, support meetings, recovery coaching, and family involvement.

- Discharge when patient develops and demonstrates ability to work his/her personal recovery plan.

Professionals trained in one setting often have difficulty adapting to or accepting the differences in other treatment approaches. It is imperative to seek treatment from healthcare professionals who are comfortable with the differing demands of the coexisting disorders in dual diagnosis.

Another treatment issue is insurance coverage. Some health insurance packages do cover both substance abuse and mental health problems – dual diagnoses – but caregivers often are forced to modify treatment to meet strict insurance guidelines.

Todd Barlow, Director of Drug and Alcohol services in Sellerville, Pennsylvania, says most insurance companies cover dual diagnoses, but they often "ask caregivers to treat patients for one or the other (illness), not both at the same time. First a person gets their addiction problem treated and, once they're stabilized, they get mental health treatment." Barlow says. "This can't work. It's the reason for the phrase dual diagnosis—the two are interactive. A person is clean for three months, and then the insurance company says go ahead and switch to mental health treatment, but not everything fits into that neat little box. Both disorders must be treated together to have the best chance of a positive outcome."

In dual diagnosis cases, extra and special education must be given to the recovering patient. According to Nancy Conover, clinical outpatient therapist at Hyland Behavioral Health Services in St Louis, "Patients with dual illnesses need substantial education concerning their medication needs, a particularly challenging situation in these cases. Because recovery from chemical dependency requires abstinence from mood-altering chemicals, many chemically dependent patients have a difficult time accepting medication therapy as an aspect of their psychiatric treatment. It's crucial to help them realize the importance and necessity of their medication and how it must complement their therapy and recovery program components. A patient with a dual diagnosis can relapse just as easily by getting off the medication necessary to treat his or her psychiatric disorder as a chemically dependent individual can relapse by going back to active drinking or drug abuse."

The duality of diagnosis and treatment must also be addressed in support groups. Chemical dependency support groups sometimes exclude recovering addicts who take medications for a mental illness. These groups, understandably wary of any and all addictive drugs, believe that any medication interferes with or precludes recovery by definition; they consider the use of any medication as a relapse. They lack the knowledge of psychiatric therapy necessary to evaluate and supervise people using prescription drugs. Among support groups, Prescriptions Anonymous and rehabilitation treatment facilities recognize dual diagnosis and teaches the recovering prescription addict how to live with the complexities of dual diagnosis, cross-addiction, and prevention of relapse.

The single diagnosis of addiction can be difficult enough, but for those who have dual diagnosis, life can be even more frustrating and painful. It takes time to sort things out and a lot of patience to understand everything that's going on. Some may have difficulty holding onto a job, living independently, or developing satisfying relationships. Relapse is a constant risk. For some, thoughts of suicide as a way out are never totally absent from the mind.

Dual disorders can affect virtually any area of family functioning as well, including the mood and atmosphere in homes, roles assumed by family members, rules by which the family operates, relationships and communication among members, cohesion, and the ability to confront and solve problems. Moreover, legal problems, the high risk of incarceration, work problems, and higher incidents of emergency room visits, as well as multiple admissions for psychiatric care, chemical dependency services, and acute healthcare take a toll on addicted individuals' and family members' patience and financial resources.

The good news, however, is that recognizing mental illnesses that accompany addiction and treating the dual diagnosis appropriately give the doubly afflicted prescription addict about the same chance of recovery as his singly afflicted counterpart. Stop now and consider your own mental health. Ask your addiction therapist to evaluate you thoroughly for possible additional mental disorders. You can overcome and live with dual diagnosis. I have, Shawna did, and many do every day. You can, too, now that you know that prescription addiction does not always attack alone. Knowledge is power.

> > > 7

# THE FIRST THIRTY DAYS
*"I'm ready, but scared. What can I expect?"*

The necessary decision for beginning day one of recovery is found in your heart and mind. Recovery is possible if you want it badly enough. Admitting to yourself or someone else that you have become powerless over your addiction and that you need help is a good beginning.

But making the decision to get help in a treatment facility, hospital, clinic, or at home on your own can be frightening. Your heart is troubled with self-doubt, and your mind is racing with questions such as the ones below, which pill addicts often ask themselves.

- **What's going to happen to me physically and mentally without my pills or other mood-altering substances?**

In the case of addiction recovery, fear of the unknown is more debilitating than fear of the known. The truth about withdrawal from addictive substances is daunting, but you will be tougher if you know what to expect. Physical symptoms vary; the longer you have been abusing and misusing your drug of choice, the longer and more severe the symptoms you may experience. Detoxification and withdrawals can last from three to seven days in its acute form. You can experience chills, sweats, nausea, vomiting, shakiness, anxiety, fatigue, restlessness, headaches, muscle pain, seizures, depression, and rage. Lesser symptoms can last for weeks or even months. Depression, varying in degree from mild to severe, is common and normal for most people going through withdrawal. Withdrawal from certain chemicals, opiates, for example, can be deadly if done too quickly. In a treatment center, detoxing is done in a way that is safe for you. Also, some of the worst withdrawal and craving symptoms can be somewhat alleviated with supervised medication that does not contribute to our addiction. This is a definite advantage of detoxing in a treatment center versus on your own.

- **How can I stand the discomfort of withdrawal and not give up?**

Don't think, "Oh, I'm in this pain and suffering for days and I can't make it." Instead, think only about the next three minutes: "I'm in this pain and suffering for these three minutes. I can stand it for just three minutes." Then at two and three-quarters minutes, think, "I got through two and three-quarters minutes, so I can stand it for another couple of minutes." Keep on congratulating yourself on the few minutes you have lived without pills and extend your goal to cover the next few minutes. Soon you can do this for hours instead of minutes. For every chunk of time that is behind you, you are closer to your goal of sobriety, responsibility, self-respect, and living a happy life on your terms. If you give up and take pills now, you will have to go through this same painful chunk of time again the next time you try to kick the habit. You don't want to do that! Remember the suffering, keep a journal, call your sponsor, recovery coach, therapist. You do not want to have to do this more than once.

- **How can I trust strangers in a treatment facility or recovery coach at home to give them control over me?**

**First, trust the process.** It has worked for many, many people who have been just as addicted and just as fearful as you. A treatment facility gives you a safe environment to help improve your chances for success. It removes you from all outside pressures and triggers associated with the bad habits that you now have. A treatment facility, addiction recovery coach or clinic gives you a "time out" from the outside world until you are strong enough to face it alone. This could last anywhere from seven to twenty-five days. Live-in programs may allow for further support, continued supervision, and monitoring of behaviors for as long as six to nine months.

**Second, trust the motivation of the recovery professionals.** Trusting strangers at a treatment facility can be hard at first, because addicts usually have not trusted others for a long time, instead choosing to isolate themselves from family, friends, co-workers, and marriage partners for months, perhaps years. Staff counselors and recovery coaches are sensitive to issues of trust and trained to help patients and clients cope and adjust to this difficult time in their lives. They are very kind, patient people who show empathy and sincerity. Many have overcome addiction themselves and, in the process, acquired invaluable insight they can pass on to those seeking help. Trusting people doesn't usually happen overnight, but it does and can happen, gradually, at your own pace and in your own time.

**Third, keep on trusting the recovery process.** There is no need to trust anyone blindly now that your judgment is less clouded. Whether it is a self-help group, a mentor, or a coach, decide who is most helpful in your struggle to maintain recovery; avoid anyone you feel tends to lead you toward relapse. Good choices for help include a Certified Addiction Recovery Coach, addiction therapist and support groups. You may try one of these and then another until you find the best person, one you feel you can trust, or the group in which you feel the most comfortable.

Addiction Recovery Coaching is a form of strengths-based support for people with addictions or in recovery from alcohol, other drugs, codependency, or other addictive behaviors. While "rehab" can be difficult and challenging, the most troubling time for a person attempting recovery is often the first 90 days after leaving treatment. When you return home, familiar sights like drugs and alcohol left in the home can be triggering, while the realities of life—job pressures, family tension, bills piling up—can all be overwhelming. This is when a recovery coach can be most helpful. Recovery coaches help you make decisions about what to do with your life based on your goals and make plans to achieve your goals. They can help you find ways to stop addiction and maintain abstinence or reduce harm associated with addictive behaviors. Coaches can also help you find resources for harm reduction, detox, treatment, family support and education, local or online support groups, and sober escorts to events. An Addiction Recovery Coach can help you create a goal and activity plan to continue recovery on your own. You make your own decisions; the coach is not trying to control but to guide you in your recovery journey.

Addiction Recovery Coaches do not offer primary treatment for addiction, do not diagnose, and are not associated with any particular method or means of recovery. They support any positive change, helping people coming home from treatment to avoid relapse, build community support for recovery including goals not related to addiction such as relationships, work, or education. Recovery Coaching is action-oriented with an emphasis on improving present life and reaching future goals.

Recovery Coaches are not therapists, counselors, clinicians, or doctors, and they do not engage in the diagnosis or treatment of addiction. While they can encourage you to attend support meetings and read recovery-oriented literature, Addiction Recovery Coaches goal isn't to eliminate all negative thoughts and feelings, it's to change your response to them.

No matter how or where you get through withdrawal, it's the recovery program aftercare treatment that keeps you in recovery.

- **I'm too embarrassed and ashamed to show my weakness, stupidity, or illness to anyone. I haven't shown anyone my real self in months, maybe years. How can I do it now?**

When I was admitted into the treatment facility, I was embarrassed, rebellious, and angry because I felt that I was smarter than other addicts there. After all, I felt I knew better than they did how not to abuse or misuse my prescription drugs. I somehow had just gotten caught up in prescription addiction through no fault of my own, and now I had the tenacious disease to deal with. I was angry. Later I learned that other prescription addicts had similar feelings, and some felt worse. After covering up addictions for so long, most recovering addicts aren't sure who they are anymore. It takes days for some, weeks for others, to begin to shed their feelings of anger, weakness, stupidity, and embarrassment. You have to try very hard not to believe that you're a bad person for being biologically vulnerable to this disease. Family, friends, and marriages do heal from such an upheaval, and people do forgive in time. Your efforts will pay off in the long run. Life can be good again if you want it strongly enough. My therapist tells me that I am my own worst critic and extremely hard on myself, as are most addicts. "I can forgive everyone but myself," I hear many addicts say. Discovering and achieving recovery makes us the smartest, strongest, and sincerest people.

- **The thought of explaining my disease to my unsuspecting spouse, family, or children breaks my heart and might break theirs, too. How can I deal with that?**

My own way of life while an addict consisted of manipulating, lying, and stealing from people to maintain my secret habit. It included hiding my prescription addiction from my spouse, family, children, and friends. This negative, secret lifestyle had become normal to me. This is not uncommon among those of us who have abused substances. Our spouses are often the last people to know; they often never suspect the fact that their wives, husbands, or partners could have such a disease. Some unsuspecting spouses don't find out until they receive phone calls from therapists or hospitals telling them their loved ones had overdosed and been rushed to hospital emergency rooms. In other cases, addicts have been able to break the news to their spouses, families, and children at home or in another quiet meeting place. There they nervously tell their loved ones they have been abusing prescriptions drugs and confess that they need to get help.

Most prescription addicts are quite surprised and pleased with their loved ones' reactions. Family members often say they suspected there was a problem but didn't know how to ask or approach the person about it. Many express relief to learn what the problem is and to know that their loved one is ready to get help. They usually offer to support the addicted person in any way. However, some addicts have had loved ones who are taken by complete surprise and are quick to judge their addicted relative harshly, accusing them of being dishonest and lying. Yet even when family members react negatively at first, they often become supportive later and offer help with recovery.

- **I'm scared and angry. What can I do about that?**

I was very angry and scared when I realized that I was not in control of my own life. Pills that were once prescribed to me to improve my health, including those that I had misused from the pharmacy shelves, were now in control, and that frightened me. My sponsor, coach and therapist told me to get my feelings out. Don't carry the burden alone. You don't have to be angry or scared alone. Millions of other people feel or have felt the same way you do. Sharing with other prescription addicts, sponsor, therapist, friends, family, and spiritual advisors can help you in recovery. Also, expressing yourself in a private journal can let your feelings out without risk. Physical activities like aerobics, sports, martial arts, or walking provide a good release of emotion without harmful consequences.

- **Will I be cured of this disease?**

Unfortunately, the disease of addiction afflicts millions of people who have inherited or acquired addictive personality traits that make it extremely dangerous for them to use any mood-altering substance, even short term. Supervision from your healthcare provider, recovery coach, sponsor, or support group will be very important should you be prescribed controlled substances during or after surgery or for other medical reasons. You can live as happy and healthy lives as other people, as long as you never forget that you have a disease that can destroy your life in a minute if you let it. A disease is nothing to be embarrassed by or ashamed of.

- **Does everybody have to go to a treatment facility? Can I withdraw on my own?**

Making the decision to go to a treatment facility, clinic, recovery coaching, or hospital can be a difficult one. This decision is best to make with your family physician or therapist.
Treatment facilities and Addiction Recovery Coaches are very thorough in their assessments of clients to determine exactly what the best treatment plan should be for you. If you decide that inpatient therapy treatment is best for you, the therapists, staff counselors, and nurses, in individual and group therapy sessions together, will be able to monitor your progress to determine any changes in your treatment or medications.

Treatment center staff know what's best for you while in a crisis situation even if, at the moment, you don't agree or understand. Addicts have tried doing it "their way" with disastrous results, so we must have faith that specialized treatment facilities know what has worked with others and trust they can apply their wisdom to us.

Not everyone goes to a treatment facility, however. Some undergo the process of withdrawal successfully with strict supervision from their recovery coach, therapist, addictionologist, or physician. With the exception of the recovery coach, these professionals will gradually taper down the dosage of pills to minimize the physical withdrawals. Frequent follow-up visits allow professionals to monitor blood pressure and any side effects to treatment. Counseling helps with any psychological problems that need to be talked through.

Here again is a diagram showing advantages of receiving care at a treatment facility and the disadvantages of trying it on your own.

| **Advantages** of a Treatment Facility | **Disadvantages** of Withdrawing at Home Without Professional Supervision |
|---|---|
| Medication management | No medication for withdrawal symptoms |
| Support groups | |
| Safe environment | Health risks |
| Detoxification supervised | Depression and isolation |
| Suicide watch | No guidance or support link |
| Non-judgmental environment | Anxiety |
| Vitals monitored daily | Dangerous environment (triggers) |
| Depression supervised | Confusion and fear |
| Not feeling isolated or alone | Lack of Self-esteem |
| Changed behaviors learned | |

- **I've heard of rapid detox where you go to a hospital and in a couple days you're rid of the drugs. Isn't that a way to do it quickly without suffering or missing work?**

Rapid detox is a medical treatment for addiction to opiates only. Two million Americans had a substance use disorder due to prescription pain relievers in 2015 alone. Moreover, there were over 20,000 overdose deaths related to prescription pain relievers that same year, according to the American Society of Addiction

Medicine. Besides heroin and methadone, this family of drugs includes the prescription medication Lortab, Vicodin, Darvocet, Percocet, codeine and others. Going "cold turkey" from opiates without medical treatment can damage the cardio-pulmonary and the central nervous systems, so detoxing by conventional treatment has required days or weeks. Rapid Detox offers a new, quicker alternative by chemically reversing the effects of opiates in your brain which "require" an ever-increasing amount of the drugs. The procedure must be done in a closely supervised medical setting while the patient is under anesthesia for several (3 to 6) hours. The anesthesia prevents the patient from feeling the worst of his withdrawal symptoms.

Rapid Detox **is not**, however, "an easy way out." The patient can experience moderate withdrawal symptoms such as nausea, vomiting, muscle cramps, and shaking for several more hours and nervousness and insomnia for several weeks. It does not deal with dual diagnosis at all, so symptoms of other mental disorders such as depression will persist if untreated. The most important thing you should know is that Rapid Detox in no way eliminates the need for a recovery program. Its success, like that of other treatment methods, depends on the patient's motivation and a full program of counseling and possible medication therapy. Abstinence is supported by Addiction Recovery Coaches, peer groups, sponsors, and understanding family members, just as abstinence following any other withdrawal method. Do not have this treatment without a full recovery program in place. The average rapid detox cost in the U.S. is a minimum of $5,000 with an average cost closer to $10,000. Although very few studies or surveys have been done on rapid detox, as a relatively new treatment, it is said to have an 80% relapse ratio. While health insurance will often cover traditional detox, rapid detox is still considered experimental. There are no reports of effectiveness or proof that it's safe so most insurance companies don't cover rapid detox.

It's worth repeating: It doesn't matter how or where you get through withdrawal; it's the recovery program after treatment that keeps you in recovery.

- **If I detoxify at a treatment center, how long will I be there and what happens when I get out?**

The therapist and staff counselors determine the number of days a person stays in a treatment facility. The average length of time is seven to ten days. If you're on suicide watch, it is a law in most states that patients be observed and not released in fewer than seventy-two hours. Your insurance policy may also determine how many days of inpatient treatment you will get. You will need to pay out-of-pocket if you want or need treatment beyond what the insurance will pay for.

Once you are detoxed and emotionally stable enough to be discharged, you will meet with staff counselors and your therapist to make plans for your continued care on an outpatient basis.

Some patients may choose to live in a halfway house or residential treatment facility where supervision and group therapy can be continued. Live-in programs have female and male residents who are supervised by addiction technicians, therapists and medical staff. Residential treatment facilities make sure the rules are followed as well as provide residents with guidance in attending support groups and transportation to healthcare appointments. Here patients in recovery learn to become independent, ask for help, and begin to get back into life with a new outlook. These programs deal with the physical, the emotional, the mental, and the spiritual aspects of life. With or without an initial stay in a residential treatment facility, halfway house, many individuals greatly benefit from an Addiction Recovery Coach at home for ongoing support in a stable, structured environment working together on preventive relapse measures, goal setting, and accountability for themselves.

Discuss your after-treatment options with your therapist and family, but most important be honest with yourself. Do you feel safe from the danger of abusing medications again? Are you emotionally stable enough to handle any other co-occurring illnesses?

When you do go home, your spouse, partner, or a family member must also be counseled on how to best help you through the adjustment period. You will be particularly sensitive and insecure in the days, weeks, and perhaps months after your discharge. Those around you need to learn to take care of themselves and not get caught up in trying to "fix" your troubles, a behavior known as co-dependence. It's up to you to help yourself. Taking this responsibility makes you stronger, healthier, and happier.

Once at home, keep busy with support group meetings and healthy living activities. Stay focused and driven to succeed. Try not to be by yourself for long periods of time. Being alone can lead to feelings of depression, loneliness, and temptation. The longer you stay in a program of recovery, the simpler life becomes as you learn and grow.

**Recovery starts here.** Making the decision to improve your quality of life by realizing your powerlessness over your addiction to prescription drugs and mood-altering chemicals is a gigantic step toward change. Putting yourself in the hands of professionals, far from imprisoning you, leaves you free to rebuild self-worth, self-esteem, and self-confidence in a protective environment.

The following testimonials posted by addicts on www.prescriptionsanonymous.com during their first days of withdrawal show a variety of attitudes and experiences as well as the feelings of desperation mixed with hope that all of us who have attempted recovery have shared and felt. Can you relate to any of these?

*I wouldn't say that I am recovered. I am dry but there is not a day that passes that I don't wish that I had just a few, you know, to get me through the day… God has to give it to you hard so you will never want to go through the pain and suffering of withdrawals and cravings.* CASEY, 28

*I believe I surrendered to my disease of addiction while at an inpatient treatment center. I prayed that God would send to me the people who could help me learn to live my life clean.* JAN, 43

*My recovery is just beginning. I am keeping a journal. Believe me, it has helped me a lot already knowing that others feel so much like I do.* JULIE, 28

*I was addicted to hydrocodone for over a decade and I overcame it. First of all, I didn't try to do it alone. I entered myself into a treatment center. When I detoxed, they told me what I was feeling (massive headaches, irritability, shakes, fear) was normal. If you're down to half a tablet, it won't be as severe for you. I went from twenty to nothing.… Everyone and everything else need to be put on the back burner temporarily. I had to give up my kids for a month and a half to go to inpatient drug treatment. But let me tell you what a blessing it has been in the long run. My life is better than I ever dreamed it could be.* SHAWNA, 50

*I want to quit so badly but the withdrawals are so bad. I (have tried) to handle the withdrawals, but it's so hard that when I am almost done going through the withdrawals, I find ways to get more and have to start the process all over again. Well, today I told my husband. He is very supportive. I have about 20 pills left and I gave them to him so I can get off of them this time without the withdrawals. He's going to give me one every 8 hours.* RONDA, 63

*I returned home from vacation in July and when my husband went to work the next day, I began to call treatment centers. They told me that, with the amount of pills I had been taking, it was dangerous for me to quit cold turkey. Since I was afraid I would lose my job if I took any more time off, I went to my doctor and asked if I could speak to him off the record. He said "yes" and I told him the WHOLE truth about my using and that I was desperate to quit. He told me I would need to cut back a pill per day. He also told me I would feel awful. I was up to 10 Vicodin a day and 20 Soma, and I really didn't want to spend 30 days detoxing, so without my doctor's consent, I stopped in 5 days. It was really rough for the first couple weeks. I felt as if I were a child again, I was afraid of everything. I got a sponsor and called people. When I thought I was losing it, I reached out for help. I was also fortunate that the meeting provided a list of side effects of detox, so I knew what I was going through was normal.* MICHELLE, 39

*I went to my OB/GYN and told him my story. He suggested a psychiatrist that was also an addictionologist. That was the best thing I ever did. That day, I went to a place at the hospital and made an appointment. They tried to get me to admit myself immediately, but, it being a Tuesday, I knew I had responsibilities at home to get in order first. I promised to come back on Thursday. Initially, my Dad and husband*

*were against treatment of that sort. They believed I should just be able to "give it up" with my own willpower. But my mother convinced me otherwise. I went into treatment and what a blessing it has been so far. It was a hard decision to make, but it was the best thing I've ever done, both for myself and my family. I was diagnosed as bipolar and now take Depakote to stabilize my moods and Paxil for the panic attacks. So far, this treatment has been successful. We don't know if the bipolar came first, and I tried to medicate with drugs, or if the bipolar came after all the drugs…go figure. But now I am taking care of myself first. If you cannot take care of yourself, you cannot take care of your family.*
PAT, 27

*Today, I had my addiction history and health assessment and I am now in treatment with other healthcare professionals that have had our physician licenses suspended for controlled substance addiction and prescription forgery. I am hopeful for a full recovery. Two weeks prior to my intervention, I would not have believed that there was a way out. This will be a tough, long, hard road, but I think that I'll make it.*
ROBERT, 42

Perhaps the best way I know to tell you what to expect, now that you have made the decision to recover, is to tell you exactly what happened to me. Your experience and mine will differ in detail, but, after talking to many, many addicted people, I believe that you will find a commonality in my account that binds us together—you, me, and all those who fight this fight.

## My First Thirty Days

### Day 1

My therapist had justification for admitting me to the hospital after seeing how depressed and high on pills I was both on that day. I was so high on pills that my therapist wouldn't let me leave his office. He asked me if he could make a call and take me directly to a treatment center for controlled substance addiction.

It's scary looking back on that time because I have very little memory of it. I remember only snatches of events, like stumbling down the hall in my therapist's office and sitting next to his desk, crying uncontrollably, unable to speak in complete sentences. I barely remember asking him to call my friend Angie and ask her to pick me up. While waiting for Angie, my therapist walked me out to the parking lot to make sure my car was securely locked. I couldn't remember the color, make, or model. We walked around the office complex for about twenty minutes until I recognized it—parked nowhere near my therapist's office.

Six months earlier, Angie had expressed concern over my deepening depression and signs of weight loss. She has since told me that she was not surprised by the phone call from my therapist.

"I was afraid I would get this call one day," she said. Since I remember little of that day, Angie has filled in the gaps for me. She told me when she arrived at my therapist's office, she was shocked at my appearance. Limp, pale, withdrawn, and angry, I looked to her like a stranger. Gone was the independent and strong person she knew.

My therapist gave her my admitting papers for the inpatient treatment center before we left his office. On the drive there, Angie asked me what she should tell my husband Michael. She also asked why I hadn't called him in the first place. I apparently told her I was afraid Michael would be angry and wouldn't understand. Angie promised to call him that night to let him know where I was.

On the way to the facility, I apparently kept trying to convince Angie that I needed to stop by home for a few things—a change of clothes, a toothbrush, and other essentials—but my therapist had told her to take me directly to the treatment center. He was concerned that, if I got the chance, I would try to commit suicide or run away. His concerns were right. I do remember feeling like that car ride was my last trip anywhere. I'm grateful Angela was there to help and kept me from sabotaging my chance for recovery.

Walking through the front doors of the treatment center, I felt butterflies in my stomach. Thoughts of running away to escape the unknown and the inevitable filled my head. I felt like everyone was looking at me, pointing fingers and judging me.

A pleasant receptionist greeted me and asked me to fill out admission forms. She also instructed me to give her my purse to be inspected for pills, alcohol, and sharp objects; then it would be returned to me. A staff admissions counselor came to escort me to her office to be interviewed and to assess my emotional and physical condition. When I said my good-byes to my friend, I felt alone and again abandoned. I was in tears and scared. Thoughts of wanting to take more pills kept rushing through my head. Instead of listening to the counselor, I was trying to think of how I could manipulate this person into giving me the pills that were in my purse.

I felt frail and weak. I was weeping and trembling in fear when I realized that my unsuspecting husband didn't even know yet where I was. Forgetting that Angela said she would call him later, I told the counselor this concern, and she said someone on the hospital staff would notify him of my admission and why I was there.

I soon became too exhausted and lethargic from the dozen or more pills I had taken to move from the chair to the couch where I wanted to lie down. The counselor attempted to continue her interview despite my overwrought state. She asked me when was the last time I took any pills, what kind, and how many. She asked if I felt suicidal and if I had memory loss. We discussed family history of depression. I was able to answer most of her questions until my speech became very slurred and I felt myself passing out on the couch. She immediately called in the admitting physician, who determined very quickly that I had overdosed. They transported me to the emergency room of the public hospital nearby.

After examination, the emergency room doctors realized that I was suicidal and that I had overdosed on several different types of pills as well as alcohol. Doctors quickly inserted a tube down my throat into my stomach. I gagged on the tubing and the charcoal used to induce vomiting. Emergency room doctors and nurses monitored my pulse and breathing for two to three hours while my counselor from the drug treatment facility stayed by my side. My wrists were shackled to the bed so I couldn't run away, an idea that had definitely entered my mind.

By the time I returned to the drug treatment facility from the hospital emergency room, seven hours had passed since my last pill or drink of alcohol. Staff counselors escorted me to a specialized treatment area where patients begin their detoxification and where their conditions are monitored for any health emergencies that may arise.

The detox part of the facility had a very large carpeted sitting area with a television, a nurse's station, a meal room, and bedrooms. Each bedroom had two beds and a bath and shower. I noticed the steel guard bars on the windows and doors with alarms that would sound if a patient tried to open any outside door in an escape attempt. I was completely exhausted from my ordeal at the hospital and more than ready to go to my own room and sleep.

Or so I thought. After the staff counselors escorted me to the specialized treatment facility, more strangers from the nurse's station came to me. They asked me to urinate into a cup to further check for drugs. This needed to be done with an open bathroom door, observed by female staff. Then they took my blood pressure, pulse rate, and temperature and gave me an alcohol breathalyzer test. Then two female staff counselors escorted me to an examination room where they explained to me that they needed to do a search of my clothes, bags, and purse for any drugs, alcohol or sharp objects that could put me or others in danger. They even took out my shoelaces. While I felt as though I was a jailed criminal, these procedures and precautions, I learned, are all standard protocols in a structured intensive treatment facility. Once they determined that I was safe, I was ready for bed.

I thought I would be escorted to my room but, because my therapist had left instructions that I was to be on suicide watch until further notice, I was not allowed to sleep in my room. I watched tearfully, too exhausted to argue at 3:00 A.M., as two staff counselors carried my mattress out of my bedroom to a well-lit hallway near the nurse's station for 72 hours of constant surveillance. There, along with loud noises, phone ringing, chatter and machines running, I tried to sleep.

## Day 2

I finally managed to get about two hours of sleep, only to be awakened by the 7:00 A.M. morning shift and early rising patients roaming the hallway past me. I could only use the bathroom if escorted by staff counselors, so I had to wait until it was convenient for them to take me. Everyone else was awakened shortly after 8:00 A.M. to start the day with breakfast, showers, and dressing. Then followed group therapy, counseling and lectures on addiction. Patients too ill from withdrawal were excused from group therapy to be cared for by nurses and staff. Medications were dispensed at the nurse's station by orders from a physician to help ease patients' withdrawals, cravings, physical pain, anxiety, and depression.

On this day, my withdrawal symptoms began in the form of extreme nervousness and migraine headaches. I felt chilled and clammy. I couldn't get comfortable in my own skin. I paced the floor and didn't want to converse with anyone. When the staff counselors noticed that I couldn't sit still and was crying uncontrollably, they asked my therapist to give me medication to calm my anxiety and help with my migraine. Having empathetic staff counselors with me in this time of crisis helped to ease both my pain and my feelings of hopelessness.

As I sat in a chair feeling worthless, my self-esteem in the gutter, a patient approached me who had been in the detoxification facility for a week. She said, "Hello, my name is Annie and I'm an addict." Annie put her arm around my shoulders as I cried. She told me I wasn't alone in this struggle and that I should focus only on this minute, hour, or day. "We take it one day at a time," she said. "We will love you until you can love yourself."

Annie had learned this wisdom in only a week through group counseling with other recovering patients and individual therapy. Now that she was to be discharged soon, she needed to apply what she learned to others. After Annie, other patients came to introduce themselves without judging my past or how I got there. I had already judged myself as being a bad person that didn't deserve anything good in my life. I had lost all respect for myself. I had jeopardized my marriage and lied and manipulated everyone I knew in order to get pills. Still, the pills were on my mind, the only way I knew to "fix" the hell I was in.

## Day 3

On day three, my withdrawal symptoms began to lessen, and I silently sat in on a group therapy session.

## Day 4

By day four, I was taken off suicide watch. I was relieved to have a room with a bed and bath that I could use without supervision.

## Day 5

I went to a group therapy session, but I wasn't ready to share my feelings or trust anyone with my "secrets." It did me good to listen to others who did want to share stories of how they became addicted to their drug of choice. They told when, how, and why they had felt drugs were needed. They told stories of emotional pain related to their marriages, children, and other family members. They described job-related pressures, depression, and loss of self-worth as well as physical and verbal abuse they had suffered. Tears rolled down my face as I thought how much I had in common with these strangers. It was as though we all lived the same life, same nightmare, same disappointments and fears. I was no different from these people, not any better, not any worse. I felt a new sense of belonging and acceptance.

## Day 6

Today was a good day. It can help boost your self-esteem so much when you become aware that your story is not so different from everybody else's.

## Day 7

I woke up feeling very irritable, jumpy, angry and anxious. I was discovering how one day I could be up and the next day I could be down, just what the others said happened to them. This day the food didn't even look good. I looked in the mirror and didn't like the image looking back. I looked frail. I had no makeup on, and my hair needed styling. I was tired of wearing the few clothes I had brought with me.

Today I was to have a family counseling session with my husband Michael to discuss an "aftercare" plan before being discharged from the treatment facility.

This was not a good day physically for me, but emotionally I felt I was strong enough to continue my therapy at home as suggested by my therapist. Our family counseling session, however, left me feeling nervous, scared, and unsure how Michael felt about having me back.

My husband asked what he could do to be supportive. I nervously watched him for any sign of distrust or anger toward me. Our communication skills had diminished over the years largely because I had been more interested in pills than in our relationship. I was very unsure of how he felt about having a wife who was now labeled as a pill addict. Michael did not show any empathy for me simply because he didn't understand how someone could become an addict from prescribed medications.

## Day 8

My first day home I felt as though I had entered into a dark cave. I felt claustrophobic in my own home. I felt like I was a stranger, and I wasn't sure I belonged there. I saw through a kind of tunnel vision, as if I had a blind spot around all sides of my head and body. I could see only a few feet ahead of me. I could only concentrate for a few minutes at a time. I feared being alone, and I was scared of doing something wrong now that I had been detoxed and was "alarmingly" sober.

I asked Michael to manage the medications my doctor had prescribed for anxiety and insomnia. My husband hid my medications from me and gave me my pills only as instructed on the bottles. I couldn't trust myself not to misuse them again.

### Day 9

I was following the recommended treatment plan that had been written out for me on the discharge forms. I attended support groups every night as well as individual therapy. I still felt angry about allowing myself to get into this mess in the first place. I could not yet talk about my anger in therapy. But I was determined not to give in and relapse.

### Day 10

My husband began to attend Al-Anon, a support group associated with Alcoholics Anonymous where family members and loved ones of addicts share their stories, gain strength, encouragement, and support from each other and learn about the disease of addiction.

### Day 11-15

With five more days behind me, I was now free of drug abuse for fifteen days! Fifteen days can feel like months to someone newly in recovery. I had such feelings of pride and accomplishment. I had done what I was told to do, went to meetings, saw my therapist, stayed busy with activities, and hadn't abused my prescriptions.

So why was I still depressed and anxious?

My withdrawal symptoms, like those of many other recovering addicts, continued after I returned home from the treatment facility. I would feel happy one minute, crying the next, and snapping at my family and friends after that. I went from hyperactive to sluggish and back again. I felt angry that I wasn't feeling better faster. My emotional needs weren't being met, and I didn't know what to do. The more physical and emotional pain I felt, the angrier I was for putting myself through this misery.

I didn't return to work after being discharged from the treatment facility. I was advised by my therapist to rest at home for a few weeks. I cleaned the house over and over, watched television, and isolated myself from friends and activities. My husband and I were not getting along, and we weren't communicating about anything "important." We didn't talk about my addiction or depression, and I didn't know where to begin to explain to him what had happened to me. I felt very alone, and feelings of abandonment overwhelmed me. I couldn't understand what was happening to me.

### Day 16

Today I was restless, confused, and severely depressed with little hope of getting out of this tunnel of doom I felt trapped in. Michael was at work, and my thoughts were muddled as to what was reality and what was not. My therapy sessions weren't helping me anymore. I wasn't talking about the emotional pain I was feeling from my past traumatic experiences. I had shut myself down, hiding how I was really feeling. I was drained from life and feared I wouldn't get my life back on track. Feeling very isolated and alone, I roamed the house looking for things to do to keep myself busy or amused. Then I found my thirty-eight-gauge revolver hidden in my closet.

I had taken lessons a long time ago and had enjoyed going to the shooting range, feeling the power of the gun as I aimed and shot at the target. I sat on the floor to open the case and took the pistol out. I looked at it for a long time, then stood up and walked down the hallway with the pistol in my hands, barely aware that it was there. The house was quiet and still. I walked to the kitchen and sat on the floor, then leaned up against the wall. I remember thinking how pretty my pistol was as I held it in both hands.

After several minutes I finally stood up, placed the pistol back into its case, and put it back into my closet. I didn't tell my husband about this surreal experience when he came home from work. I pretended everything was fine.

### Days 17-22

I attended my meetings for several days before divulging my secret experience with the pistol to my aftercare support group. My aftercare counselor notified my therapist of this episode with the gun. My therapist called me at home to check on me and do a phone assessment of my emotional stability. I was able to convince her that I was doing all right. I said I'd been feeling depressed and unable to communicate my fears to my husband. The therapist tried to convince me that perhaps I needed to be readmitted into the treatment facility for severe depression. I declined and told her I could work out my depression at home.

### Day 23

I had gone twenty-three days without abusing or misusing prescription drugs! This is a monumental feat for anyone who has been addicted to anything. Support group members acknowledge each other when they have been clean and sober for any length of time. The show of support from friends, family members, sponsors and church members can encourage the prescription addict to keep doing the next right thing to stay alive.

Twenty-three days of experiencing life again can make a person sharply aware of his surroundings. My hearing became clearer, flavors in foods were tastier, air smelled better, even water tasted cleaner. Things that most people take for granted became spectacular now!

A week had gone by without incident, and I had put the gun scare out of my mind. I enjoyed going to my support meetings. I felt I fit in with the others who attended, even though I didn't fit in anywhere else.

Even so, I wasn't happy with myself or my marriage, and I had difficulty sharing my feelings with my group or anyone else, including Michael.

## Day 24 through 30

Another long week passed without incident, without misusing or abusing any mood-altering chemical. Twelve-Step support groups have a "chip" (poker chip) system that acknowledges the number of days a person has been clean and sober. A person can receive a chip for new members, thirty days, ninety days, six months, nine months and twelve months. The day I received my thirty-day chip in my support group, I was over-whelmed with pride and accomplishment.

> > > 8

# FACING LIFE WITHOUT ABUSING Rx DRUGS

*"Now that I'm clean and sober, I feel a void in my life."*

The expression "get a life" seems made for the recovering addict. Once in recovery for a few months or even weeks after abusing (Rx) prescription and over-the-counter drugs and no longer spending every waking moment trying to figure out new ways to get pills, recovering pill addicts are amazed how much spare time in a day they have. When you quit any habit, you immediately feel something is missing, and boredom fills its place. Boredom is one of the strongest and most dangerous triggers for relapse. You must learn to recognize boredom before becoming prey to the cravings that inevitably accompany it.

It is understood that you are going to your therapist regularly and to your support groups often and you are in frequent contact with your sponsor or recovery coach. These interactions themselves take up time, and at this stage that's good. Moreover, I cannot emphasize enough that therapy and support groups can be lifelines to peace and understanding without judgment or criticism. Your therapist will continually support and encourage your work toward recovery and your related achievements, no matter how small or large. He or she will listen when perhaps others won't. An experienced therapist and Addiction Recovery Coach do for you what you cannot do for yourself and what you will not be able to do for yourself for quite some time. You will face issues that you have avoided until now by misusing pills, and you will learn skills necessary to live a life that doesn't require prescription drug abuse to get you through the day.

At first, that's all you need to do—get through the day—but as soon as possible you need to start rebuilding your everyday life. For many, that means starting from scratch. As for any building project, you need a plan, materials, and some professional help to do the things you've either forgotten how to do on your own or things you can't be expected to do by yourself.

You may be thinking that you should just go back to work (if you worked before) or get a job if you haven't had one. Be cautious about this. Some, if not most recovering addicts are not emotionally strong enough to go back to work during the first vulnerable weeks or months. Another consideration when deciding to return to work is where you worked during your addiction period. As for me, I worked in a hospital healthcare center with countless mood-altering pill samples in cabinets and prescription pads easily accessible. I chose to quit my job in healthcare and eliminate the triggers I could control to keep my recovery strong. When deciding to go back to work, consider whether or not your place of employment will be a huge trigger for you or source of countless possibilities for relapse. Even if you need the money, try to make-do without going to work until you are truly ready and safe, even if you have to beg or borrow money from family or take out a second mortgage on your home. If you go back to work too soon, you could be jeopardizing your recovery.

If you can't stay sober under the stress of work, you will be back where you started and have to undergo treatment all over again. Please try to wait until you and your therapist or Addiction Recovery Coach decide you can handle the challenges of going to work every day.

Just as rebuilding your life does not mean going back to work, it does not mean making unnecessarily drastic changes in your world. No matter how tempting it may seem to reinvent yourself at this point, this is not the time to get married or divorced unless your safety is in jeopardy, buy or sell a house, move, get pregnant, get a new job unless necessary for recovery reasons. Research shows that even healthy people will get sick if the total life-changes they experience within a year exceed a certain threshold. And an addict in recovery for less than a year is not a healthy person. Getting clean and sober and giving up the habits of addiction are all the major changes you can take this year without risking other health or stressful problems.

### Filling the Void

In making a plan for new possibilities and dreams, the first step is brainstorming your options. So sit down either by yourself, sponsor or with a recovery coach and work on a strategy goal plan: one that is reasonably obtainable and to which you can commit yourself every day.

List activities that you once enjoyed before you became addicted. List the ones you did for fun—like ice skating, boating, playing guitar, walking on the beach, sketching, or fishing—and the ones that were more like work, for example, studying a school subject, cleaning the house, pulling weeds, or tinkering with your car. If you have trouble making a list, try to remember your likes and dislikes before you became addicted. Ask yourself, are you good at making things with your hands? Do you like using words, reading, or writing? Do you have musical talent? Do you like working with numbers and computers? Do you prefer talking with people throughout the day? If you've been addicted all your adult life, you may need to do some exploration to find your talents. Your recovery coach can help you by suggesting exercises, hobbies, and activities that might guide you in finding areas of interest. Fortunately, there are also books, classes, and consultants to help you determine what you are good at and where your interests lie.

Approach these issues in different ways. Try writing out sentences like these below and then fill in the blanks.

*I am a person who likes to…*
*I used to like to…*
*I don't want to do that now. I would rather…*
*Here's what stands in the way…*
*Here's how I could remove this obstacle…*

Then list all the goals you remember having in the past. How many of these have you fulfilled? What are your goals now? Your number one goal, of course, is to remain clean and sober. But what is your second goal? And your third?

Chances are you don't know the answers to some of these questions right now. You haven't been in recovery long enough. It's not too soon, however, to play with these ideas, see what gives your heart a little bounce, and see what makes you sigh in despair. What turns you on, what turns you off? Make the effort to know yourself again. And write your thoughts down in a journal. Writing helps clarify feelings, especially right now. You will also probably want to look back at your journal to remember your journey someday.

Don't wait for your whole life's plan to be formulated before you start living. Get busy now, keeping the idea of making a plan loosely in mind. Choose activities that soothe and strengthen your body, your mind, and your spirit so that your whole self will heal.

Whereas at first you were just filling time with anything but drugs, now almost every activity should involve three key elements: **people, skills,** and **purpose**. As you will see, one element leads quickly to another.

## Meeting People

You need to be with people because social interactions drown out the cravings in your mind as well as the doubts and negative thoughts. Spending time with others will also alleviate the fear and loneliness you feel as you continue on the bumpy road to recovery. The presence of friends and loved ones keeps you from looking around for drugs. Also, as you interact, you are possibly making up for years of hiding behind underdeveloped social skills. Your new interactions will help you learn to care about other people, share, be open, tell stories, listen, laugh and empathize.

You can choose activities that involve people by design (team sports, classes, workshops) or by invitation (walking with a friend, seeing a movie with your spouse, going to an art exhibit with your sibling.) You should do things in which you can be so engrossed (reading, sewing or balancing the checkbook) that you don't get bored and let your mind wander. If you are bored, depressed, or tempted, seek out people. Call a friend, call your sponsor or recovery coach, go to a group support meeting, go somewhere where you can join an activity, even if it's only taking your clothes to the Laundromat and washing them with the other coin-pushing folks. Approach someone else who looks bored, ask a question, start a conversation, or offer to help someone fold their clothes while they are waiting. Interactions with people are your safeguard against boredom, the chief cause of relapse.

And don't forget that one special person in your life—your spouse or boy/girlfriend. Put "your song" on the stereo and ask, "May I have this dance?" Buy roses, cook a favorite dish, or go to a restaurant you both enjoy. Buy a special nightgown; give a backrub. Remember the romance you had before your world revolved around pills? Try to return to that time.

## Developing Skills

An activity that builds a skill takes your mind off drugs; at the same time, you build confidence and gain satisfaction from being productive again. As you practice a new skill, you'll find that something you don't do very well (e.g. draw a picture, writing, start a conversation with a stranger) will become easier each time you do it. Simply having a skill gives you confidence. It is important to track your progress so you can see evidence of your increasing skill level, whether it means scoring higher, going farther while jogging, or lowering your blood pressure. Keep a record of your progress in your journal.

A skill is a joy. A skill makes you proud. When you do something well, don't take it for granted; instead, say to yourself, "Wow, kid, you are not bad at all!" Besides the boost to your self-esteem, a new skill has practical value as well. You can use the skill around your house or on the job, and you can share it with others.

Some of the best ways to combine learning a new skill with social interaction include taking a class at a community center, or continuing education program, joining a sports team, and lending a hand on a volunteer project. Nothing warms the heart and lifts the spirit than volunteering for a cause or organization you feel passionate about while helping others less fortunate than you. You will not only learn new skills and gain new information, you also will benefit from spending time with **people**. More importantly, the new people you meet don't know your old untrustworthy self; so you can begin fresh to rebuild trustworthiness within yourself and show others you can be trusted again.

### Gaining Purpose

At first, your activities will be chosen just to get you through the day while staying clean and sober. Being with people and learning skills help you do just that. As soon as possible, however, you should choose to do activities that also include the third element of recovery: **purpose**. This key element includes both short-term and long-term purpose. Thinking about purpose, write your ideas down under the headings of the big areas of your life: **work, home, health, social life,** and **spirituality.**

**Work:** Do you need new work goals? You may need less stress and therefore need a plan for changing jobs or for reducing stress in the job you have. Your activities could include or lead to courses necessary to change fields or jobs. For example, first, you might arrange for career guidance. This might mean going to a library or bookstore or online and searching for an old standard like Richard Bolles' *What Color is My Parachute?* What other books are on the same shelf or page? Or you might hire a career consultant. Getting career guidance might mean finding an educational program or class on choosing or changing careers. It might mean finding a training program that leads to a new job skill or certification in a field you think you would find satisfying.

I chose to leave the medical healthcare profession for my own personal recovery, knowing early on that the triggers of sample medications in hospitals and doctors' offices posed a great threat to my sobriety. I made the wise decision to change my direction to something I felt passionate about: I wrote this book which has given me more satisfaction and joy than any job choice I've ever made.

**Home:** Now that you are clean, you can begin to take pleasure in color, order, and artistic arrangement. Do you want to make some changes in your environment to reflect your new upbeat take on life? Make a list of things you want to change around the house. For example, repair the ceiling and install a new light fixture, clean out and organize your closets, and start a garden.

For each project, write down the steps involved to accomplish your goal. Then break these steps down one by one. Break down the first step into little manageable steps you could do in one day. How about today! For fixing the ceiling, you could call your neighbor (Step 1) and ask who did their recent drywall work. You could go to the lighting store (Step 2) and look at fixtures. You could call the drywall contractor (Step 3) and ask him to come give an estimate. Or you could enroll in a class to improve your own dry wall installation skills. In the same way, you can break down the steps for reorganizing the closets or planting a garden. There are books in the library, consultants, specialists and classes to teach you to do just about anything you want to know how to do. Or you could team up with a friend with different skills than yours and do your projects together.

**Health:** Getting clean and sober was such a huge step toward better health that you may think you'll never need to do another thing. But building a life is about progress and improvement and reaching a higher level. It's time to revel in your new physical self.

Take an interest in your diet, read about healthy foods, go to a market that sells the freshest, most beautiful products, and learn some new, healthy ways to prepare them.

Exercise is paramount. Lying around for too long can bring on what we addicts know as 'Skinkin Thinkin', which can lead to depression and relapse. Vigorous exercise actually changes your physical chemistry, giving you an adrenaline surge, lifting your spirits, and lightening depression. Regular exercise reduces stress and tension. Aerobic exercise, like running, swimming, tennis and, of course, aerobics classes, lowers your blood pressure and heart rate. Other exercise like yoga, dance, and stretching increases flexibility and mobility. Weight training enhances strength. With exercise you will feel more energetic and sleep better.

But how do you get yourself to do all—or any—of these things? How do you stay motivated?

Start an exercise program with other people. Join an aerobics class or hire a personal trainer. Buy a step-exercise video and invite someone to exercise with you in your home so you both stick with it. Join a rowing club; enroll in a martial arts class. Take up a sport you never tried, like ice-skating, roller skating, water or snow skiing, tennis, pickleball. Take up a sport you used to enjoy, like softball. There are "geriatric leagues" as well as youthful leagues in just about every sport. Buy a bike and explore the biking paths in your community.

All or most of these activities cost some amount of money. If that's a problem, walk. (Ask for a gift of walking shoes for your birthday, Valentine's, anniversary or thirty days clean day.) Many clothing consignment shops have a variety of sportswear and shoes at very low cost to you. Invite a friend to walk with you and get in a good visit while you walk. Walk to the library, walk to the bus stop, walk to work, walk around your community. Walk or bike pedal to the grocery store every day with a little pack on your back to bring your purchases home. Even if you have a perfectly good car, this daily routine—oh, so European—can provide the exercise and routine you need. If you live in a rural area or where the library and the store are too far away to walk to, go instead to the nearest mailbox to mail your bill payments or walk to your neighbor's house and take her something you baked. Walking just for the exercise is extremely good for your health; walking with someone provides the key element of being with people, and walking for a purpose provides an additional key element.

Remember that exercise is not solely rigorous activity like aerobics, weight lifting, and hiking. Exercise can be going up the stairs instead of using an elevator or walking from room to room. Exercise can be vacuuming, sweeping, gardening, or even dusting. Whatever forms of exercise you choose, get in the habit of doing something physical every day. Exercise will help keep you healthy, focused, and toned.

Sometimes it's good to just pamper your body to relieve stress and make physical discomforts fade. Whether you indulge in a warm bath with scented candles or a treatment by a chiropractor, anything you do to keep yourself relaxed helps ward off stress-related discomfort and can sooth minor aches and pains so that you don't feel the need to take a pill.

Some healthy alternative activities and treatments that heal your body while involving your mind and spirit include chiropractic, yoga, meditation, homeopathy, massage, acupuncture, aromatherapy.

- *Chiropractic* is the practice of healthcare management, primarily dealing with the recuperative powers of the body to heal itself without the use of surgery and/or drugs if at all possible. Chiropractors are the nation's third leading healthcare providers, exceeded only by medical doctors and dentists. The practice of chiropractic emphasizes the connection between structure and function. The chiropractic approach is based on the theory that adjustments to return the spine's alignment to its normal, healthy state will permit the nervous system to regain normal function, allowing the body to heal itself and eliminating pain and illness. Some chiropractors may supplement adjustment therapy with applications of heat, cold or electrical stimulation. They may also suggest lifestyle changes. Unlike doctors of osteopathy, chiropractors cannot prescribe medications.

- *Yoga* is the practice of mental and physical exercises to improve health. With yoga you use your mind, body. and spirit to overcome obstacles both physical and mental. The word "Yoga" actually means, "disciplined," and it is through this disciplined practice that many people have seen great results. Yoga encompasses specific behaviors, different breathing techniques, and body postures.

- *Meditation* is the process of quieting the mind in order to spend time in thought for relaxation or religious/spiritual purposes. The goal is to attain an inner state of awareness and intensify personal and spiritual growth. In practice, meditation involves concentrated focus on something such as a sound, image, or feeling. Age is not a factor when it comes to yoga and meditation. It's good for all people, regardless of their condition.

- *Homeopathy* is a two hundred-year-old practice of healing by the application of certain natural substances in minute amounts. The efficacy of tiny amounts of active ingredients is enhanced by a process of "shaking with impact" at each stage of dilution thus releasing the "dynamic energy" or healing information of the original substance. While the mechanism for healing cannot be demonstrated, healing effects from homeopathy have been documented by traditional medical research. Side effects, drug interactions, tolerance, and addiction are unknown among users of homeopathic medicines.

Homeopathic remedies are best when prescribed after a thorough interview of the patient by a homeopathic practitioner. A diploma or certificate from any homeopathic program by itself is not recognized as license to practice homeopathy in the United States. However, healthcare professionals, pharmacists, podiatrists, and others are permitted to use homeopathy within the scope of their state license to practice. Self-treatment with over-the-counter homeopathic remedies is safe, although perhaps not as effective as individualized treatment.

- *Massage therapy* consists of rubbing, kneading, striking, tapping, and stroking the skin and soft tissue for the promotion of health and the feeling of well-being. These techniques are great for the alleviation of headaches, tension, physical pain, injuries, chronic conditions, and muscle soreness. Massage therapy stimulates blood flow and releases inflammatory or pain-producing substances, such as lactic acid, from the muscles. It helps reduce pain by relaxing muscles; by increasing lymphatic circulation, thereby reducing inflammation; and by promoting a sense of calm and relaxation. Techniques include acupressure, Swedish massage, rolfing or other deep-muscle massage therapy, and reflexology. However, check with your doctor before receiving any deep-muscle massage because massage should not be performed on inflamed areas or on individuals with cancer or infectious conditions.

- *Acupuncture* is an ancient Chinese procedure of relieving pain and treating an array of diseases through the use of needles. Specialists in acupuncture insert needles into specific points on the skin to relieve symptoms ranging from headaches to chronic pain to drug dependence. Researchers have demonstrated that the use of acupuncture produces an increase in natural painkillers within the human brain and is useful in pain management and the maintenance of health.

- *Aromatherapy* is a form of herbal healing. Scents and fragrances have been used for healing and mood change for thousands of years. Fragrant potpourri not only stimulates your senses, but lifts your mood, changing a bad mood into a good one in minutes. Simply by smelling or inhaling the active ingredients, you experience a physical change inside. Aroma consultants have recommended the following scents to alleviate depression and nervousness: melissa, narcissus, almond oil, sandalwood, and lavender as relaxants, and chamomile, lemon oil, peppermint, spearmint, pine oil, and rose as natural mood lifters.

When choosing an alternative therapy or practitioner, remember knowledge is power. Research credible healthcare information about any therapy you are interested in trying. Talk to people who have utilized the treatment method you choose to get recommendations for practitioners. Find out the practitioner's education, philosophy, and years of experience. Inquire beforehand about charges for service, insurance coverage, and policies on fees and payment. Call your insurance company, and ask if your policy covers the alternative treatment.

Be responsible for your health and recovery. Evaluate your treatment and take part in deciding what should change and what should stay the same. Seek guidance from your healthcare provider, therapist, sponsor, recovery coach, and peers for their viewpoints. Remember that not all treatments work for all people.

**Social Life**: Often, people don't think about how they got their friends. It may seem that the friends were made willy-nilly, as if chance threw them together. But each friendship starts with some kind of meeting. Write down all the friends you have and how you met each one of them. Now, **purpose** must be added to this activity. What is it you want to accomplish in your social life? Do you feel you need different friends or more friends? Perhaps the old ones have drifted away or they aren't supportive of your addiction recovery. Maybe they are old drinking or drug buddies, who reinforced the bad habits you are now trying to avoid.

If you decide you need to make new friends and develop your social life, you may worry that people you make an effort to meet aren't "real friends" because your relationship wasn't spontaneous. You may feel you need that spontaneous spark of connection to ignite a real friendship. However, after all the wasted time spent getting high on drugs, the recovering addict must put forth a serious, concerted effort to develop new, healthy friendships that aren't centered around drugs or alcohol.

Most important in your new circle of friends will be your support groups. They will meet the requirement of understanding and accepting your addiction and recovery, and they will take up a lot of your time. Pick and choose among this group the individuals with whom you want to spend more time outside of support group meetings and whose company your spouse or partner might also enjoy. Once you feel you have made a connection, you can develop your friendship by inviting the person (or persons) to a movie, out to dinner, or to join you for coffee before or after support group meetings.

As you move beyond needing every friend to be aware of your addiction, join unrelated interest groups. Take a variety of classes and when you find an area that really interests you, join an organization that promotes that interest, for example, a hiking club, a civic group such as Jaycees or Kiwanis, community theater, spiritual affiliation, or a pottery studio.

Friendships aren't the only damaged relationship in the lives of recovering addicts. Often, the most important relationships—those with spouses and family members—are badly in need of repair. First, you should tell your loved ones that you realize what your actions have done to them and that you are profoundly sorry. Then build your relationship just by being a healthy person when you are with them. It sounds simple, but it works. You don't have to do cartwheels or beg on our knees for forgiveness. Just be the person you wish you had been all along. Treat your spouse and family as well as your new friends with honesty and be authentic with them. Invite them to join you in your activities or for a pizza. Walk with them, go to a performance play with them, go to yard sales with them. Simply spend time with them. When they see the healthy, positive changes you have made in your life, trust will begin to return, and relationships will blossom.

If your purpose is still not clear, remember that you are still seeing your therapist or recovery coach while trying out these new ideas.

You should talk to your therapist or recovery coach about how these new activities make you feel. Maybe the new activity brings about some new anxiety, maybe a person you chose to become friends with didn't want to be your friend or perhaps you find yourself skipping the new activity and sliding backwards emotionally. Share your feelings with your therapist or recovery coach. These are the kinds of things he or she is there to help with.

**Spiritual Life:** People who have undergone treatment for substance or alcohol abuse often come through with a feeling of "renewal," a sense of well-being and inner strength. Some return to their original faith. Others question their original religion and find it doesn't seem to fit anymore. They may choose a new faith.

If you belong to an organized religion or at least did before your addiction, now's the time to strengthen it. Worship with your congregation. Read scripture or a daily devotional. Sing. Make a joyful noise. If you didn't have a spiritual life in the past or don't now, be open to the spiritual possibilities around you. Spirituality need not come only from organized religion. It may come from a philosophy, point of view, or activity different from anything you have considered or been exposed to before. Over a hundred different religions and beliefs in this world offer support, wisdom, and guidance to those reaching out for inner peace.

In any case, religious or not, you should recognize that there is something more powerful than you are and that "something" is good. Any spiritual connection that comforts you and calls for a positive response on your part will lead you to grow spiritually. In twelve-step support group meetings, an expression often uttered is, "Let go and let God." The message behind the expression is that you must learn to let go of your anger and problems and turn them over to God or whatever other higher power your believe in. Spirituality comes in many forms and can be very important to addiction recovery. If it gives you comfort, love, peace, and strength, stay with it.

But if you are not there yet, don't despair. Readiness comes in its own time. Just be open to other beliefs, seek new experiences, learn from those around you, and grow as a person.

All these activities of body, mind, and spirit cross-connect, serving multiple purposes so that the whole healthy effect snowballs. To illustrate, here's one possible scenario: Your religious goal leads to singing in the choir and doing a helpful project for others. The one you choose is Habitat for Humanity, an organization that involves people like you building houses for the working poor under the direction of a skilled foreman. You are learning a new skill and getting hands-on experience. Your Habitat building skills and experiences lead you to take up carpentry as a hobby and then to do carpentry for money. Next you leave the stress of your present job in a big office and become a carpenter working for yourself. Your new friends include the friends at church, the friends in Habitat, the friends in carpentry class, and the people who hire you to do carpentry work.

Here's another possible chain of events: You decide you'd like a pet to ease loneliness, give purpose, etc. First your effort is very small. You read about pets and their care. You think you'd relate best to dogs. You read about breeds of dogs and their particular characteristics and temperaments. You choose one that you feel is best suited to your lifestyle. You read books on training and care of the breed you chose. After visiting the humane society and a few animal shelters to look at dogs available for adoption, you find one you want to adopt. Training begins. As you walk your new dog around your neighborhood and the local park, you meet a lot of other dog owners. You're getting exercise and dogs attract people!

You decide to go to a higher level of social engagement and sign up for an obedience class and then a course on agility training. Always you are making friends, practicing sobriety, and learning skills that help you face life without drugs. The dog loves you in your good moments and your not-so-good times.

You are forced to get out of bed every day because you have a purpose, you decide to become a dog groomer or trainer, or you and Fido visit the elderly nursing homes for pet therapy. And it all started with reading a book on pets.

In these two examples, it is clear how one can go from filling time to getting exercise, learning skills, interacting with people, and helping others. Though it takes time and dedication, you too can take the journey from nothingness to purpose. Every activity you engage in during your recovery has the potential of creating for you a social life, a growing skill and a new step on your purpose list. Life can be so joyful when you aren't thinking about escaping from it.

Maybe you're saying, *that all sounds very good, but I'm still lying in bed reading this book and I don't feel like getting up.* Yes, starting can be the hardest part. The first step needn't be a huge, overwhelming challenge. It can consist of simple picking up a sheet of paper and a pen or pencil. Now, with that small step out of the way, write down three goals. Then, for each goal, write down three activities that relate to that goal. Each activity should involve people, skill, and the purpose of fulfilling your goal. For each activity, write down the first few little steps necessary to get started on that particular undertaking. Then get out of bed and do just one of those little steps. And then another...

You can use every activity you plan to do to make you feel more in control. Whether it's taking the clothes to the dry cleaners or just getting out of bed when you feel like lying there all day, if you plan to do it and follow through with your plan, your self-worth grows. When you have planned three things and accomplished those three things, you are three steps closer to your goal and three steps higher in self-esteem. Write down what you have done in your journal; mark the steps you have completed on your list with big red checks as you go. Reward yourself with simple pleasures like a hot shower, lighting a candle, or calling a friend for a chat. You don't even have to wait for three completed steps to congratulate yourself. Do it after one step! It doesn't matter how small the step, it's the direction you go in and the regularity that count. You will get there. I know, because I have been where you are.

If and when you do go back to work, should you go back to the same job? Every situation is different. Are drugs available at work increase temptation and cravings (e.g. in a hospital, pharmacy or doctor's office)? Were coworkers an enabling part of your drug-focused world? Is the stress of work such that you felt and still might feel you have to have a pill, a drink, or some other mood-altering substance in order to deal with it? If so, this job is not for you—not now.

Think hard about the stresses of your job that made you feel you needed a pill. What were the conditions at work? Were there personality clashes? How much responsibility was put on you in a day? Too much? Too little? Were there long hours and poor management?

If you answered yes to most or all these conditions, then your risk of relapse could be high at that job, and you should consider a change.

When you feel you are ready or you absolutely must work, look for a job, first of all, where drugs are not available. Also, seek a position with the right stress level for you. Low stress is often necessary, especially, for the newly sober. This may mean less responsibility or—if low responsibility represents boredom to you—more responsibility. Many drug users are looking for more risk and stimulation, higher activity levels and tighter deadlines, rather than less.

Maybe your most recent job was one you "stumbled into" without thought just because the job was available; don't do that again. This may be a good time for you to explore your job needs by reading books on choosing a career, taking a course on evaluating your work needs, or seeking career counseling to determine just what kind of work environment you are best suited for.

Whether in a new job or an old one, now that you are focused and clear minded, you can perform your duties with greatly improved organizational abilities you never thought you'd have back. Your energy level will improve radically with this new and healthier attitude on the job.

Nevertheless, every job comes with some stress. Think about possible changes you could make at work to reduce or avoid stress. This could include delegating duties to others or talking to your boss about working in a different department. Once you've made all the changes possible to reduce stress in your workplace, you must deal with whatever tension or pressure remains. You have to learn how to diffuse the stress and release your overwhelming emotions instead of letting them build up. Obviously, you can't use your stress-busting method of the past—using drugs or alcohol—so you must find an outlet for times of extreme stressful anger or anxiety every day, like pounding a punching bag at the gym, doing aerobics, running, jogging, walking or dancing. Even yelling at the wall can release stress so you don't take it out on others or yourself. Take short (five minute) breaks at your desk for deep breathing exercises, stretching, and meditation to refocus and relax your mind. Stress management is a learned technique that doesn't come naturally to everybody, which is why many people benefit from taking classes on the subject. Instructors teach students how to evaluate themselves and assess their feelings. They teach organizational and management skills that help individuals focus more clearly and make better decisions in stressful situations.

As for myself, even though I stayed in the healthcare field after my treatment, I chose not to return to the same medical clinic where I had worked before. That setting would have brought back too many memories of wrongdoing on my part, such as stealing sample medications and the treadmill incident, that caused me such intense shame and guilt. Also, on that job I had to work under extremely stressful conditions with ten physicians and twelve employees I was supervising and managing. I decided not to return to a position that clearly could not be changed, and no other position was available for me to transfer to. Another reason for my decision was that I would always have felt guilty for letting them and myself down and for not giving them 100 percent. I couldn't look my old employers or colleagues in the face. I still felt ashamed of myself and, perhaps, I still felt guilty. I have since gone back to apologize for my wrongdoing to a particular cardiologist I worked with for three years. I have found that letting go of the past is sometimes a good way to open your life to new possibilities and dreams.

After taking some of the basic steps outlined in this chapter, I decided to volunteer for the American Red Cross. As a volunteer, I established relationships within the organization and proved myself as skilled, competent, and reliable. When I was ready, I took on a new job as CPR/First Aid instructor for the American Red Cross where I worked for many years on a part-time basis in Atlanta, GA. When I moved to Naples, FL in 2016 I continued to volunteer with the American Red Cross volunteering on the Disaster Action Team and Services for Veterans' Armed Forces program.

In my spare time, I pursue my passion, which is to help other prescription drug addicts recover and to educate people about prescription and over-the-counter drug abuse, recovery coaching for addicted individuals and families in recovery, including my own efforts in 2002 to lobby for a new "Bill of Rights" requiring selected controlled substance medications to place warning labels on medication bottles about their addictive natures.

These interests and activities have filled my life with positive stimulation and a sense of peace, so I no longer need uppers, downers, or chemical mood alteration of any kind. The fullness of my life makes me feel that I have come a long way in my own recovery by continuing my efforts to give back to those in seeking my support and guidance.

Write to me through Prescriptions Anonymous website and tell me how you have achieved success, too.

> > > 9

# Relapse

*"I'm in recovery, but I'm still fearful."*

Relapse is a constant fear for the recovering addict. I believe it is a healthy fear because that sense of dread keeps you safe. You never want to forget the chaos and pain this disease has brought you, keeping it in a safe place in your consciousness so it doesn't command you to relapse. Relapse is **not** a part of recovery, but should this happen to you, it can become a learning experience that makes you even stronger and empowers you to work harder at underlying emotional pain for life-long recovery.

My unfortunate relapse occurred after I had been released from the treatment facility and detoxed from my various drugs. After a while, I realized I had suffered the pain of withdrawal without winning back happiness. This realization made me quit caring about recovery. I began to talk myself out of my new state of sobriety. Then I talked myself out of life altogether. This was before I was diagnosed or realized I was suffering from depression, post-traumatic stress disorder, as well as addiction, and I needed to be treated for all three illnesses. When a half-hearted attempt to kill myself failed,

I took some pills I had squirreled away before my "recovery." Only when I was in relapse, did I call my therapist.

    A relapse is something that occurs when a person who has gone through drug rehabilitation treatment and has been in recovery then goes back to using, but it's more complicated than this. Modern addiction science views relapse as not a single event where a person goes back to using, but instead it's defined as the setbacks along the road to recovery. The prescription addict's definition is stringent: the use of any mood or mind-altering substance or medication, over-the-counter or prescribed, not taking the medication exactly according to a fully informed physician's directions. It's a zero tolerance definition. There is no judgment factor such as "too much" or "too often," or even "unknowingly." Note, however, that some people, even some addiction support groups, say that if you're on any kind of mood-altering pill even if its prescribed by a physician for surgery or serious illness, you have relapsed. This is not true. Just as diabetics need their insulin, people with elevated blood pressure need medicine to control it and people with heart problems need their stabilizing medication, so prescription addicts with a dual diagnosis often need prescribed drugs to combat depression or anxiety, combined with behavioral therapy. If left untreated, such mental illnesses greatly inhibit the addict's recovery. The point is that any medication taken must be prescribed by a competent physician to whom you have told the truth; then you must follow his or her directions for use. Medication taken under any other circumstance constitutes relapse.

    A relapse does not undo previous progress made in an addiction recovery program. Signs of a drug relapse can be broken down into three stages: emotional relapse, mental relapse, and physical relapse.

The coping mechanisms and strategies you learned during a recovery program will still help you overcome a relapse. Try to remain conscious of your emotions, moods, and behavior throughout the recovery process to reduce your risk of experiencing a full relapse.

Lack of motivation could also be an obstructive factor in long-term recovery if the person was forced into treatment and did not come of his own volition. He simply wasn't ready. While many who are forced or persuaded by a loving intervention to enter a treatment center do "come around" and commit themselves to recovery, many others are just going through the motions to satisfy someone else.

Marilyn, one relapsed addict, speaks for those like her: "In treatment we were always doing what was expected of us to make everything 'alright' again. We did what we thought others wanted us to do—our spouses, family, children, or employers. We were in recovery for everyone but ourselves. When we tried it again *just for us*, that was the turning point."

Some recovering addicts relapse, even though they are motivated, because they are motivated to do too many things. Unfortunately, recovery takes so much of your energy and attention that concentrating on other things in your life causes you to neglect recovery. Often, addicts don't realize they can't successfully go through a recovery program and at the same time do all the other things they are motivated to accomplish.

"When you put everything before recovery, you will lose to this disease," says Marie, a member of Prescriptions Anonymous. "I put everyone else first—my husband, kids, in-laws, business—thinking that if I made them happy, I would be doing the right thing. I knew I had turned the corner when I put recovery as my first priority."

Some enter into treatment knowing they have a stash of pills hidden at home "just in case." This kind of doubt gnaws at the recovering addict's commitment. One woman who felt she couldn't go into a treatment center had worked it out with her husband that he would give her the pills less and less frequently until she was taking no more. "I really want this to be the end of it for good," she said, explaining the procedure, but adding, "I still have three refills left that I can always get from the pharmacy if it doesn't work out." She is setting herself up for relapse by even thinking about those refills. Truly sincere commitment means flushing your remaining pills down the toilet or telling a responsible person where all your reserves are hidden so they can dispose of them before you come home. That way the drugs aren't even there to see or think about.

Even if an addict was motivated during treatment and felt positive about his future free of drug addiction, he may suffer from overconfidence coming out, thinking, "I'm recovered." This individual will not be prepared for the difficulties that lie ahead, because he is inexperienced. Inexperience is the cause of poor judgment in any area of life, so why assume it will be different for addiction recovery? It takes learning, then trying, making mistakes, and correcting them before any new process is mastered.

Overconfidence may also indicate a newly recovered addict's deeper layer of denial. In this case, the individual thinks she's learned all she needs to know to say clean and sober, so she is careless in her behavior. She may not observe all the necessary precautions. The likelihood of relapse for this person is great.

Addiction specialist John Wallace, M.D. from National Association of Addiction Treatment Providers says, "Recovering individuals must gradually change their patterns of thinking. Just as denial has enabled addicts to persist in self-destructive, pill-taking behavior counter to their values, its continued use after they stop their abuse can leave them vulnerable to relapse. Sometimes, after a prescription addict has been detoxed and is beginning to feel better physically, he mistakes a craving for pills for a reasoned assessment that he can now take charge and medicate himself as needed. With this deception, he fools even himself."

One forty-four-year-old relapsed addict, Scott, explains how he deceived himself into believing he could take controlled substance pills and still be in control:

*I stayed clean for nearly two years. Then, just when I thought I had it licked and had all the answers, I relapsed. I thought I had been cured! I thought I could use just a 'little more' and not let it get out of hand. Well, my thinking got me right back into the living hell of drug addiction.*

*I am working with a recovery coach from home getting back on the road to staying in recovery. I have faith that, if I stick with it, I can live a life free from the insanity of drug addiction. I have learned a valuable lesson: recovery from drug addiction is not easy. It requires honest effort. The rewards, though, are priceless!*

Scott's reason for relapse is now clear to him. He won't make that mistake again. His motivation is great, probably greater now, after relapse, than the first time around. It is a signal that more change is necessary. If relapse is approached appropriately, it results in a renewed and refined effort at change. Part of the relapse process is to obtain more knowledge about addictive behavior patterns and to learn the new behavior patterns necessary for a healthy, sober life.

Studies indicate that most people treated for any type of substance dependency relapse at least once and a significant number experience two or more relapses. Between one-half and two-thirds of addicts in treatment will relapse within one year. According to Terence Gorski, founder of The Cenaps Corporation, a prevention training organization, "One-third of all patients are recovery-prone and maintain total abstinence. Another third are transitionally relapse-prone and have a series of short-term and low-consequence relapse episodes prior to finding long-term abstinence. The final third are chronically relapse-prone patients who can't find long-term sobriety no matter what they do." The belief that relapse is an indication of weakness or failure belies the fact that, for many people, successful recovery often involves a series of relapse episodes. Relapse can happen, but remember that relapse is **not** a natural part of recovery treatment and should not be viewed as an excuse to start abusing drugs again simply because others have.

Treatment after relapse feels different from the original treatment. The first time an addict enters treatment, he usually doesn't have any real idea of what will happen, including how withdrawal will feel. All he knows is that he wants to feel better and end his dependence on drugs. He is fearful but hopeful about the future. First time recovery treatment is a "learn as you go" process.

On the other hand, treatment for relapse feels worse than the first time in several ways. Now the addict knows what's going to happen to her. She dreads the aches, shakes, and nausea. Moreover, this feels even more like failure because she has not only let herself down, but she has let the loved ones down who supported her through this ordeal once, twice or six times before, only to have to do it all over again. The unhappiness over her failure increases the risk of depression for the addict receiving a repeat treatment. When she went into treatment the first time, she may have thought that all she needed to do was detox, go to a few meetings, say the right things, and that's all there was to it. It's a rude awakening when she finds she has relapsed.

The good news is that the second treatment can make the addict stronger, more focused, and more determined to make sobriety the first priority. Relapsed members of support groups say that, when they returned to treatment or worked with a recovery coach, they learned something new and valuable about themselves and the process of staying in recovery. They listened harder and retained what they heard. As if watching a movie for the second time, they picked up new information they had missed or forgotten.

This is not to say that you should try to relapse! Relapse is having to repeat detox and emotional pain you had the first time. But if you do relapse, try to consider the reasons why you relapsed, forgive yourself, and learn from the experience. Whatever you do, don't assume relapse means you've failed. The odds of maintaining life-long sobriety are still in your favor. Keep fighting!

Whether they realize it or not, recovering addicts set themselves up for relapse days or weeks before it actually happens. A series of changes in behavior and thinking in recovering addicts allows relapse to happen. In response to a gradual progression of "warning signals" that herald emotional pain, addicts talk themselves into the inevitability of abusing prescription or over-the-counter drugs again. As a result, they believe they are unable to function without pills or some other mood-altering substance. By self-medicating, they return to what they know will diminish or mask the emotional or physical pain. Here are some of the self-defeating thoughts that, given a few hours or days to torment the recovering addict, will often result in relapse:

- **I don't deserve to be happy**

As the recovery process begins to make you feel better about yourself, you may start feeling a little guilty about being happy. After living in a world of self-destructive behavior then changing for the better, you will feel different, both physically and mentally. Many addicts and alcoholics have difficulty dealing with change and, as a result, they question why they should be happy.

To answer this self-defeating question, tell yourself that you deserve to be happy because you faced your addiction and are working hard to be a better person. Then, do something good, productive and worthwhile, so you can show yourself in a tangible way why you are deserving. This exercise is especially effective and meaningful if you do something for someone other than yourself, so that the other person's gratitude and appreciation will act as external validations of your worth.

- **I can't go another day; it's just too hard.**

There will be times when you feel like you can't stand another day of being miserable. When you feel like this, get out of the house. Visit a friend, do some gardening, see a movie, etc. The worst thing you can do is be alone. No matter what the cause of your unhappiness, share it with others. Call your therapist, sponsor, recovery coach, or close friend. Allow them to help you shoulder the burden of your pain and sadness—at least temporarily. Most importantly, banish the words "I can't" from your vocabulary. Every time these words enter your consciousness, stop what you're doing and tell yourself, "Actually, I *can* do it and I know I can because I have been drug-free for seventeen (or however many) days already and I am proud of it."

- **I feel like I'm in a dark tunnel of depression. I hate it.**

Depression can be a very difficult emotional problem to deal with, whether a person is a recovering addict or not. Depression makes you feel utterly alone, as if the world has forsaken you and left you to live in a dark tunnel. You believe there is no relief in sight for your sadness and pain. If you are in extreme distress, call 911 immediately.

Usually though, the following process will begin to pull you out of your funk: Take it one minute at a time; try not to focus too far in the future because it is often too overwhelming to handle. Look on your calendar and find your next appointment with your therapist or recovery coach. Say, "Only three days until I see her. I can make it until then." If there is no such appointment on your calendar, make one now. In fact, it's good to always have an appointment out there in the future so you can plan accordingly. The dark tunnel does eventually open wide and disappear, letting light in and allowing your mind to become clearer and more focused. When good feelings begin to overtake the bad, you will feel more confident about yourself and proud of every hurdle you get through. The light at the end of the tunnel is closer than you think.

## Common Triggers

"Other factors can be entangled in relapse," the National Institute on Drug Abuse states, "including difficult life experiences, lack of a support system, and an inability to handle stress. The inability to learn skills to manage stress is a major relapse factor in recovering individuals."

We can increase our chances of not relapsing by recognizing the dangerous feelings we call triggers and knowing actions we can take to cope with them. Triggers will be different for everyone depending on their backgrounds, childhoods, self-images, how and why they started taking drugs, etc. To give an idea of the different triggers that have preceded and caused relapse in real people, I came up with the following list of the most common triggers: **cravings, boredom, depression, anger, bad habits, low self-esteem, criticism, family disapproval, facing people, not going to meetings or therapy, guilt and shame, physical pain, and availability of mind-altering substances.**

Let's look at each of these triggers one by one.

- **Cravings**

It was the cravings that got me. I couldn't get them out of my head. Once I was back home from treatment, I didn't have anyone there who understood how I felt.

Sometimes relapse is a simple response to intense cravings. Emotional memories are our deepest, most powerful recollections. They can often be evoked by some sensory cue like a taste or a smell, and they seem to shortcut the process of rational thought.

Everyone who has engaged in addictive behavior will experience uncomfortable cravings ("I want it badly") and urges ("I have to do it now"). They are normal. For many people, the urges and cravings to use drugs or alcohol trigger automatic responses. They are without conscious thought: I want [fill in the blank] = I get it. Learning to say NO to these intense, ingrained desires is one of the biggest challenges in recovery. The good news is that you can understand these desires and learn to resist them. You can make cravings and urges decrease in strength and frequency over time by adopting the coping strategies that work best for you as part of your plan for relapse prevention.

Randy Lindel, Facilitator at SMART Recovery in Boston suggests five practical strategies on how to cope with urges and cravings after you have decided to abstain from drugs and alcohol. These are summarized with the easy-to-remember acronym DEADS. Each letter stands for one useful approach: Delay, Escape, Accept, Dispute, Substitute. Here's how they work:

**D = Delay.**

The mental activities of cravings and urges disappear over time unless you actively maintain them with your attention. Given time, they will run their course and disappear. If they aren't gone in 10-15 minutes, then chances are you are still exposed to the stimulus that cued the urge in the first place. Just don't give in no matter how bad the urge is, and it will pass. All the urges you have ever had have passed. Once you have denied an urge, you know you can do it again and again. And after a short time, there will be fewer cravings, and the ones you have will diminish in intensity. Waiting them out is a great step to recovery.

**E = Escape.**

Just leave or get away from the urge provoking situation. Run away from it. Leave the pub so that you can stop staring at the beer taps. Leave the supermarket or pharmacy where all the bottles of wine are so nicely displayed and medicines are neatly placed on shelves. If there's an alcohol or pharmaceutical ad on TV, switch the channel. Just the act of escaping the trigger will focus your mind on something new—which will quickly lessen the urge.

**A = Accept.**
Put your urges and cravings into perspective by understanding that they are normal and will pass. It's important in the recovery process to learn to accept discomfort. It won't "kill" you and will be gone pretty quickly. You'll feel good about what you're learning and achieving.

**D = Dispute.**
If you've worked through the disarm exercises listed above, you may have developed a rational "effective new belief" or counter statement to help you attack your (irrational) urges and cravings. These exercises help you productively diagnose past addictive situations and develop useful tactics for disputing them when they occur again—which will help them pass much more quickly.

**S = Substitute.**
When you get an urge, quickly substitute a thought or activity that's more beneficial or fun. Take a walk or any other form of exercise. Pick up something new to read or turn on something to listen to. The possibilities to substitute (and lessen the craving more quickly) are endless. Think about and write down some possibilities to have a list on hand when an urge occurs. Then, when an urge arises, just pick one thought or activity as an effective substitute.

Keep a log of when and how often the cravings come. Write in your journal where you were and what you were doing when each craving hit. For example, what sights, sounds, smells and tastes were your experiencing when the craving hit? What mood were you in when your/ craving began? Then, write down what you did to alleviate the craving or get your mind off it. How did you avoid giving in to the craving each time? Once you have a record, you can study it and learn to recognize the dangerous mood and sensory experiences that trigger cravings and the most effective ways you've been able to ward them off. You can then start to develop a system to intervene when the craving strikes and do what works to help you avoid giving in, whether it means calling a friend, recovery coach, therapist, or going to a support meeting or just getting out of the house to take a walk.

- **Boredom**

*I had too much time on my hands while I was at home. I was left alone all day, feeling bored and lonely. I had all this free time and nothing to do to replace my thoughts of abusing again.*

Stay busy with hobbies, meetings, and exercise. Seek out people with whom you feel safe or enjoy socializing with and who make you feel like reengaging life again. Contact those friends who have a positive influence on you or call friends from your support network.

- **Depression**

*I can't seem to snap myself out of this dark tunnel I feel I'm in. I cry and isolate myself to the point that I have difficulty motivating myself to do anything.*

Some people know the reasons for their depression. In the past, they may have used pills to mask feelings they didn't want to think about or deal with. While in recovery, they had to face up to those negative emotional problems without the aid of a pill. That can be incredibly difficult and painful for anyone to handle, even those who aren't prescription addicts. It is important to talk about these feelings and problems openly and honestly with people who care about you. Ask your therapist to help you resolve the underlying problems.

Sometimes, however, people don't know why they are depressed, they just know they are. They know of no specific problem that needs solving and thus don't know what to do to feel better. When this vague depression strikes, one of the best methods of dealing with it on our own is to use relaxation skills learned through activities like yoga or engage in some activity that you know from the past will provide peace and satisfaction. In addition, safe, appropriate doses of medication, prescribed and supervised by a physician, may be necessary. Talk to your psychiatrist, therapist, or recovery coach for goal setting and medication therapy.

- **Anger**

*I felt angry all the time. I was angry with my wife, kids, neighbors, co-workers and even the family pets, everyone but myself. I wanted to blame others for my addiction.*

Anger kept bottled up inside is a relapse waiting to happen. Anger can not only cause relapse, but it can emotionally destroy you, your marriage, your family, and other relationships. Nothing positive can come from misdirected anger. Work through it with your therapist, recovery coach, sponsor, support network, spiritual advisor, or good trusted friend *you respect*. When an attack of anger strikes, go for a hard workout at the gym or a brisk walk, clean the house or mow the lawn. Burn off some anger by putting it to good use rather than by letting it fester until you hurt yourself or others.

- ***Bad habits***

*I went back to the same friends I had before. They were still using drugs. When I wasn't with them, I found myself going through other friends' medicine cabinets and purses to steal their medications. It was so easy for me to do.*

Socializing with the same crowd of people who also misuse pills, illegal drugs or alcohol can only make things worse for you, and you will probably relapse because of it. Make a list of these people and put them off-limits! Bad habits also include lying, manipulating and stealing. To hide your drug addiction in the past, you probably became very adept at lying to your spouse, boss, co-workers, friends, physician, dentist and pharmacist. Now, every time you go to a healthcare provider, before you are even tempted to lie, you must tell them up front that you're a prescription addict or that you have an addictive personality. This will help them see through you, if you slip into your old lying habit, and they will make every effort not to give you any mood-altering medications.

- **Low self-esteem**

*I had a difficult time restoring my self-esteem and self-worth and I didn't get any help or support from my family. I felt so ashamed of what I had done to myself and others.*

When you have very low self-esteem, it is difficult to be motivated to improve. And, though self-worth comes from within, it certainly doesn't help to be surrounded by negative, critical people. It is important to make an effort to spend time with positive, supportive, happy people. Perhaps, if you have difficulty finding positive people in your current everyday life, you can reestablish a relationship with a friend from years past who was always upbeat and positive. By attending support groups you'll find the most supportive, understanding friendships that can be as meaningful as anyone else in your life; they can help you rebuild self-esteem at your own pace. Healthy relationships can help to restore your self-worth and motivate you. Another simple activity you can do is write down a list of all your good qualities and all the things you have done that you're proud of. Read this list when you are feeling really down about yourself. Self-esteem can get a boost from affirmations and acknowledgment of your good points. But the straightest, strongest route to self-esteem is to earn it: Do a task well, be kind to others, stay clean and sober. It won't take long for people to notice your efforts and let you know how much they appreciate you. These are the reinforcements you need to increase your self-worth. Win them by good behavior.

- **Criticism**

*I never get positive feedback from my spouse or family. I always hear, "You'll never amount to much in life" or "Why can't you be more like your brother? He's successful." I got high on pills so I wouldn't have to think about their comments. It was easier to not feel anything.*

Criticism is tough for anyone to take. It's especially easy for prescription addicts to believe the negative things said about themselves and not hear or believe the positive ones. It is as if they don't feel they're worthy of any positive things said about them. Instead of feeling bad and inwardly agreeing with people when they say negative things about you, consider how unhappy those people must feel being burdened with all those negative thoughts. Think of criticism as one of *their* bad habits! As you build a healthier lifestyle, the happier and more worthy of positive remarks you will feel and the easier it will be for you to shrug off criticism.

- **Family disapproval**

*My family members are my biggest triggers. They can depress me, anger me, frustrate me, bore me, and accuse me of God knows what, all within seconds after I walk into a room. Before, I'd take a pill to protect myself against them. They still make me think about taking a pill.*

Distance yourself from anyone who cannot be positive and supportive—even if it's a family member. You are not punishing them; you are just protecting yourself. Once you are well into your recovery and you feel that you can help negative people to be more understanding, then approach them—with caution. Don't expect miracles, but in time they may listen and be supportive as they see the changes in you. If they don't ever approve of you or agree with you about your changed positive behavior, that is their choice and right. While you're around them (if you choose to be), change the subject from your illness to the wonderful things happening in your life. The more energized and happy they see you are, the more they will let go of their disapproval and admire the person you have become.

- **Facing People**

*People at work kept looking at me like I was going to lose my cool or sell them drugs. I couldn't stand being treated as if I was a criminal. My best just didn't seem good enough.*

Facing people who knew you before recovery can be difficult. You feel like you're walking on eggshells, not knowing how to act or talk around people, fearing their judgment and criticism. Be patient with people. They have seen your bad behavior in the past, and they are not sure how your new behavior is going to work out. Can you blame them? Just keep doing the right things by going to meetings, and showing that you are truly worthy of being trusted. Remember, they may feel as though they're walking on eggshells, too, because they don't want to say or do anything that might upset you. Communication is the key. Keep everything out in the open and help each other understand what's going on.

- **Not going to meetings or therapy; not utilizing my sponsor, therapist or recovery coaching**
  *I got tired of going to meetings, counseling, and having to meet with my sponsor and recovery coach all the time. I felt like that was all I had in my life: everyone else telling me what I should do, where I should go and when I should do it.*

Discontinuing your support group attendance, therapy sessions, or frequent contact with your sponsor or recovery coach will undoubtedly push you to relapse. When you are new in recovery, you need close supervision, support, and structure, whether you like it or not. You need to learn how to change bad habits into good habits. Recovery and staying in recovery is hard work because changing old behaviors doesn't come easy for anyone. You need feedback, encouragement, and guidance. "Working a program" alone—without any help whatsoever—didn't work for me and likely won't work for you, but meetings, sponsors, therapy, recovery coaching and good friends do help if you let them.

I cannot emphasize this enough: You must stick with a recovery plan to succeed and rebuild a healthy, happy lifestyle you deserve and want. The people telling you what to do have at one time been right where you are now. They know what lies ahead for you. They have only your best interests in mind. You will come to know how important they are and learn to enjoy being around them. People in support meetings not only learn about their disease and get to share their concerns with each other, they also find new friendships. These people become your "partners in recovery" and your friends. You will always need a support system to help with the bad days and to share the good days. The goal of a recovery coach isn't to eliminate all negative thoughts and feelings, it's to change your response to them.

- ***Guilt and shame***
  *I was consumed with guilt and shame over what I had done to my family. I hurt my wife so much by lying that I couldn't face her. Also, I was in a car accident while under the influence of opioid prescriptions and injured two people. I can't forgive myself for that.*

The predators of guilt and shame have been living inside you for months, maybe years, and they will gnaw at you to the point of destruction if you let them. Talking about your guilt and shame in meetings, with your recovery coach or counselor, and attending family counseling can help you work through these feelings until you find the answers you need to put the past in the past and move on to a better future. Don't let guilt and shame destroy you, as many have. Learn to ask for help and open up to others who want to see you succeed. Beware: guilt and shame don't go away overnight; you must be patient with yourself and others while you work through this. As you do, be gentle and respectful to those you feel you have hurt.

Making amends is a powerful step in the recovery process and is a part of many twelve-step programs. Even if you are not in a twelve-step program, making amends will give you relief that you have confronted your mistakes. You can't change the past; you can only change the present. Guilt and shame will diminish as you begin doing more things of which yo*u can be proud.*

- **Physical pain**
  *My physical pain was so intense that I felt justified taking extra pills. I followed the instructions on my prescription bottles, but I also went to the pharmacy and bought sleeping aids so I could get through each night without pain. That caused my relapse.*

When confronted with pain, prescription addicts often associate their discomfort with an immediate urge to take a pill. They think, "I can't stand this feeling any longer. I have to have a pill." In fact, since pain in the past has led to the sweet relief of medication, addicts are often conditioned to feel discomfort or pain in order to justify taking the medication. This is a connection addicts need to unlearn. When that first sensation of discomfort hits, you need to engage in a distracting activity to disrupt the unhealthy link between pain and your desire to pop a pill.

That said, I believe no one, not even a recovering addict, should have to suffer intense physical pain. You can have medication for pain—the right medication, prescribed by the right people and taken as directed. Your therapist, addictionologist, and pharmacist understand addictive medicines. They should be the people who tell you what medication to take and how much to take so that the risk of relapse will be low. Listen to their instructions, and do what they tell you without deviating. Until you have proven you can trust yourself, ask your spouse or some responsible person to keep your prescribed medications locked up and to administer them to you only according to the doctor's instructions. **Never** self-medicate without supervision and that includes over-the-counter medicines!

- **Availability**

*Going to any healthcare provider, dentist, or pharmacy was like going to a candy store and pressing my nose against the glass. Everyone has a medicine cabinet in their house just asking to be opened. Every medicine cabinet has got something that looks good to me.*

Availability of drugs is a real problem, especially since all your friends and even the people you live with probably have dozens of medications they legitimately need or that are left over from a previous illness. Here's the solution: Ask your spouse, partner, or whomever you live with to clean out the medicine cabinet now or before you come home from treatment. This is not a do-it-yourself project for you. Ask someone to comb the house for pills you may have stashed away. Tell this person to check behind the window blinds, in the toilet tank, in your clothes pockets, purses, in jars in the kitchen, and in other places only you know about. You don't want to stumble upon an old cache of pills when you are newly sober.

Ask others in your household to put their own medicines in a locked container and to keep the key with them. That's an inconvenience for them, but nothing compared to the inconvenience of living with an addict in relapse.

And I repeat, tell your doctors and other healthcare workers that you are a recovering addict or that you have an addictive personality. Admitting your pill addiction to your healthcare professionals won't be the first time they've heard confessions from their patients getting addicted to prescribed medications. It's essential for you to communicate with all healthcare professionals about your addiction and to feel confident these professionals know how to prescribe non-addictive medications. Ask your doctor for your diagnosis, not just a list of your symptoms. Ask that you be involved in the decisions for any necessary prescriptions. We live in a world where it has become automatic to be seen by a healthcare provider and handed a prescription without even discussing the addictive components of the medication or whether your symptom is one that is "short lived" and can be managed without drugs. Doctors have become accustomed to writing out prescriptions for tolerable symptoms without patients even asking for them. Make the choice be yours. Can you treat your symptom without running the risk of relapse? Is the prescription offered written for a passing symptom or for the root cause of a significant disease? Remember, don't let your addiction "trick" you into unnecessarily putting a pill into your mouth.

- **Understanding Over-the-counter Drugs and Possible Relapse**

Many people never think that over-the-counter (OTC) medicines are as addictive as controlled substance medications. Yet over-the-counter stimulants such as diet pills, caffeine tablets, nose sprays, sedatives that contain alcohol, sleeping aids, and cold remedies all can be potentially dangerous. Nan Davis, R.Ph., M.S., pharmacist and founder of Pharmacy Counseling Services, says, "It is difficult to live drug free in a society flooded with quick-fix drug advertising. Sometimes, it seems almost un-American to endure aches and pains without doing something about them. Breaking the pattern of impulsive drug use may necessitate the removal of all medications from the home. Unfortunately, long-standing, compulsive drug seeking and supply procurement behaviors make it difficult for an addict to clear the home of drugs. Common excuses for keeping drugs include: "I might need it someday," "It's for somebody else," and "But it's not addicting."

Davis explains that pharmacists, like physicians and dentists, need to be aware of the potential dangers of prescription medication and over-the-counter drugs for their patients in recovery. Any mood or mind-changing drug taken to relieve an addict's anxiety or other discomforting symptom results in relapse an unacceptable percentage of the time. Pharmacists understand and can explain the mechanism of non-drug and drug-minimum alternatives, though some may need education updates on how their drug knowledge applies to addiction and recovery. As respected professionals, pharmacists and dentists, as well as physicians, have a special responsibility to assist recovering alcoholics and addicts to use medication appropriately. For example, if a pharmacist is asked, "Can you help me find medicine without alcohol that will treat my cold?" he should take time to explain the potential psychoactive side effects in both liquid and solid dosage forms of any medicine he recommends. Rather than resorting to a systemic agent with potentially undesirable side effects for a recovering addict, the pharmacist could recommend a vaporizer and explain the effects of increased fluid intake and even inhaling the vapors of hot chicken soup.

The risk of adverse drug effects is generally acceptable only if the disease being treated is very serious. Use of a potentially addictive drug for a trivial illness, however, is unacceptable, considering the high risk of relapse.

This is not to suggest that people in recovery should never medically use over-the-counter drugs again. Many have been safely used with proper precautions. The trick is to use the least addictive form of necessary medication that will be effective and to follow your doctor's or pharmacist's instructions carefully. OTC drugs are typically safe if used at recommended doses. Although less potent than other substances, OTC drugs still pose a risk for developing an addiction.

Abusing OTC drugs can lead to health problems including memory loss, kidney failure, heart problems and death. Some people abuse over-the-counter (OTC) drugs to self-medicate for mental illnesses like anxiety and depression. Abusing these medications can also give users a euphoric "high" or hallucinations. Any use outside of what's recommended is considered abuse. Someone abusing OTC drugs may move on to more dangerous or illicit drugs in search of a better high.

Some commonly abused OTC medications include:

### Cough medicines (Dextromethorphan, or DXM)
Cough medicines can cause hallucinations and a potent high when abused. Cough medicines are popular among young people, as they're often readily accessible in medicine cabinets at home or at a friend's house. High doses can cause vomiting, rapid heart rate, blurred vision, shakiness, and even brain damage.

### Cold medicines *(Pseudoephedrine)*
Pseudoephedrine is a stimulant and the active ingredient in many cold medicines. People may abuse pseudoephedrine to experience hallucinations or an intense "body high."
Pseudoephedrine is often used to produce illicit drugs like methamphetamine. Abusing pseudoephedrine can cause irregular heartbeat, shortness of breath, high blood pressure, dizziness and seizures.

### Motion sickness pills *(Dimenhydrinate)*
Dimenhydrinate is properly used to treat motion sickness and vertigo. In high doses, the drug can cause hallucinations, ringing in the ears, nausea, irregular heartbeat, seizures, coma, and even death. The drug is often abused for its psychedelic properties.

### Pain relievers (Acetaminophen)
Acetaminophen is the active ingredient in pain relievers like Tylenol. High doses and long-term use can lead to serious health problems such as permanent liver damage. Other side effects of acetaminophen abuse include diarrhea, sweating, nausea, and stomach pain. Acetaminophen is generally taken for its pain-relieving properties. Many people abuse acetaminophen to treat chronic pain.

### *Sleeping Pills*

Most over-the-counter sleeping pills are intended to be used for only two to three nights at a time. Taken too often, over the counter sleeping pills may cause rebound insomnia (sleeplessness that returns in full force when you stop taking the over-the-counter sleeping pills). In the worst case scenario, the user will begin to abuse and develop an addiction to these over-the-counter sleeping pills convincing themselves they can't sleep without it. Brand names of abusable over-the-counter sleeping pills include Excedrin PM, Unisom, Sominex, Tylenol PM, Zzz NyQuil and pharmacy brand sleep aids.

The most addictive prescribed and non-prescribed medications fall into three categories: stimulants, narcotics and sedatives. Stimulants cause the central system to speed up, and they also suppress hunger. Narcotics can cause a momentary rush or pleasurable feeling as well as pain relief. Sedatives slow the body down, cause drowsiness, and temporarily relieve anxiety, worry, depression and nervousness. Stimulants, narcotics and sedatives are all available in small amounts in certain over-the-counter medicines.

As a recovering addict, you should never purchase an over-the-counter medication on your own unless instructed by a healthcare professional about which medicines are "safe" to purchase. A mouthwash you might consider harmless can contain alcohol, a mood-altering drug you may not be able to have even in small doses. Diet pills often contain stimulants to make the dieter burn off extra calories; these often lead to the use of stronger stimulants like amphetamines. A cold or sinus medication may contain pseudoephedrine, an effective decongestant that also acts as a stimulant. Banned for Olympic athletes, pseudoephedrine should also be banned for the recovering addict.

If your healthcare provider or therapist has diagnosed a symptom that requires an over-the-counter medicine and has <u>prescribed this medication to you,</u> then and only then should you purchase it.

Realize that for prescription addicts there can be no absolutely safe list of medicines. Listed below, however, are a few non-addictive medicines, suggested by pharmacists as reasonably safe for you, and the symptoms or ailment these medicines treat.

### Safe Over-the-counter (OTC) medicines

| | |
|---|---|
| Headache: | Aspirin, Extra Strength Tylenol, Bufferin, Advil, Aleve, Ibuprofen |
| Stomach acid, nausea: | Pepto-Bismol, Emetrol, Nausetrol, Emecheck |
| Nasal congestion: | Ocean, Humist, Ayr, Saline, Nasal, Salinex |
| Sore throat: | Vicks, Chloraseptic, Sucrets lozenges, Vicks cough drops |
| Mouthwash: | Cepastat |
| Cough, cold: | Naldecon Senior EX, Robitussin (not DM), Breonesin capsule |
| Insomnia aids: | Camomille Tea, Sleep-time Tea, warm milk |

I have devoted pages to the use of over-the-counter medication by the prescription addict because, while a great many relapses are triggered by such factors as boredom and anger, prescription addiction still is a disease of drug abuse. Having clear rules about what substances you can have and what to stay away from is basic to recovery. Using medications not prescribed for you or misusing any similar substance is relapse.

When will you know you are out of the woods and you will not be facing relapse again?

One answer is NEVER.

As Teresa explains after several years of recovery, "I still go to support groups and meet with my recovery coach because I am still petrified that one day I may take a Percocet and I'll be back where I was years ago." Fear of relapse is a good thing when it comes to keeping yourself in recovery. Remembering where you once were and how you see yourself today is a great place to feel and live in everyday.

Another answer is SOME DAY.

Remember Carol, who detoxed and recovered under a doctor's supervision without her husband ever knowing she was addicted? Here, Carol reveals how she knew she'd "made it:"

*My husband had dental surgery recently and will have to have it again in a few weeks. The dental surgeon gave him a prescription for the same painkiller I had been addicted to. I had to go to the same drugstore where I had gotten many of my refills to have his prescription filled. Then I had to carry the pills home, bring them to my husband with a glass of water, and watch him swallow them. He has no idea these pills might be a temptation for me. He didn't take all of the pills this time. He is saving the rest for his next round of surgery. Every time I go in the bathroom, I know they are there in the medicine cabinet; I see them often. I think about them, but what I think is, "I'm never going to take another one of those in my life!" That's how I know I've made it.*

As part of my professional work, I conduct virtual recovery coach group meetings of Prescriptions Anonymous by Skype. One day I asked the group what it would take in their lives to be able to move successfully through the steps to true recovery. Here's what they said:

- Have faith that a solution is possible if you keep searching for it. Adopt an attitude of positive expectations, allowing yourself to be lifted up, to be happy, to grow, to laugh, to cry, to feel all there is to feel.

- Learn to **forgive yourself.** Forgiving yourself means getting back the good that has been lost and moving forward with a new outlook on life. It means freeing yourself of resentments, embarrassment, guilt, anger, and shame. Forgiving yourself means getting another chance, changing your behavior, and releasing your past.

- Take responsibility for at least part of the past so that you have strength over the future. Responsibility means no longer blaming others for the mistakes you made.

- Attend support group meetings frequently to maintain your mental and physical health. Through sharing and listening to others, we learn to be honest with others and ourselves while building self-worth and self-respect.

- Seek "partners in recovery" and mentors to ensure their support. Concern, support, and input from others are essential to the recovery process. Others can identify our fears and resentments better than we can, as well as our addictive behaviors. Partners in recovery and recovery coaches can be a link when you need comfort, understanding, and structure to minimize the risk of relapse.

- Learn to take charge of your time. Plan your day. Make decisions and choices that serve your recovery and make them early in the day so things don't come at you haphazardly (causing stress) or so you find yourself with nothing to do.
- Stop looking for magical answers and participate fully in solving your own problems. Magic didn't get you into this, and magic isn't going to get you out. You have to work at recovery every day.
- Live each day with your head held high and as much joy, honesty, trust, and serenity as you can.
- Share with others, as those have before you, the courage, wisdom and serenity you have received through your recovery program.
- Live, Love, and Laugh again!

In the spirit of courage, wisdom and serenity, I asked the group to tell me what activities, places, or states of mind they seek when they are tempted to relapse. You could ask your own support group the same question. Here's what they shared with me.

- **I love taking time for myself away from distractions to sort things out.**
  Solitude gives you a chance to reflect on your day and helps build inner strength and peace. Learning to love solitude means you like being alone with yourself in a healthy way. If solitude allows you to become depressed or think negative thoughts, you're not ready for it yet. Seek the company of others instead.

- **I enjoy lighting aromatherapy candles and curling up on the sofa with a good book.**
  You should do what makes you feel peaceful when the bad urges or negative feelings hit.

- **I love to laugh. It makes my heart and stomach feel good!**
  Laughter promotes physical and emotional healing. Just ask Hunter Doherty, M.D. "Patch" Adams, an American physician, comedian, social activist, author of a Patch Adams movie, and founder of Gesundheit Institute in Virginia. His work demonstrates what studies have found, that laughter stimulates the immune system by increasing antibodies. So call a funny friend or rent a sidesplitting comedy such as "Patch Adams," starring Robin Williams, to help raise your spirits.

- **I enjoy painting and drawing. It helps me express my emotions in a healthy and creative way. It also gives me a sense of accomplishment that is very personal and private.**
  Artistic endeavors, like drawing, painting, sculpting, writing poetry, craft-work, dancing, and acting help to release stress and other negative emotions while fighting boredom and providing a sense of pride and accomplishment.

- **Hugs give me a sense of security, belonging, support, and calm.**
  Touch is very therapeutic and healing. It's intimate and personal. Humans need touch for emotional and spiritual growth. A simple hug can reduce stress and can make someone

feel loved and accepted unconditionally. Ask for hugs from your loved ones and urge them to give them liberally. Sometimes you may have to hug them first. Hug a family pet! They love unconditionally and ask nothing in return.

- **I enjoy the rejuvenated feeling I get after taking a yoga class. Yoga helps me to focus on myself. The meditating, stretching, and breathing exercises turn off all outside influences and help put spiritual balance in my day.**
  There are so many different types of yoga—Hatha yoga, Bhakti, Jnana yoga, Karma yoga, Tantra and others—that you should be able to find one style that is tailored to your needs and goals. Classes can be found in the newspaper, on the Internet, in bookstores, in schools, or simply by word of mouth.

- **Falling in love heals me.**
  Love is a most powerful tool for healing. Allow yourself to be open to love and freely, unselfishly share it with others. When you open yourself to love, your spirit blossoms. Love should not be selfish, possessive, abusive or jealous. These are neurotic forms of love which are destructive, draining, and dangerous to your recovery. When you open yourself up to true love, you open up a world of wonderful possibilities.

- **I ask for help from God through prayer.**
  Prayer allows you to connect with your higher power (who or whatever it may be), allowing you to ask for forgiveness, offer thanks, and ask for healing, courage, wisdom, and serenity.

When something feels too big for you to handle alone, you can always ask for God's help because nothing is too big for Him/Her to handle.

- **I've found that when I reward myself for the hard work I've put into staying sober, I reinforce my success, and I stick with it.**

    Rewards are a great way to congratulate yourself and keep motivated. However, this doesn't mean you should buy out the store (remember that shopping can be a cross-addiction). Limit yourself to one or two small items as a way to say, "Keep up the good work." You can also reward yourself by getting a manicure or pedicure, or by going to the movies or to a sporting event.

- **I call my therapist and recovery coach.**

    This is an often-repeated suggestion. If your therapist or recovery coach discourages calls when you feel you are in danger of relapsing, get a new therapist or recovery coach with whom you feel good and who understands your needs for support and encouragement. My own therapist and recovery coach have been lifelines to peace and understanding without judgment or criticism. They continually encourage me in my addiction recovery and support my achievements no matter how small or large. My therapist LISTENS where other people have not. She guides me as I work through my shame and guilt of my past. She allows me to get my anger out and, if I'm feeling especially vulnerable, she will suggest that I go to a support group meeting or spend time with people I enjoy. She will also suggest activities to help me work through my vulnerability. If I were close to "using" again, my therapist and recovery coach would strongly suggest that I be admitted into a treatment center for observation until I worked through the reasons for wanting to use drugs again.

A good therapist or recovery coach does for you what you can't do for yourself, whenever you need his or her help and until you can stand on your own. A Certified Addiction Recovery coach can also be available for overnight observation including sober companion escorting for special events to ensure you don't relapse and stay in recovery.

Whether you never relapse or relapse once or a dozen times, all recovering addicts have several goals in common: to live drug-free, to find happiness, to move on with their lives as whole individuals, and to leave their pasts behind without resentment or blame. In the beginning, the recovering addict focuses on being alive for just one minute at a time. Then minutes turn into hours, hours into days, days into weeks, and, finally, months into years of accomplishments and contributions to family, marriage, and career. Reaching out for help is the first step, then reaching out again and again if you slip, until finally you are the one to whom people reach out for your wisdom, strength, and hope.

Finally, let me quote from Richard Taite, CEO and Founder of Cliffside Malibu in California, his viewpoints on relapse:

> "Recognize that relapse temptation is short-lived. The thought or craving to use generally lasts no more than thirty minutes.
>
> "Know your triggers. In therapy, you'll learn about your personal triggers. What are the hard things that get you

to want to use? Is it driving down a particular street, a certain time of day, or a situation at work? If you know what your triggers are, you can learn to avoid them. If you cannot avoid them, have a plan for when you are triggered and know what you can do to keep yourself safe.

"Meditate. The more you practice meditation, the more you will change your brain in positive ways. Meditation is one of the most grounding activities you can participate in. Although it is difficult to do at the beginning, keep practicing until you are doing at least 30 minutes morning and evening. Once you have bulked up your practice, you'll find that it is one of the most important aspects of your day.

"Exercise– Exercise activates your body chemistry in ways that tell the brain that using is not important. If you want to drink or self-medicate every day after work, instead, make a habit of going to the gym. This change will quickly supplant your desire to use and you'll feel and be healthier for the effort."

# >>> 10

# A Family Disease:

*"My addiction stressed my family to the breaking point."*

The addict, as long as he is not caught, may think he's not hurting anyone else but himself. However, a person who says her pill addiction or alcoholism is not hurting her family is engaging in a form of denial. Addiction **is** a family disease. Addiction affects all members of the family, and their behavior—whether it is ignoring or enabling—allows the addiction to continue.

If you, the reader, are an addict, here is a moving story about what families go through. If you're a family member or friend of an addict, here is an example of others who have suffered in your role.

David, the husband of Shawna, who first described her addiction in Chapter 2, tells his story:

## David's Story

*When I first met Shawna at a church activity in 1991, her beauty, intelligence, and charm immediately caught my attention. Shawna was everything that I had been looking for in a woman. We began dating and fell madly in love. One thing that I quickly learned about Shawna was that she sometimes suffered from poor health. She had frequent headaches and fainting spells. In addition, she told me that she had experienced numerous surgeries at a young age, including open heart surgery, back surgery, stomach surgery, and gynecological surgery. I thought this was a bit unusual, but knowing about her medical history increased my admiration for her because she had kept such a positive attitude in the face of adversity. After some careful thought and prayer, I knew in my heart that I loved her enough that her medical problems would not scare me away. Seven months after we met, we were married in Oakland, California. What I did not know at that happy time was that my new wife, the girl of my dreams, was a controlled substance addict.*

*The first year of our marriage passed as we went through the normal adjustment period that most newly married couples go through. During this time, Shawna continued to have health problems and frequently went to the doctor for a variety of complaints. I was very naive and never questioned the validity of her problems. The doctor bills were mounting, and I began to be concerned, but I never questioned whether or not her problems were real. I trusted her.*

*One day, out of the blue, Shawna approached me with an anxious look on her pale face. She said that she needed to confess something to me that might cause me to hate her and ruin our marriage. Nervously, I told her to proceed. She said, "You know the medical problems I have been having.*

*Well, I have been faking them...for my entire life." She then added, "And I think I have a problem with taking too many medications." I was devastated. My world would never be the same, and I knew it. She explained that she could not take the pressure of living a lie anymore. She said, "I know I am going to hell if I don't make changes in my life."*

*Not knowing what else to do, I asked her to go speak to our pastor about these problems. He was very kind, but he really had no idea how to deal with the issue. As amazing as it now seems, I still was unable to put two and two together. I thought that her admitted problem with faking illnesses was based on something psychological—perhaps the need for attention—and I didn't connect it with her comment about taking too much medication. I considered the faking of illnesses to be a much more serious problem.*

*While she was in counseling with our pastor, I went to the library and began researching psychiatric disorders related to faking illnesses. I came across some information on a rare disorder known as Munchausen syndrome. This mental illness causes the victim to seek attention from medical personnel and others by feigning sickness. All of the symptoms seemed to fit my wife perfectly. I thought I had discovered her problem. I copied the research and took it to a well-meaning psychiatrist, who met with my wife and confirmed the diagnosis. He informed me that, while there was some hope that she might be cured of this problem, it was unlikely. Most Munchausen patients haunt hospitals, undergoing numerous unnecessary surgeries, for the rest of their lives. Shawna accepted the diagnosis and agreed to go to weekly psychiatric counseling. The doctor also told us that Shawna was suffering from depression, and he prescribed antidepressants.*

*I was so horrified by the Munchausen diagnosis that I completely forgot about my wife's statement that she was taking too much medication. I knew little or nothing about prescription drug abuse. I trusted her doctors and believed that they would never prescribe more medication than she could handle. We did attend one Narcotics Anonymous support group meeting together, just to find out what the program was all about. I was turned off by the appearance of the addicts and the foul language that was being used in the meeting. I figured these were street-drug users and junkies. My wife and I did not belong among this group of society's outcasts. I now realize the foolishness of this judgment, but, at the time, I wanted nothing to do with these addicts. So we stopped going. I figured that having her admit to the problem with pills was enough. Now that it was out in the open, I believed she would never do it again.*

*Shawna continued her counseling and seemed to be improving. We did our best to move on and put our marriage and our lives back together again. Our first child, a healthy baby boy, was born a year later and brought a great deal of joy to our home.*

*Despite this wonderful event, something still seemed wrong. Shawna continued to have numerous medical problems, which, of course, made me suspicious. However, despite my concerns, I was unable to prove that any of her problems weren't genuine. She would sometimes have a difficult time getting out of bed to take care of the baby, but I rationalized these incidents away.*

*Shawna's second pregnancy was a nightmare. She went into early labor and was in and out of the hospital for three months. During this time, she kept pleading for painkillers because she said the contractions were hurting. Eventually, she gave premature birth to our second child, a little girl, ten weeks before she was due. The baby weighed a little over two pounds. As a father, I cannot begin to describe the terror caused by this event. This is not the way to have a baby. She looked like a little doll except she had countless tubes and wires attached to her small body. A large machine breathed for her.*

*Our baby survived, but she spent almost two months in the hospital. Meanwhile, Shawna was getting worse. Her depression came back with* a vengeance. The pressure and strain of having a baby in the newborn intensive care unit was unbelievable. The cause of the premature birth was never determined.

One night, Shawna came to me and told me that she was going to kill herself. She said that I would be better off with another wife and that she had a plan to end her life with pills that she had hidden. I tried to reason with her, but she would not listen. She seemed to be in a daze. I immediately took her to the hospital, where they admitted her for severe depression and suicidal ideation. She was confined to the psychiatric ward for a week. During this time, I moved in with my parents who, like angels of mercy, helped take care of my children, so I would not lose my job.

Shawna's depression was so bad that her doctors performed electrodeconvulsive therapy (ECT) on her. This was a frightening procedure that caused her to lose her short-term memory each time it was done. One time, as she was regaining consciousness, she mumbled to me that she was to blame for our daughter's premature birth. The nurse told her to be quiet and told me not to believe what a person says when they are coming out of anesthesia. This seemed strange, but I believed the nurse.

Shawna was released from the hospital, and we all returned home. After a while, she started doing better and desperately wanted to become pregnant again. We consulted our doctor, who told us there was little chance we would have another premature baby and that everything should be fine. So we decided to go ahead and soon conceived another child.

The same nightmare returned. Shawna went into early labor and was hospitalized. I could not believe what was happening. Our second baby boy was born eight weeks early. He was very sick, but not as sick as our daughter had been. He was in the intensive care unit for several weeks. Our medical bills were sky high. Each premature birth cost over $80,000. We were struggling financially as a constant wave of medical bills washed up into our mailbox.

Completely worn out from her two premature pregnancies, Shawna again sank into a very deep depression. She was now seeing a psychologist and a psychiatrist. The psychiatrist was giving her some pretty powerful medications such as Xanax, a benzodiazepine. At the time, I knew nothing about benzodiazepines and was grateful for any help we could get from her doctors.

Then came that fateful night when I came home from work and discovered Shawna in a zombie-like state lying on our couch. She was barely cognizant and was mumbling something that I couldn't understand. I had a feeling that something was terribly wrong. I ran to the cabinet and began going through her medications. I found a bottle for a newly filled prescription, counted the pills, and discovered over forty pills were already missing. I could not believe she had taken that much medication. That amount should have killed the average person. I called Poison Control, and they told me her life was in danger. I rushed her to the hospital, where they proceeded to pump her stomach. The next day, she told the doctors she did not remember taking so much medication and that she must have done it by accident. I did not believe her and asked that she be placed in the psychiatric ward for her own protection. In this setting, she finally admitted her prescription addiction drug problem.

While Shawna was in detox at the hospital, I went to meet with our family doctor. He ran a check on her prescription history (using a state sponsored database) and discovered that she had been doctor shopping for many years. He told me that she was definitely addicted to painkillers and anti-depressants. The pieces were all starting to come together. I was relieved to discover that she did not have Munchausen syndrome after *all. Many of her fake medical problems in the past could be attributed to drug-seeking behavior.* Shawna later admitted that the multiple unnecessary surgeries she had were done just so she could get drugs.

Concerned about the astonishingly high levels of medication that were being prescribed by her psychiatrist, I went to speak with him. I told him about her problem with addiction, and he said that he now understood. He said that he would need to taper down the medication, so she would not go into seizures. I trusted him—which turned out to be a huge mistake. At the time, I didn't realize that most physicians have no idea how to handle pill addiction.

When Shawna was released from the hospital, we both decided that she would be better off moving in with her parents (who lived about 180 miles away) until she could put her life back together. I took the kids and moved back in with my parents. This separation was painful, but I figured it was her only chance for success.

Shawna lived with her parents for a couple of months. She attended an outpatient drug abuse program and occasionally came down to visit the children and me. She said that the outpatient program was working and that it was so nice to finally be free of the drugs that had ruled her life. We started making plans to get back together. Then, it happened again.

I was at work one day when I suddenly had a distinct desire to pick up the phone and call Shawna's psychiatrist. His administrative assistant answered, and I told her that I wanted to reiterate the fact that Shawna was an addict and that the doctor needed to be careful. The assistant paused for a moment, then said, "Shawna just called us for a refill on her opioid medications." I practically dropped the phone. Shawna had told me she had not been using Lortab painkillers for months. When I asked to speak to the doctor, the assistant told me that he would not talk to me because of laws dealing with patient confidentiality. A patient must sign a disclosure confidentiality form stating who is allowed privilege of information about a patient. Shawna had not signed this form, keeping her secrets confined with her psychiatrist, because she feared what would happen if I had known what was really going on. In fact, I could tell (based on her nervousness) that the administrative assistant realized that she had broken the law by giving me the information about the Lortab. I was furious that the doctor would not speak to me, but I was grateful that the assistant had told me the truth.

I immediately confronted Shawna about the painkiller refills, and she started making all kinds of lame excuses. This time, however, I refused to back down. She knew she was caught. She admitted that she had been using while living with her parents. She would have her psychiatrist phone in (long- distance) a variety of prescription drugs. I was at the end of my rope. I told Shawna I was going to leave her and take custody of the children if she did not get her life together immediately. She said she thought she needed to go to inpatient treatment if she was going to have any chance of success. We took her for an evaluation at a government-sponsored inpatient drug rehabilitation treatment center, and they admitted her the same day. I had little faith that, after all the deception, she would be able to turn her life around. Just in case, I looked up the phone number for the county divorce education clerk. This time, I was deadly serious. It was a do-or-die situation. Although I loved Shawna, I honestly had little hope that our marriage could survive this ordeal.

After Shawna went into treatment, I wrote a letter to her psychiatrist (because he wouldn't talk to me), letting him know that I would turn him in to the DEA, his professional medical board, and the state if he continued to prescribe controlled substance medications for my wife. I also threatened to sue him for malpractice because, even though I personally told him that she was a pill addict, he continued to prescribe addictive medications. I told him I would send him my wife's rehab bill that was rapidly approaching over $10,000. My threats appear to have worked. He never prescribed anything for my wife again and never returned to his practice again.

When Shawna went into treatment, I was at the lowest point of my life. I was exhausted and began to feel the icy fingers of depression closing around me. All of my hopes and dreams were gone.

One night, I had a strong feeling that I should drive to my place of worship. It was a cold night, and there was snow on the ground. I did not feel worthy to enter, so I stood outside and poured my heart out to God. My prayer went something like this:

"God, I stand before Your house. What kind of a husband am I? My wife has been using drugs for fifteen years, and I didn't know it. How can I be so stupid? Why didn't I know? Why didn't you tell me? I once believed that I could 'fix' my wife's problems, that I had the intellect to diagnose and resolve her condition. I also believed that I could fight her problems with my own strength and wisdom. I have come to You tonight to admit that I have been beaten. This thing call 'addiction' is far too strong for me to deal with. You are the only power in the universe that can slay this beast. I surrender and plead with You to join the battle. Please save my wife because I cannot."

In the cold, I could see my own breath, and everything around me was silent. Then a feeling of peace and comfort began to warm my heart. I knew God was listening and this matter was now in His hands. I drove home with the feeling that a tremendous burden had been lifted. To this day, I believe God answered my prayer that night.

Shawna was in inpatient treatment for about six weeks. She was not allowed to leave the treatment center for any reason in order to stabilize her while she was detoxing and work through the history of trauma she had endured over the years.

*During that time, she experienced terrible withdrawal symptoms, including a seizure that sent her to the hospital. The counselors at the treatment center were able to break through the thick layers of denial that had built up over many years. When she was released, she began attending a mandatory day treatment program and went to support meetings every night. The counselors at a 12-step treatment facility told her that she needed to go to "ninety meetings in ninety days." This was hard on me because it seemed like she was gone so much. However, I understood that it was very important for me not to do anything that could sabotage her recovery efforts.*

*After several months of being in recovery, Shawna was able to admit that the premature births of our children were probably caused by drug use during the pregnancies. This has been the most difficult issue for both of us to come to terms with. We also discovered that loss of trust is an inevitable consequence of drug abuse; we have really had to work on that loss in our marriage.*

*I have to admit that, at first, I was terrified to live the rest of my life married to a recovering pill addict. The counselors told me there was no "cure" for the disease of addiction. That thought scared me. However, I have discovered that living with a recovering addict, as long as they are taking their recovery seriously, isn't much different from living with a non-addict. My wife is clean now, and we live a pretty normal life. She needs to go to Narcotics Anonymous meetings or Prescriptions Anonymous virtual meetings to get support from home. To me this is a small price to pay.*

*In the end, I am especially grateful to God for the miracle that He worked in my family's life. Without His help, I know there would have been no happy ending. I have discovered that God does not give up on any of us very easily. I almost hit the "panic button" with my wife, and now I am so glad that I hung in there—even when things got really rough.*

*A marriage is not a trivial thing to break up. God has miraculously restored the love and trust between my wife and me. Together, we now carry His message of hope and freedom to anyone who will listen.*

Alcohol often plays a big part with any addiction, whether the addiction is for alcohol alone or added to other controlled substance medicines. This next story comes from a grown child that endured years of abuse from both of his parents because of their alcoholism. The impact on children is sad to read and frightening to live through.

### Logan's Story

*I am a 60-year-old ACOA (Adult Child of Alcoholics). In my case both of my parents drank, and ultimately suffered, died, and were buried as alcoholics. My father was only 59 years old, my mother only 46, when alcohol claimed their young lives. I still wear the emotional scars emerging from a destructive and dysfunctional alcoholic family, and I always will. As painful as it is for me to relive and relate my story, I do so in the hope that others who suffered as I have will gain the knowledge that true happiness and a greater quality of life await you, if you haven't already found it. My story is that of tragedy, failures, successes, and survival. My upbringing, or lack thereof, has made me who I am today. In some strange way I thank my parents for the job they didn't do! In spite of it all, I have the ability to love, laugh, feel emotions and express them, to trust others, and best of all I have learned to like the person I have become.*

*I was the youngest of three children. Because of the age differences between my sister, brother, and me, I felt like an only child. As the years came and went, I saw there were other differences that set us apart. Rather than band together through strength in numbers, we were driven apart to fend for ourselves. Each of us established our own attempt at survival. Some of us were more successful than others. I instinctively learned, at a very early age, how to play the game and avoid the beatings my siblings got on a regular basis. Once the alcohol took over my parents' minds and bodies, which was usually by 7:00 o'clock each night, they sought out fights, which consisted of both mental and physical abuse of each other, my siblings, or both. An ongoing scenario, played almost nightly, would be for one of my parents to holler down from the top of the stairs and ask if someone was on the phone. Regardless of what the answer was, my parents, already under the influence, just needed an excuse to beat somebody. One of them, usually my father, would storm down the stairs and often beat whoever he thought was on the phone. It didn't take a rocket scientist to know that all I had to do was to stay away from the phone to avoid the physical abuse. I don't know when I became aware that alcohol was the driving force of our family. I just know it was always there. My parents' daily routine was simple: work all day, drink all night, mentally and physically abuse each other and their kids. I recall each day as a carbon copy of the previous one. My parents never hugged, kissed, or showed any affection for each other or us. My mother's face always had a look of sadness, withdrawn into her own world. Her battle scars showed on her face, evidence left behind from previous nights' beatings, wounds not yet healed. Her eyes remained black and blue from prolonged years of beatings. I thought it was her normal skin tone. I was with my mother frequently as a young child and rode with her to pick my father up from work in the evening. Their first stop was the liquor store where they purchased their "drug of choice," Seagram's 7. To this day I can't stand the smell of this brand of liquor. Before leaving the parking lot, the top was off the bottle, and they would pass the bottle back and forth with the brown wrapper still on it, as if people didn't know what it was they really were drinking. It was the only time of the day they got along, the one thing they had in common.*

*I quickly learned how to be the "perfect child" for fear that I would be killed if I ever received a beating like those my siblings endured. When my father administered punishment, he used a razor strap, a four-inch by three-foot long piece of leather just like the ones once attached to the side of a barber's chair, used to sharpen razors. I witnessed welts, indentations, and bloody wounds on my siblings' bodies, and I wanted no part of it! I decided it was much better to be a friend rather than an enemy to my parents. When my mother asked me to do something, I did so happily, or at least had the appearance of being happy. That led to a life of co-dependency. It was much easier to please my father. All I had to do was stay away from him. There was no ball playing on the weekends, no family vacations, no "How was your day, Son?" I never really knew my father, except to know he was an angry person. He breathed anger, and I could smell it on him.*

*Every night until the night my mother died, she had the same evening routine. Once the drinking began, I knew I had about an hour before "show time." She would stumble or fall down a flight of stairs on her way to the kitchen. Even though she had dinner just an hour or two before, she raided the refrigerator in her drunken state every single night without fail. Instead of kitchen implements, she used her hands. Mayonnaise and other food were spread everywhere, on herself, on the walls of the dining room, living room, and stairway as she made— or attempted to make—her way back to the bedroom after the feeding frenzy. It was a virtual guarantee that every few nights she would be so drunk that she passed out on the kitchen floor or failed to negotiate the stairs and fell down the entire flight. There were nights I cleaned blood, vomit, and urine off floors. There were trips to the hospital and the occasional visit from the police, when my parents' fights spilled out into the front yard. All of it scared the hell out of me. My brother and sister were probably smarter than I was. They usually locked themselves in their rooms and refused to get involved. There were times when I acted as a human shield, standing between my mother and father so he would not strike her.*

*I had a glimmer of hope when I turned fourteen. Little did I know then that in just a few months my mother would be dead. My best friend Todd lived down the street. His mother was a recovering alcoholic. His family introduced me to the concept of AA (Alcoholics Anonymous), and I attended an open AA meeting without my parents' knowledge. For the first time I heard and spoke with adult alcoholics who told their life stories. In spite of their lifelong ordeals with alcohol, I viewed their overall lives as success stories because they found sobriety. I was so happy for them, and it gave me hope for my parents. I did exactly what I was supposed to do. Without accusing my parents of anything, I simply brought information home and left it around the house. That was the first time I ever saw my mother so mad that she wanted to hit me. She was angry that I would even infer that she had a problem with alcohol. I was told under no uncertain terms to never bring up the subject again. Even at the tender age of fourteen, I knew that, unless she or my father wanted help, it just wouldn't work. I never brought it up again. I never had time. The last year of my mother's life was a living hell for all concerned. That year I did poorly in school, unable to focus on what should have been important, like grades, sports, girls, parties, and just having fun. Instead, I was consumed with thoughts of how will I get through this day, where will get my next meal, will I have to carry my mother from the kitchen to the bedroom again, or will my parents fight to their death tonight. I lived in constant fear and was a virtual prisoner in my own home. I was afraid that, if I left, something terrible would happen. The one time I did, for just a couple of hours to visit with friends, I came home to find the window in the front door broken with wet blood smeared on the door. My father kicked my mother and locked her out of the house. Her only recourse, with the mind of an angry drunk, was to break the glass with her bare hand to gain entry. She cut her finger so bad I thought she would bleed to death. The role reversal was complete. I didn't go out of the house except to go to school for an entire year. I corrected my parents when they misbehaved. I sent them to their rooms when I thought it was necessary. I prepared meals, and I broke up their fights. The only thing I couldn't control was their drinking. I stopped trying a long time ago. Death came for my mother suddenly and without warning. Within days of my brother's return from Vietnam and my sister's arrival in the area, we, the siblings, went to a coming home party for my brother. I will never forget this night. We returned home several hours later to find every light in the house on. I knew something was wrong. I felt it in my bones. I ran to the house; my father was standing at the door.*

*When he said she was "gone," the rage in me ignited, and I struck him and demanded to know where she was. She was dead. She had gotten drunk, raided the refrigerator, and fallen on the kitchen floor, as usual. Only this time, she choked on a piece of bologna and suffocated. It was the mix of alcohol and missing or broken teeth from falling and fist fights with my father that made it impossible for her to chew properly so that ultimately she died an excruciatingly painful and frightening death.*

*I blamed my father and myself for many years. In reality, I had taken care of myself and parents for years. I eventually drew strength from this realization and began to see myself as a survivor. I was growing up much too fast, but my fate had been mapped out, and I had to "roll with the punches" and make the best of my life without good role models to learn from. My father died two years later on Christmas Eve. Cirrhosis of the liver, pure and simple. My father's drinking increased after my mother's death, and he attacked me while I was in the bathroom one day. Once again, the rage of my youth was ignited, and I nearly killed him. I left home that day and swore I would never return. I was true to my word. I was only fifteen. When he died, I didn't shed a tear. It wasn't until my thirties, going through my first divorce and psychotherapy, that I removed the blinders from my eyes and allowed myself the pleasure of standing over his grave and telling him angrily what he did to all of our lives. I cried that day and thought the tears would never stop. It has taken me years, but I have learned to forgive both of my parents. Without excusing their behavior or lack of parenting skills, they loved us the best they could and the only way they knew. They gave us what they could; it just wasn't what we needed for a normal, happy, and healthy life.*

*There has been additional fallout. I have been through three failed marriages and have made my fair share of mistakes along the way. Because of the life I have lived and the memories of dysfunctional living, at the age of 60, I look ahead to each day as a new beginning. I draw as much goodness out of each day as possible. There is still so much life to live and experience. Right at this moment I am looking forward to the events of today, no matter how simple or difficult this day will become. I am determined to make the best of it. If I can help just one person understand that he or she is not alone, the way I felt for so many years, and survival is not only possible but actually sweeter because of our life's experiences, then this story is a success and my hopes have been realized.*

Here is the story of another child who suffered greatly from the addiction of a parent. Brandon's mother Marjorie was addicted to prescription drugs. What happened to her was bad enough, but an additional tragedy was that the children in her family thought their unhealthy family dynamics represented normal family life and behavior. Her children grew up without normal social skills, using deceit to avoid being close to other people. Her story shows how deeply the illness of addiction affects the entire family. Brandon described for me how the family coped with his mother's addiction.

### *Brandon's Story*

*My mom's addiction started early in her life. When she was twelve years old and her parents divorced, her grandmother gave her sleeping pills to help her rest. It was the 1950s, and America was in the era of Mother's Little Helper, in which doctors, delighted with a new array of pharmaceuticals designed for stress disorders and panic attacks, were handing out serious mood elevators like candy to depressed patients. My mother, like other children in this era, grew up in a pill happy environment. No one could foresee the effects these pills would have on families for generations to come. By the time I was born, my mom had a bent for pills, often in combination with alcohol, that would take the edge off her mounting responsibilities. Her marriage to my dad during that time was all fun and games. They had friends, a nice house, my newborn sister, and myself. Life for my mom was consistent. She was the model housewife. My dad was an up-and-coming salesman, who went to school at night to secure a bright future. The first danger signs I remember coincided with a move to the country. Big parties on weekends, which were fun for all us kids, usually ended with my mom having to be put to bed. My first glimpses into the vortex of disaster were those moments of uncertainty, not knowing the problem or why Mom was acting so funny. And so it went year after year with me not understanding what was really going on until the birth of my baby brother, when I saw the intensity of her illness growing. My dad by now was on the road a lot with his job, so the job of "watching Mom" became a normal thing for me and my sister. We learned the art of trickery to keep my mom out of trouble and her problem a secret from the outside* world: we hid the pills, watered down or poured out all liquors and, most importantly, hid the car keys. Dad's wrath for letting her drive the car away was harsh, so we were very efficient at our job. Protecting the image of the family became the status quo. I was a master liar by age ten. For example, I concocted stories to deceive friends and teachers when my mother didn't come to pick me up from school. That kind of nightmare was our normal family routine.

Meanwhile, the country doctor, who essentially was her dealer, didn't read the signs, or maybe he did and found it easier to look the other way. Besides, he probably had a new car from all the money that my dad paid trying to make mom well. Everybody knew about Mom but didn't know what to do except give her a different kind of pill.

Therapy seemed logical, but it brought out more destructive patterns. The more psychiatrists pried into the hurt resulting from the divorce of Mom's parents, the more she would shut the door and hide in her little inner world of hurt where she used the only thing that would take all the pain away—PILLS!

Mom learned to speak "The Language" which enabled her to get any kind of pill. One memory comes to mind: When I was with my mom at the doctor's office and she explained her symptoms, the doctor proceeded to pull out a physician's pharmaceutical pill book that looked like the kind of tablet that Charlton Heston held in his film role of Moses. I'd never seen anything so big in my life. And when he opened it up, it was nothing but pages and pages of colorful rows of pills. The doctor would flip through the pages, all the while listening to my mom, and, finally, like pinning the tail on the donkey, he would point to a specific pill and say, "Let's try this one!"

It was absurd to me that she even bothered visiting a doctor to get more pills. She already had a mini pharmaceutical storage room in our kitchen cabinets. Every time we opened a cabinet door to find some food, *a small, caramel-colored bottle with a white, childproof cap would come tumbling out.*

*The real challenge came in my years as an adolescent female in the role of being a Cinderella in a school play. Hell, I was forced to grow up so fast that I felt like a twenty-five-year-old in a fourteen-year-old body. I had seen things no child should ever see, and it had made me skeptical of those who really did seem to care about my family and me. The ability to enjoy my youth was tainted with dread. I was always wondering if bringing home new friends would turn out to be like a scene from the Addams Family. Therefore, the desire to make friends was hampered, and I started to hide within a shell of books and adolescent fantasy.*

*By this time, the relationship that had seemed somewhat normal between mom and dad began to deteriorate. My dad's frustration and inexperience dealing with emotions that came from the heart fed the fire. He started to distance himself from her and us. Physical fights between them were becoming more and more frequent. Then we had to lie to cover up the reason for my mom wearing sunglasses around the house. Craziness erupted in the middle of the night as my mom fought off the demons in her sleep. Every day my mom had a new problem; every day was a battle to hide whatever we thought was the problem. A never-ending series of cyclonic episodes destroyed our home life. The peaks and valleys of alternating good times and bad times were slowly killing a little part of all our hearts. We were learning about the true definition of addiction, and we didn't even know anything about pill addiction. We learned to distance ourselves from the turmoil and create modes of operation that were escape mechanisms. Temporary ploys of entertainment took us away from the reality of our lives, where things could turn on a dime.*

*My out, my escape, came with a scholarship to college. Eager to experience a new life, I hoped that the tumult that filled my home would disappear and I would have a chance to have a normal life. What I soon realized was the modes of living at home were far less cruel than the ones that awaited me in the real world. I had spent so much time at home absorbed with Mom that I hadn't learned the social skills needed to protect myself. Instead, I had learned a set of skills that were now inappropriate.*

*Learning quickly how people operate was a new hobby: watching after my mom had chiseled me into a master of details, and I was a virtuoso of deceit. College soon became a snap. I made it through without people really knowing me or my past. In order to have true friends, I concluded, you have to take on a lot of their baggage, help them, pamper them, give them a lot of time and effort. Frankly, I didn't have the time or heart for others.*

*I was relieved to no longer have the responsibility of dealing with my mother. My relationship with her was reduced to a random series of phone calls. I would sit and listen to her idle chatter, tell her how much I loved her, and say goodbye. I had become hardened and didn't want to deal with all her problems.*

*I had become self-absorbed, not really trying to understand my moods. I went through my life intensely wanting to be part of something; however, I never really made an effort to be part of anything.*
*It was a debilitating circle. I went through my life in a series of near successes, never grabbing the brass ring, but learning a lot of hard lessons along the way.*

*My second chance came with meeting the person who would help me heal. My second husband took the time to listen and not judge. He and my mom bonded immediately with the birth of our first child. It looked like things were finally changing. Mom had become fairly stable. There was still the occasional binge, but everyday life had started to improve when she began giving her time to teach Sunday school at a lovely Unity*

*Church. Her search for something more in life was finally being realized. What she was so intently looking for had been there, right in front of her face. She was fighting addiction with a new confidence and renewed vision. Just as my mom had finally turned toward the light, it was as if she decided she had endured enough and, without warning, died in her sleep at the age of fifty-four.*

*My mom is dead, and it had everything to do with what she had put into her body over the years. There is no one single person to blame, although I have tried to find one. The only person who could have changed the story was my mother herself.*

*I will always be angry that my mom won't be here to see my family grow, and I will always be angry that she wasn't strong enough to say No to prescription drug abuse. I will always be angry with the doctors who never really tried to cure her but instead tried out another medicine* du jour. *I will always miss the beautiful smile that welcomed me into this world. I am angry that I will never again be able to say, "I love you," to her face and hug her and tell her how proud I am that she finally found some relief from the talons of her addiction. It is too late.*

"Too late" are the saddest words. Could Brandon's story of her mother Marjorie's addiction to alcohol and pills followed by her early death have been changed? Maybe. Truthfully, we'll never know. And that is one of the hardest parts of "too late"—the finality of death, not getting the chance to say all the things you wanted to say, and not knowing what the future might have held if things had turned out differently. But such a tragedy did not have to be.

The next chapter illustrates how families—the addict and his or her loved ones—can recognize addiction, intervene, support, and participate in recovery so that their stories do not end like Logan and Brandon's did.

## >>> 11

# RECOVERY AND FAMILY
### *"I Can't Fix it!"*

When I was in treatment for my dual diagnosis, searching for any means to fight my way back into this world, I found myself confused by multiple crossroads on the road to recovery. Much of my treatment was decided by various therapists who kept me alive by telling me what I needed to do in order to "feel" better about myself. Even family members voiced their opinions about what I should and shouldn't do in order to get "my life" back in order. Friends told me what books to read for advice, and a husband that told me that he could "fix-me" so we would have a normal life together again! Is it any wonder with everyone else telling me what I should and shouldn't do that I felt like I was the only person in the world that was too dysfunctional to make my own life whole again. With everyone else knowing what was best for me, why did I relapse? Everyone else had the answer to that question, too!

The sobering fact about recovery is that the choices I make for myself, by myself, are the only ones that matter. I found myself surrounded by well-meaning co-dependents or enablers who only knew what was best for *them* to feel better and not was best for me.

Co-dependency or enabling is a progressive disease that includes an array of psychological and physical symptoms. The heartfelt caring behavior shown by the co-dependent is an unconscious effort to keep repressed pain at bay. As long as the co-dependent cares for and takes care of the addict by protecting him from consequences of his addiction, the addict can continue his addictive behavior; at the same time the co-dependent continues the caring behavior in order to gain a sense of his or her own self-worth. Each participant in co-dependence reinforces the other. Recovery from co-dependency requires major attitude and lifestyle changes.

Anyone reading that last paragraph one might feel annoyed or relieved to think about pinning all the problems in the family on the co-dependent. Don't be too quick to judge. A co-dependent's intention in the beginning is to help an addicted loved one, not to make matters worse. Co-dependents themselves can be their own worst enemy in that they don't know how to allow the addicted one to take responsibility for their own frustrating lifestyle. Accountability for our own happiness and recovery is a scary thing. Empowerment to achieve success for ourselves is of far greater value than allowing that power to be turned over to someone else.

Whole families may fall into denial when one member is addicted to prescription or over-the-counter medications. Usually it's the addict's spouse who has to deal most intimately with the addiction. Yet that person likely knows little or nothing about the signs of addiction. Even though he or she may be closest to the addicted individual, a spouse often doesn't see what is happening or is in denial about it. "My wife couldn't be addicted to prescription drugs; she would know better," the unsuspecting husband might say.

At the same time, the addict lives in denial of the effects that addiction has on family and loved ones. "I never realized the pain and suffering I caused my family," says Ellen, a recovering addict, recalling her denial. "Once my addiction to pills took over my life, I never thought I was hurting anyone else. I was the sick one; what effect could this have on them?"

Former first lady Betty Ford, who became addicted to pain pills following surgery and who founded Betty Ford Treatment Center after her recovery, calls prescription addiction "a hidden epidemic." Abuse, she said, "is swept under the rug by the prescription addict and by desperate families and friends. They can't accept the reality of a mother or aunt or sister who may be abusing pills or is addicted to pills and they simply don't know what to do about it."

If the addict can hide his addiction from himself, he can hide it from others. It takes a person who is aware of the possibility of addiction to look at the signs and recognize them.

Here are some warning signals that might indicate that a loved one has an addiction problem.

The person:
- Has a substantial increase in visits to doctors, pharmacies and dentists.
- Schedules surgeries that may not seem necessary.
- Has unexplained increasing medical bills.
- Frequently cancels plans with friends or family.
- Has a difficult time on the job or is losing a lot of time from work.
- Doesn't look you in the eyes while talking.
- Has a range of physical symptoms, for example, is hyperactive; has quick weight loss or gain; is bloated or flushed.
- Sometimes will call someone to "just talk" but can't remember the conversation the next day.

- Keeps prescription pills handy at all times and offers them freely to friends.
- Runs out of prescribed controlled substance prescriptions earlier than a pharmacist can refill.
- Roams around the house lethargically and without purpose.
- Is moody, irritable or restless; sleep patterns change.
- Spends most of his time alone and screens phone calls.
- Has money problems, borrows cash, and runs up charges on her credit cards.
- Acts contrary to his values, such as stealing, lying, and having extra-marital affairs.

Even when family members or friends do begin to get the picture, not knowing how to help, they often continue the behavior of denial. A family member or colleague may say, "Don't you think she's acting peculiar?" or "I know for a fact she's not supposed to be taking so many of those…"

Then someone else says, "Have you talked to her?"

And the first person replies, "You know you can't talk to her, she'll just get angry and say…," "Besides, it's not my place," or "I don't want to ruin Christmas or other special holiday…"

Spouses in particular often feel responsible for their partners' addictions just as parents feel responsible for the addictions of their children. Families feel a need to keep the addiction a secret out of shame, fear of criticism, pride, a desire to protect the addict, and fear of financial consequences. While trying to keep this secret, family members often become controlling, angry and rigid, yet at the same time they often feel powerless, hopeless, and depressed. It is quite common for the family to become as disabled by the addiction as the addicted person does.

What's more, family members may be playing into the disorder, a behavior known as "enabling." Enabling is any act that interferes with the natural consequences of destructive behavior. Although enabling is born out of caring, love, and concern for the addict (as well as self-protection), it perpetuates the disorder by reinforcing the addict's behavior and keeping an individual from recognizing his or her problem and getting help.

Examples of enabling:
- Making excuses to cover behavior. For instance, a spouse might call the addict's job and say he/she is ill, when the addict is actually incapacitated by substance abuse.
- Pretending not to notice destructive behavior.
- Consoling the addicted loved one by blaming others for the problem.
- Giving assurances to family members that the behavior is normal.
- Agreeing that others are wrong to worry.
- Keeping silent ("speak no evil, hear no evil, see no evil").

Matthew, the child of an addict, now an adult, recalls, "As far back as I can remember, I have always covered up for my father, looking the other way. I always looked up to my father. How could I confront him with my suspicions that he was abusing his pills?"

Recognizing an addiction but failing to act against it, going along with it, or accommodating it is a form of denial. It enables the addictive behavior. I am not blaming those who enable addiction, certainly not children. Enabling is a normal reaction. People naturally think, "What can I do? I don't know how to fix this." Not enabling—that is, letting the addict feel the natural consequences of his actions—may mean the addict will lose his job or worse, and the spouse and children may suffer from such a disaster as much or more than the addict.

Joe, the husband of an addict, says, "I know I am enabling her when I make excuses to her boss so she won't lose her job. But the mortgage is based on both our incomes, and we just can't do without it right now."

Beth now realizes she was enabling her husband's addiction when she took a job she didn't want in order to earn more money so he didn't have to work. "At the time, he couldn't work. Who would hire him? He couldn't pass a drug test. What choice did I have?"

It's clear that enablers are often in just as much of a bind as the addict. It seems difficult or impossible for either to bring an end to the problem. However, it is important to realize that the self-protective behavior of the enabler allows an individual to continue his or her addiction without severe consequences. Which brings up The Big Question: What will you do down the road if the addiction continues? Divorce? Kick the person out? Suffer as you do now? Bury him or her? Are those long-term consequences worse than the immediate consequences you would face if you stopped enabling and let nature take its course?

When something happens to force the issue of addiction out into the open or when an individual takes the brave step of admitting the problem and seeking help, the rest of the family is suddenly thrust into a struggle as threatening as if they had fallen into the strong current of a roaring river. If you are suspicious or aware of the plight of a loved one who has not sought help, you may be trying to come up with a plan of assistance before you are suddenly thrown into the icy water. I support your desire to intervene. But don't confront the addicted individual until you have a plan.

If there are prescription bottles, over-the-counter medicines, or alcohol that the person you are concerned about uses, copy all the medication doses, directions, refill information, prescribing doctor, etc, for each bottle and count the pills in each one. Keep a record of the rate at which they disappear and do the same for any additional bottles that show up. You can keep track of alcohol bottles by listing in your journal any empty bottles left on the counter and in the trash or by taking a picture of each bottle to see how fast the amount in the bottle is decreasing daily. Take note of how often your spouse or partner gets up in the middle of the night and whether you can smell alcohol on his breath returning to bed. Does your partner hide alcohol bottles around the house, garage or in the car? These may not be all the pills and alcohol the person is using, but you may be able to record a pattern of abuse for the ones you do see. Having the facts will help you bring the person out of denial. Again, don't confront the addicted individual until you have a plan.

Sometimes, a well-planned family intervention or an Addiction Recovery Coach can help a person examine her life and decide that she does need help. While even the best intervention and Addiction Recovery Coach offer no guarantee, there is a better chance of getting positive results from an intervention and recovery coach if the entire family supports their services. Enlist the help of sympathetic family members, best friends, and even a supportive boss who is aware of the problem. Ask them to join you, but do not try to persuade someone who is unwilling. Ask everyone involved to read about addiction and recovery. You could hand them this book. You could also ask them to go to a meeting of Al Anon for family members, Prescriptions Anonymous support network, Narcotics Anonymous, or Alcoholics Anonymous support groups.

An intervention requires planning on the parts of all the people involved. Ideally, you would be able to ask a therapist or Addiction Recovery Coach with intervention experience and training to help you design the intervention and to be present to guide you through the process. After all, when those involved meet to plan the intervention, things may not go as smoothly as you hoped they would. One relative or friend may blame another. They may say: "You should have seen this and stopped it; you were the one who was with her every day," or "This problem comes from your side of the family." Others may complain about having to be involved, asking you why you can't stop this nonsense by yourself. A trained therapist can help bring people together and teach them how to be respectful of one another and of the person you are trying to help. An intervention professional or Addiction Recovery Coach can set up guidelines and help each person plan his or her part of the script. There should be at least one practice session with the professional interventionist or recovery coach. Anyone who cannot join in respectfully or follow the rules must be asked to excuse him or herself. More about formal interventions guided by professionals can be found at www.prescriptionsanonymous.com and www.intervention.com. Whether or not you have a professional interventionist or Addiction Recovery Coach to guide you, do not schedule an intervention until you have a treatment plan in place. You'll find wonderful treatment resources in this book and on www.prescriptionsanonymous.com to consider when choosing a treatment plan of action for your loved one.

Collect information about any professional treatment center of interest for professional assessments based on your needs and location. Call and ask about admission policies, costs, insurance, in-patient versus out-patient care. Get recommendations for therapists with training and experience in pill addiction, alcohol, and dual-diagnosis treatment. As you gather this information, keep it and this book handy for the moment when you need them.

If the person you are trying to help observes your efforts to collect information, you will likely be propelled a little faster into confrontation, which may mean having an intervention a bit before you are ready. Confrontation occurring sooner than you planned is no reason for panic. If it happens, it happens. Whether you choose the timing or not, if you have gathered all the information and kept it handy, you are more prepared for the confrontation than you may realize. If necessary, let the addict rage. At some level, she knows the truth, and she knows things can't go on the way they have been.

Are you scared? Of course. Do you hesitate? Naturally.

Just remember this: If a loved one or friend were sick with a physical disease, you'd do everything you could to help, wouldn't you? In fact, prescription addiction like any other addiction is a medically proven physical disease just like diabetes, cancer, and heart disease—and it's just as life-threatening if untreated. One difference is that your beloved addict may be resisting your efforts. But this is when he needs your help the most. The silent cry you cannot hear says, "I need you to do for me what I can't do for myself."

By confronting a loved one and telling him in a caring manner how his behavior has affected his family and friends, you may be able to break through the wall of denial and greatly increase the likelihood that he will get professional help. Regardless of the outcome, the person with the disease will never be able to engage in the unacceptable behavior in the same way again, knowing you know. Once everything is out in the open, the situation is changed forever. If you're concerned, talk now. If you wait, more harm will come to your loved one, even a loss of life.

If you are searching for the words to get started, borrow one of the following:

- Nancy, we love you very much. But we have noticed a change in your personality, and you've been isolating yourself from us. We're worried about you. We know you have been filling a number of prescriptions lately, but you don't appear to be sick. We want to help you in any way we can if you'll let us.
- Gail, I'm not a professional, so I can't tell if you have a problem. But I can see that something is affecting you. Remember the wedding we all went to where you cried uncontrollably at the table? Or the numerous times you have forgotten conversations we had only days before? You might want to have a professional assessment done to find out just what the problem may be, whether emotional, physical, or both. I know the names of some good medical professionals I'd be happy to share with you.
- Steven, you're my best friend and I care about what's been happening to you. I've noticed you're taking more pain pills than instructed and drinking more heavily every day. You've always been there for me when I had a problem, so I would like to help you, if I can, without judgment or criticism.
- Seth, I can only go by what I see. I do know something is affecting you that has me worried. Remember the night you called me at 2:00 A.M., and you didn't remember that call the next day? Or the day you yelled at the waitress for not refilling your water glass? You used to not act out this way; you were always in control of yourself. You might want to seek help from a professional, someone who can help you work

through whatever is going on. I'll even make an appointment and take you myself if you will let me.

Once the ice is broken and the confrontation has been gently begun, add progressive pressure. Here's how:

- Confront the addicted person with your suspicions in a calm, loving and caring manner, saying, "I have a concern...." Use "I" phrases such as "I noticed" or "I'm worried" about the incident instead of "you" phrases, as in: "You never take pills as directed." A person can't argue with your feelings. The word "you" places blame, criticism and judgment.

- You're intervening because you care, not to make her see how bad she is.

- Don't worry if you don't say things perfectly. The most important thing is to express your concern in a caring and honest way with an open mind.

- Be specific. Bring up incidents such as "When I saw you take more pills than instructed this morning at breakfast..." or "I heard you make appointments with two different doctors on the same day for the same complaint" or whatever evidence of abuse you have personally witnessed.

- Be prepared for the addict to deny that he or she has a problem with addiction(s). This is one of the unfortunate symptoms of this disease. Don't take it personally.

- Talk about the effects of addiction on whatever the addict cares about most: this could be his children, spouse, family, appearance, or job. He very well may not be concerned about himself right now, but he may care deeply about his children or marriage; or he may not care about his health but is very appearance-conscious. In fact, if you are the spouse and you have made up your mind that you will leave the marriage and take the children if the addict doesn't seek treatment, tell him that. Or if you are the boss and you know you must fire this employee unless she recovers fast, now is the time for the ultimatum. Don't deliver it in anger, just state the consequences of a failure to seek treatment. Tell him, "I love you, but this behavior has to end," or "I value you as an employee, but I can't risk the consequences of keeping you." Or, in extreme cases, "I will call the police or 911 if you do not permit me to drive you to a treatment center." If the addicted person refuses to seek help, make sure you follow through with the consequences so that he or she will know just how serious you are.

- An addict will sometimes be hesitant to enter a treatment center or fear having to talk to an addiction recovery coach because, on top of feeling guilty, ashamed, angry, and embarrassed, she also feels guilty about taking time for herself and spending less time with her children, on her job, or taking care of other personal responsibilities. Remind her that most treatment programs are short-term, support meetings are an hour, and aftercare recovery coaching can be conveniently scheduled at the recovering addict's home or other local community location. By taking time to recover and get healthy, she will actually be more available to her family and other activities she used to enjoy. Remind her that focusing on herself for the first time in a long time is not only okay, it's a necessity.

- If and when the addict agrees to go to a treatment or rehabilitation center, offer to sit with her while she makes the arrangements. Offer to drive her to the treatment center, therapist, or addiction recovery coach who will decide whether the addict needs intensive outpatient or inpatient residential care. Reassure her over and over that she is doing the right thing and how proud of her you are for making the decision to recover from addiction. Tell her how supportive you will be and that you will stay with her while she is being assessed if she chooses you to be with her in the room while she talks to the treatment intake counselors.

- If the addict is impaired, visibly ill, suicidal, dangerous to himself or others, call 911. Do not attempt to drive the addict yourself to the treatment center or hospital. This could be dangerous for you and the addict if he or she becomes unconscious, stops breathing, or physically threatens you.

A mental health treatment facility is required by law in most states to hold an addict for seventy-two hours for evaluation to determine if the afflicted person is suicidal or a danger to himself or others.

Regardless of the outcome of your family or friend intervention and your offer of support, you as a spouse, friend, or family member are likely to feel tremendous relief in the knowledge that you have done all you can do to help your loved one and yourself. Exposing the problem means you will never again have to pretend that nothing is wrong.

## Telling the Children

In families with children living at home, a parent going into treatment requires explanation and comforting. Ideally, both parents discuss between themselves what and how much they will tell the children. Talking to your own children about going away for treatment requires an understanding of their maturity level and their needs. Decide what you are comfortable telling them as long as it's truthful and something they will be able to understand based on the children's age. Then bring it up together in a family meeting so everyone will know what has been said and how everyone reacted. This sharing of information openly tells the children that this is not a family secret they must hide and never talk about. Let them know you all are dealing with the problem together, each helping the other out.

What you tell the children should have four parts: If you are the addicted parent, tell the children first that you have a problem; second, that you are going to get help for it; and third, that you will get better. Fourth, ask them if they have any questions about the situation and answer them honestly.

Throughout the four explanations and forever after, talk to your children honestly. Don't give them false information about your problem that will keep them from understanding your addiction. Later, when they may want to understand the whole picture more clearly, they will need to be able to rely on the earlier information given to them. When you feel you must withhold information because the children will not be able to understand or deal well with the particulars due to their age or level of maturity, generalize rather than give misinformation. For example, it is all right to tell a young child that you are sick and are going to a hospital because addiction is an illness. You may also say you feel sad rather than depressed because this concept will be better understood. You might explain to an older child that you are having trouble giving up painkillers and that these medications are not good for you anymore, so you are going to go to a special treatment hospital where you can be more comfortable learning to give them up. With an older child, you might tell him you have been feeling very depressed, also, if that is the case. People who are afraid it will be harmful for a child to know about a drug addiction should be aware that giving a good example about facing and curing addiction may prove to be a very important lesson for that child. It will teach him to be wary of any drugs including alcohol, to know that these addictions can cause problems, and to know that it is good to take charge and seek help for his own problems in the future.

Reassure children that the treatment you are seeking will be very helpful and that they, along with the whole family, will benefit from your becoming well again. "I won't seem so sad anymore, and we will have more fun together," you could say. Explain to older children about sobriety and how you will work hard to resist temptation.

Ask the children if they have questions. The questions they ask will give you insight into how much they understand, about how they feel, and about what else to tell them.

As I said, having the type of conversations discussed here are ideal. However, the departure for a treatment facility center or even jail does not always allow such a measured approach. Moreover, the addicted person may be incapable of talking calmly and reassuringly to his or her children. In that case, it is best that the other parent or caregiver say these things on behalf of the parent who is going for treatment. The conversation should follow the same four steps. First, you could calmly say that Mom or Dad has a problem with pills or alcohol and is going away to seek help. Second, reassure the children that their parent will get better and be a better parent when he or she returns. Next, promise your attention and support during this time. Finally, invite the children to ask questions for you to answer honestly and as fully as is appropriate for their level of understanding.

**You're In This Together**

Just as the family's denial shadows the addict's denial, so does family chaos mirror the chaos in the addict's life when she first admits she has a problem and seeks help. For every step the addict takes, from denial on, there is a family counterpart as addict and family struggle toward recovery together.

During treatment by choice, persuasion, or intervention, the addict will change for the better if they are committed toward finding and keeping their recovery. If you are a family member, what you may be less prepared for is that you also will change as you learn about addiction and support versus enabling. If you had a part in the addict's life before, you will have a changed role in his life from now on. We live through personal interactions, and if one person behaves differently, the other will have to change. If you confronted your loved one about his addiction, he had to react. When he comes home sober, you may find you are living with a stranger. The whole family is in recovery now. I call this a "Family Dis-Ease."

That is why I strongly recommend that everyone in the family go to an Al Anon support group meeting, consult a Family Addiction Recovery Coach (resources found at www.prescriptionsanonymous.com) or attend a family support group of any addiction organization. Also, I strongly urge spouses of addicts to get therapy, both individual and couple's counseling from either a qualified family counselor or Family Addiction Recovery Coach.

Couples and family members from Prescriptions Anonymous and Al-Anon support groups have suggested these helpful hints for recovering addicts and their partners.

## DOs AND DON'Ts IN RECOVERY

### Do

- Do learn as much as you can about prescribed addictive controlled substances, over-the-counter medications, and alcohol addictions as well as dual diagnoses (i.e. addiction along with depression, anxiety, suicidal tendencies, and cross-addictions such as gambling, shopping, or sex).

- Do go to couple's therapy, both private counseling and individual support groups, for feedback from others who have experienced what you are going through and how recovery has made a difference.

- Do talk to others in the addict's family, like her parents and siblings and even her closest friends, to keep them updated if the addict can't bear to talk with them herself. Be sure you ask the recovering addict for permission to talk to others about her addiction. Showing support also means respecting the addict's privacy and sharing only what she is comfortable for others to know for now. Ease the stress by communicating with them until the addict can face these people. She should not be rushed or pushed. She will know when she is ready.

- Do go to the pharmacy to fill and refill prescriptions in the beginning when the recovering addict returns home from the treatment center, and for a few weeks or a month into recovery. Make arrangements for someone other than the recovering addict—neighbor, therapist, recovery coach, or friend—to dispense the medications until you and the addict feel he can manage them without temptation.

- Do listen, listen, listen to your loved one in recovery without interruption. Don't just hear the words, absorb them.

- Do freely communicate your feelings in a positive, honest, and respectful way without harsh criticism or judgment.

- Do allow others to express opinions different from yours. Keep an open mind.

- Do have a lot of patience with your loved one's mood swings, irritability, and sudden unexplained crying.

- Do make time to do fun things together again. It may have been a while since you've laughed and enjoyed each other's company doing the simplest activities like walking hand in hand, exercising, gardening, playing at the beach, or sightseeing.

- Do give constant reassurance that everything will be okay and that you will work together on getting through this time of crisis. Make the recovering addict feel less alone in his own home. After a few months pass, you both will no longer feel like you are walking on eggshells.

- Do remember hugs, kisses, and romance. Re-ignite the romance. It's a brand new beginning; make the most of it! Changing the way you live doesn't mean forgetting what it was like to be happy with each other. Rekindle all the things you both once enjoyed; sobriety makes everything more fun and enjoyable, including food, romance, and socializing with family and friends.

**DON'Ts**
- Don't blame each other for all the problems not being faced. Both of you are feeling hurt enough already. Don't try to figure out "how we got into this mess" but "how we are going to get out of this mess together."
- Don't make judgments or criticize each other. Think before you speak.
- Don't keep medicines—yours or your spouse's—out in the open for easy access for a month or until the addict feels healthy enough to manage his medications alone.
- Don't keep alcohol in the house or allow others to drink around the addict until she feels that it is no longer a trigger or temptation.
- Don't leave your loved one alone if you suspect that she is not feeling "safe" from the temptation to misuse or relapse. Ask a friend, family member, or addiction recovery coach to stay with her for a while when you are out, until she or her recovery coach says she's ready to be alone.
- Don't close yourself off from the problem. Isolating yourself will only stop all communication. The addict needs all your support and understanding now more than ever.

The impact family and friends can have on the addict's success—or failure—in recovery should not be underestimated. Shawna, whose story appears in several places in this book, relates a touching anecdote of what family support did for her. After she pretended to be in recovery, she secretly continued using pills. When her husband found out, he told his mother what Shawna was doing. Shawna's in-laws immediately came to the young couple's home to help. This is what happened next, as Shawna remembers it:

*My mother-in-law came into my room and rubbed my back as I sobbed and held myself in the fetal position on the bed. She kept telling me how much she loved me and that she would do whatever it took to get me well. She then said, "Turn around and look at me, Sweetie." I turned around, my face drenched with tears and shame, and I looked at her and said, "How can you still love me after all that I've done to you, your son, and your family?" She replied, "You are my Shawna." I knew right then that I was not going to have to endure this alone.*

Shawna and many others in recovery learned a great deal about the benefits of supportive loved ones during their difficult struggle to end dependence on controlled substance drugs and alcohol.

Several people who have been in recovery for a few months to several years shared with me their thoughts and advice for families and friends of those in recovery:

*As a family member or friend, please be your loved one's greatest support system. What he or she is going through is pure and utter hell. You must be there for her or him, without enabling addictive behavior. Many of us in the beginning hated our spouses and family members at the time for bringing our secrets out in the open and forcing us to get help, but we are now eternally grateful for their unwavering support and love.*

>>> 12

# The Peace of Recovery

*"I look back and see where I was before and I cry tears of joy."*

You've made great progress and you think you've made it. But... how can you be sure? First, you are never completely free from cravings and triggers, and you will always be a recovering pill addict. The possibilities of relapse are real no matter how long you have been in recovery, a day, month, or years. Still, there are signs of achievement and feelings of serenity that mark real recovery.

- You know you've made it when…
- You believe in yourself because you have just succeeded at something very, very difficult where failure had always prevailed before.
- The good times have finally outweighed the bad, whereas before bad was all you knew.
- You and your spouse or partner have learned to listen with your hearts every day to better understand each other's needs.

- You have made amends with those whom you hurt during your illness, and you feel the weight of guilt lifted from your shoulders as relationships begin to heal.
- You have resolved feelings of guilt, embarrassment and shame.
- You have developed a meaningful life.
- You have rediscovered pleasure and satisfaction in your day-to-day activities.
- You have restored positive values and spiritual beliefs.
- You are able to live in peace with yourself even through unsolved problems. You have found self-soothing techniques other than drugs, and you are making healthy solutions with a clear mind.
- Concern for yourself lessens as you gain interest in others and renewed self respect.
- You intuitively handle situations that used to baffle you.
- You have begun to understand the words, "peace of mind".

Here is a different kind of "test" for recovery. It asks you to look both within and without and assess yourself at this moment. How many positive changes do you see in your condition now? The changes you can check off are a measure of your progress. The changes you cannot currently check off are benefits you will soon observe on your road to recovery.

**How many changes do you see?**
- I'm feeling healthier.
- My headaches are less frequent.
- Physical pains are less frequent.
- My stomach doesn't ache.
- My stomach is less upset.
- Chest pressure is going away.
- I don't cry as often.
- I find myself smiling more often.
- My blood pressure has returned to normal.
- I can see clearly; my eyes are bright and focused.
- I'm eating normally, healthier.
- I'm less anxious or nervous.
- My sense of humor has returned.
- I feel good about my accomplishments and goals.
- I feel I can be honest with myself and others.
- I can hold onto a job.
- I don't feel violent anymore.
- My creativity has returned.
- I have improved communications.
- I feel loved and wanted.
- I feel grateful for my recovery.
- My life is getting better and better.
- I have a desire to help others in need of support.
- I don't get as angry as I used to.

- Concentration has improved.
- Sex has improved.
- I think more clearly.
- It feels good to not want to abuse or misuse controlled substances.
- I get to work on time.
- I get more compliments from others.
- I look better, for example, my hair, skin, and/or weight.
- I feel like a winner in my personal and professional life-change.
- I feel organized.
- I feel less guilty about my past behavior.
- I have learned to trust myself and the choices I make.
- I have learned to forgive myself.
- I have many blessings to live for.
- I have a positive attitude.
- I can feel comfortable around people.
- I feel less anxious with my family.
- I have made amends with family and friends.
- My love relationships have improved.
- I'm proud of myself.
- I love myself...again.

Here are some voices of inspiration from people who have been through the worst to find life again in their souls. These people have "arrived."

- *I have found harmony and feel at peace with myself. I understand my past, which helps me to understand my needs today. My past was filled with physical and emotional pain, so I turned to pills and other drugs to avoid further hurt. Dealing with my past head-on has allowed me to move toward a healthier, happier future.*
- *I now feel worthy of a fulfilling life. I had always felt abandoned, both as a child and later as an adult. In therapy I worked through feelings of shame, loneliness, and depression, so that I now have many healthy relationships.*
- *I learned to trust myself and others. Trust never came easy for me. I always thought that it was "a given," not an earned ability. I experienced rejection and told lies in the past. I didn't learn to trust until I began my recovery, went to support groups, and listened to my addiction recovery coach where I got my affirmations, support, and the feeling of being appreciated and valued.*
- *I have learned to take care of myself for the first time. I was so codependent with my family, I thought my purpose in life was to "fix" them; instead I lost myself. I have since worked diligently at taking care of myself through Prescriptions Anonymous, Family Recovery Coaching, and Al-Anon. I found out I can take care of myself while still being supportive of others, without "fixing" them.*

- *I have developed healthy ways of coping with stress and other uncomfortable feelings. Before recovery I would find unhealthy ways of dealing with emotional problems, such as over-eating, under-eating, drugs, gambling, sex, pills, alcohol, anything to take the emotional pain away. By sharing with other recovering people, I found healthier ways to relieve the pain I was feeling on the inside—a void that can only by relieved by talking it out, not self-medicating. I have found balance in my life through my recovery journey. I never felt any kind of balance in my life before.*

- *I was always in chaos; I was always living on the edge. Now I live life feeling grateful for those that helped me find and keep balance in my life.*

David, Shawna's husband, speaks of spiritual sustenance:

*I am especially grateful to God for the miracle that he worked in my family's life. Without His help, I know there would have been no happy ending. I have discovered that God does not give up on any of us very easily. I almost hit the "panic button" with my wife, and now I am so glad that I hung in there—even when things got really rough. God has miraculously restored the love and trust between my wife and me. Her recovery has brought our family back together, a feat I feared would never happen. "Healthy" is a word we thought only other families understood and felt. Now, we are healthy. We talk, we love, and we play like we did when we dated. It's not to say things are perfect, but with each recovering day our lives together keep improving in some way. Our children have a mother again they can laugh with and talk to. A mother they can be proud of and a father who is full of pride. Together, we now carry God's message of hope and freedom to anyone who will listen.*

Kevin speaks of self-growth:

*I feel such gratitude for all the help I received through Prescriptions Anonymous support network, my addiction recovery coach, and addiction counselor. I have found new meaning and purpose in life. I've worked very hard to achieve self-respect and prove my worthiness to my family. In the beginning, I thought detoxification and treatment were all I needed to have a successful recovery. I honestly thought that just admitting myself into a treatment facility meant that staff would "fix" my addiction and problems and I would go home. I quickly learned that treatment facilities and recovery coaching educate you on addiction to work through your own recovery. I needed to make my own choices and decide to stay in recovery or go back to a life of addiction. Others further along in the recovery process helped me understand that I needed to work on myself throughout my recovery program if I wanted to truly heal and keep what I now have—a life, a family, and a career.*

Pat speaks of insight:

*I'm grateful to be alive today. I had to learn that I could survive on my own again without pills or alcohol and without being a codependent of anyone. I needed to find help for dual illnesses in order to fight prescription addiction and severe depression. I needed more awareness of how I was raised and the understanding that my behavior was a result of a need to survive in an environment over which I had no control. Through recovery, I found the hope, understanding, guidance, and structure I needed to live a productive life. My ability to survive now comes from letting go of resentments and anger and empowering my own life, the way I choose to live it.*

I want to end this chapter, almost the end of my book, with my own important discovery. *I am now actually grateful for my disease* because the process of recovery has made such a positive impact on my life, giving me self-esteem, self-worth, and a purpose in life. I think back and never want to forget who I was or where I came from. For it is my past that makes me who I am today and what I will become tomorrow. I once thought I was unique and that my story and life were very different from everyone else's. I came to learn that I wasn't so different or unique and that we are all in pursuit of personal growth and well-being. I learned to freely share my pain, fear, anger, and needs, never carrying the burden alone. I will always be aware of this illness that I carry with me, never taking recovery for granted.

I've also learned to forgive myself for striking the pedestrian in the roadway in 1973 when I was 18. The fact that the 21-year-old-pedestrian, I learned later, had actually been committing suicide by deliberately stepping in front of my car did not dull my pain. I carried with me intense feelings of guilt for being the instrument of his death. I couldn't forgive myself for 20 long years, during which I thought my only way to find freedom from guilt was abusing controlled substances to numb that pain and, indeed, any painful emotion. The irony is that the young man who died of his injuries after walking in front of my car turned out to be a young addict just released from a treatment rehabilitation hospital who suffered with mental illness and who apparently couldn't face life on life's terms. Now I see my old self in him. How I wish I'd been with him before he was released in order to share with him what I know now. But time, of course, doesn't work that way; I could not have helped him then any more than I could help myself then.

I carried my burden of guilt until February 27, 1997, when I began my recovery at a treatment rehabilitation facility in Atlanta, Georgia, support groups, and an addiction recovery therapist renewed my life again with more blessings than I can count. I learned many lessons while in therapy; the most important among them is that I am not responsible for my disease of addiction but I am responsible for keeping my *self* in recovery. Learning to forgive one's self doesn't come easy, but it does come. Accepting my disease is what keeps me strong and motivated to keep improving myself and supporting others as an Addiction Recovery and Family Coach. My promise in recovery is to offer the help and wisdom that I have received and pass it on to others. I pray for the inner strength and courage to fulfill this promise in all that I do and say.

I am hoping to hear that you have made it, too.

# Epilogue

When I was discharged from treatment in 1997 and was looking for support groups to attend, I was directed to Alcoholic Anonymous and Narcotics Anonymous 12-step based programs. The fellowship members of these groups were supportive, and their shared stories were an inspiration. Some of their stories, however, were very different from mine, and in AA or NA I felt a lack of belonging. I needed to find a support group that related to my drug of choice, that is, pill addiction, and to my dual diagnosis. When I asked my therapist and other people with problems like mine where I could find a suitable support group, I found there were none.

So I decided to form a new support group myself, inviting people recovering from controlled substances or over-the-counter medicines, and also those with dual diagnosis. Prescriptions (RxA) Anonymous was formed in 1998 in Atlanta, Georgia, and is now helping and supporting others nationally via phone, email, recovery coaching, and virtual Skype network support services.

I created my website www.prescriptionsanonymous.com for controlled substance addictions, alcoholism, over-the-counter pill addiction, and other cross-addictions for individuals and families in either active or continuing aftercare recovery coaching support. I guide others toward recovery working with aftercare pill addicts and family coaching creating healthy action planning decisions, resources for treatment rehabilitation facilities, 12-step and non-12-step programs. I also offer my own services as a Nationally Certified Addiction and Family Recovery Coach. Recovery coaching is action-oriented with an emphasis on improving present life and reaching future goals.

When I began to write about my own addiction experiences and those of others, I realized how much more widespread the problem of prescription addiction was than I had even known. In 2014, 4.3 million people aged 12 or older were non-medical users of opioid pain relievers. According to SAMHSA (Substance Abuse and Mental Health Services Administration), addiction to opioids and other prescribed controlled substance addictions has increased from 4 million to 9 million. SAMHSA also witnessed a near quadrupling of overdoses from prescription opioids from 1999 to 2016.

The feeling people expressed of being blindsided when they discovered they were addicted to a drug originally prescribed by a doctor made a huge impression on me. My contact with recovering addicts in other states led me to take on a regional and national focus. I continue my efforts to promote awareness of the growing epidemic of addiction and the dangers inherent in prescription drug abuse.

The next step was to find those who needed to become more aware and those who could help me bring attention to the problem.

The following chart shows the groups and levels of responsibility that must ultimately be addressed if we are to control prescribed and over-the-counter drug abuse.

# PRESCRIPTION DRUG ABUSE AND RESPONSIBILITY

## DRUG ENFORCEMENT

- To monitor sales
- To investigate diversion
- To enforce industry compliance with manufacturing quotas and sales

## FOOD AND DRUG ADMINISTRATION

- To set production quotas of Schedule II controlled medications
- To review and approve package inserts
- To approve medications that are safe and efficacious

## PHARMACEUTICAL MANUFACTURERS

- To maintain manufacturing standards of purity and quality
- To avoid production in excess of quotas set by FDA
- To conform to industry standards in advertising and promotion of medications
- To report sales of controlled medications to DEA
- To provide information to physicians about the medications
- To verify that customers who order medications from them are licensed to receive the medications

## STATE PHARMACY LICENSING

- To license pharmacists who meet licensing requirements of the board
- To license and monitor pharmacies

## STATE MEDICAL LICENSING BOARD

- To license physicians who meet the board's requirements
- To discipline mis-prescribing physicians

## PHYSICIANS

- To examine and diagnose a patient's medical problems
- To prescribe appropriate medications based on a knowledge of the patient's conditions and history as well as other medications the patient may be taking
- To obtain current information about the medications they prescribe, including indications, side effects, therapeutic limitations, and abuse potential

## RETAIL PHARMACIES

- To dispense prescription medications prescribed by patients' physicians
- To follow regulations regarding dispensing of controlled medications
- To provide patient information about the medications

## PATIENTS

- To be truthful with all prescribing healthcare professionals
- To take responsibility for your actions and choices

- To follow physicians' instructions
- To take prescribed and over-the-counter medications only as instructed

**Patients**

Even though you see the responsibilities of patients listed at the bottom of the chart, the patient is the first one who must be made accountable for proper use of medication. The American Medical Association states that, while healthcare providers who fail in their responsibilities to patients should be censured, the current tendencies to assign fault to physicians when patients have violated their responsibility is unreasonable and unfair to physicians. When patients are dishonest in the patient-physician relationship and deceive their doctors, or when patients use their medications other than as prescribed, society should hold the patients accountable for the inevitable adverse consequences. Because patients are responsible for themselves, my primary goal is to educate patients first so that they can make responsible choices.

**Physicians**

Next on the hierarchy of those responsible are physicians. If physicians, including dentists, knew their patients' histories and other medications the patients were taking and then prescribed wisely, the chances for prescription addiction to occur would be reduced. Moreover, requests for prescription refills of pain medications, sleeping pills, etc., should raise red flags for all doctors. Doctors should re-evaluate patients who ask for refills, so that they are aware of any changes in patients' histories and current medical conditions. In the case of children, like Shawna, who became addicted through the use of prescribed opioids at an early age, certainly they have no responsibility for use or misuse. Healthcare providers must be vigilant when prescribing powerful and addictive drugs to children, particularly those who are not old enough to understand the consequences of addiction. In such cases, doctors should inform patients about the possibility of addiction, the warning signs, and how and where to get help. When treating adults, doctors must apprise them of all potential side effects—including addiction. These newly-educated, responsible patients, in concert with well trained, responsible doctors, will be equipped to avoid addiction.

The following guide is an elaboration of the responsibilities of physicians and patients.

## RESPONSIBILITIES OF PHYSICIANS AND PATIENTS IN THE PHYSICIAN-PATIENT INTERACTION

**Physician**
- To have the patient's well-being as his or her primary concern
- To formulate a working diagnosis of the patient's problem based on the patient's history and examination
- To obtain the appropriate laboratory test or consultation with a specialist to clarify diagnosis
- To prescribe appropriate therapy (assumes that the physician is acting within his or her scope of expertise and that the physician possesses about the same level of knowledge as other practitioners in the community)
- To monitor the effect of treatment, including monitoring for side effects to toxicity
- To continue follow-up until the condition is resolved or the patient's care is assumed by another physician

**Patient**
- To seek medical attention for conditions that he or she believes a physician can cure or ameliorate
- To be truthful in relating historical information and to cooperate with the physical examination
- To cooperate in obtaining the laboratory tests or consultations requested by the physician
- To comply with the physician's instructions, such as taking medications as prescribed and avoiding activities that would complicate or aggravate the disease
- To report symptoms accurately
- To follow through until discharged by the physician

It is the responsibility of the physician to prescribe the least addictive medication possible for as short a time as the patient needs and only as necessary. It is also the physician's responsibility to warn patients if prescribed medications are addictive. Of course, some prescriptions of careful and honest physicians indicate a limited number of refills without reevaluation. Unlimited refills can be dangerous. Physicians expect their patients to follow instructions. Many physicians think that the insert enclosed in the packaging of the medication suffices, but that is an unwise assumption to make. Few patients read the inserts to learn the degree of addictiveness; their most immediate concern is relief of their symptoms. Doctors must take the time to tell patients when medications are both effective and addictive. For every addictive medication prescribed, the doctor should say, "I don't want you to suffer in pain, but I don't want you to get dependent on these pills either. Take no more than you need and try to stop using them as soon as possible. There is no reason to finish the bottle of prescription pain medication if you find over-the-counter pain medicine helps with your pain." When it comes to medications like antibiotics, patients are used to being told to take all the pills in the bottle even if they feel better. Thus, it is important to emphasize the fact that it is not necessary to do the same when taking addictive medications like opioids that can jeopardize your recovery and relapse.

In addition, all physicians and dentists should be aware of the patterns of deceit addicted patients use to get controlled substance medications. Here are some requests the addicted patient might make that should send up red flags. If physicians or dentists suspect deceit, they must review the patient's chart, noting any recurring requests for refills of medication and decide if their patient is being truthful or deceitful.

## GUIDELINES FOR HEALTHCARE PROVIDERS

**Patient to Doctor:**
- I'm going on vacation for two to three weeks (the second or third time this patient has had a similar request over the last several months); can I have enough pain pills to last me until I get back?
- I'm having pain and can't sleep at night! I heard you were the best in you field. (Flattery). I can't find anyone that seems to be able to help me with my pain, and your name was given to me by one of your patients. (The name of that patient will likely be a made-up one, but doctors often don't remember the names of all their patients.)
- I have migraines daily; I need a stronger pill!
- A family member just died and I can't sleep.

- My husband and I are having problems; my anxiety is out of control.

**Patient to Nurses or Staff**
- Can I get another refill on my prescription? Dr. \_\_\_\_ said I could call **you** if I was still having pain or I couldn't sleep. Here's my pharmacy number and Rx refill number so it will be **easy for you** to call it in for me. (It sounds like the patient is doing the nurse a favor.)

**Patient to Emergency Room Staff:**
- Same scenario as physician listed above, but Physician Assistants and interns are sometimes easier to persuade because they are so eager to help the suffering that they believe the addict and forget to ask probing questions that may reveal a red-flag.

**Patient to Doctor on call:**
- My personal doctor is not available this weekend, and I was hoping you could give me a refill. I have an appointment set up for later this month with my regular doctor. Can I have enough pills to last until my appointment?

**Patient to Dentist:**
- The tooth that you worked on last week still hurts, and the pills you gave me don't seem to be strong enough.
- I have another toothache that is bothering me; perhaps that's the one with a cavity and it needs pulling. Can you give me something for pain until I can get to your office?
- It's been three weeks since I had my root canal, and I'm still in pain. Can I have another refill of painkillers?

Healthcare professionals hear all these requests and more. Some of them may be legitimate, but it is important for professionals to consider that such requests may be the ploys of addicts. Here are some other suggestions to help doctors avoid feeding patients' habits.

- If you suspect that a patient may be drug seeking, don't leave a patient alone in the exam room. Ask a nurse or assistant to stay in the room with the patient while you leave for a minute. If there is no one available at the time, leave the exam door open a little. This may discourage a patient from opening drawers and cabinets because staff and patients may be walking by in the hallway.
- Don't ever place expired pills in an open trash basket. Have a special place for discarded pharmaceuticals out of sight and reach.
- Always document on patient charts the instructions given verbally, and copy all paper written prescriptions as well as any sample medications handed out along with instructions.
- Use prescription pads with patterns that make alterations difficult and triplicate copy forms for protection against forgery.
- Instead of prescription pads, licensed healthcare professionals now have the option of using a secure physician-based data program prescribing most or all prescriptions from their office computers or laptop brought into the exam room while talking with their patient.
- Except in cases of real emergencies, healthcare providers or dentists should not call in new or refill prescriptions over the phone.

- Be observant while talking to your patients. Do her eyes look watery or red? Look for unusual nervousness. Can he sit still? Does your patient look at you while you're talking? Is he interested in your diagnosis or just interested in getting a prescription and getting out of there? Is her overall demeanor unusually sluggish, and does she look disconnected from reality? Does he look and act depressed, anxious, or lethargic? All of these could be signs of substance abuse.

- Before meeting with or examining a patient, read previous office notes about each patient and look at medications given in the past, including the number of refills allowed. A red flag should go up if you see that an unusual or unjustified amount of pills have been prescribed without sufficient need.

- Communicate with all staff members who have contact with patients about the necessity for reporting any suspicious activity, and develop a plan of action should anyone suspect a patient is drug seeking.

- Most state laws indicate that any healthcare provider can discharge a patient with written and verbal notice with "just cause" if the provider believes that a patient has come to them under false pretense or if there is proof of fraud or forgery. Call the referring physicians, pharmacists or dentists and ask if they have ever questioned or had problems with the patient's attempts to obtain prescriptions. Ask how many addictive prescriptions the patient has been given in the past three, six, and twelve months, how many refills, and in what time frame.

- Remember that healthcare providers not only have an obligation to help their patients avoid addiction, but they must also protect the clinic or hospital they work for against liability for wrongdoing.

- When dismissing any patient who you suspect has an addiction to pills, alcohol, or other drugs, use gentleness and compassion along with firmness in your explanation. Some patients may have started coming to you with real pain and suffering only to have gotten addicted to the very substance you prescribed. Confront your patient in your office (with a witness), showing your proof or reason for suspicion. Let him know you are obligated to dismiss him, then offer referring rehabilitation treatment facilities where he or she could go for help.

## GUIDELINES FOR PHARMACISTS

Pharmacists are an important link in the chain of addiction. Customers con pharmacists as often as physicians. Here are some good policies for pharmacists and pharmacy personnel to adopt:

- Do not allow anyone to pick up a controlled substance prescription at a pharmacy without showing identification first, especially at the drive-through service.
- To avoid theft, do not leave filled prescriptions unattended on the counter within reach of anyone other than the customer the prescription is intended for. In fact, do not leave prescriptions within reading distance as information is sometime gleaned by sharp-eyed addicts who read labels of other people's bottles and claim to be that person.
- Shred all paper prescriptions before discarding to prevent addicts from getting old prescriptions or information such as DEA numbers from the trash.

- Pharmacists and pharmacy personnel should always review medications to clarify use and addictive capabilities, and make sure the patient looks at the warnings indicated on the bottle, enclosed with the packaging, or distributed by the pharmacy. Ask customers if they have any questions about the medication.
- Pharmacists should document any suspicions of abuse or fraudulent activities and notify the healthcare provider and law enforcement.
- Pharmacists should be wary of requests like these: "It's the weekend and my doctor's office is closed, can I have just a few pills until Monday or until he gets back from vacation?" or "I put some of these in a travel case and I lost it. Can you give me just a few pills to make up for the ones I lost?"

When choosing not to fill their prescriptions, pharmacists, like all healthcare providers, should confront customers whom they suspect of drug abuse or drug seeking. Again, gentleness and compassion along with information on treatment options may make a difference. It's true, most addicts will go to another pharmacy, but by refusing to fill a prescription you may be helping a drug abuser to seek help. Consider this letter I received:

*I turned in a prescription from a different doctor to my pharmacist. He caught it immediately. He pulled me over to the side of the counter and told me how dangerous and addictive these drugs were. He told me how easy it was to get addicted and that it happens to a lot of people. He suggested that I was drug seeking and addicted to opioids. That made me mad. I didn't like what he said because he exposed my addiction openly. I didn't realize I was that transparent to a stranger, and I wasn't ready to own up to my pill addiction. He made it very hard on me to cheat and lie. He really cared. When I straightened up, I realized what a great pharmacist he was. After I sought recovery and was well on my way to a healthier lifestyle, I told him everything, I even printed out my story I had posted on a drug abuse site and gave it to him. He had already looked it up. I just didn't know it. I consider him a dear friend.*

While there is no evidence that the pharmacist was responsible for this addict's recovery, his diligence was probably one of the important factors that pushed her to admit she had a pill problem and seek help.

## REPORTING TO LICENSING BOARDS

You should report to the state medical licensing board any doctor who blatantly contributes to addiction by over-prescribing or prescribing without sufficient oversight or while ignoring clear signs of patient abuse. Drug abuse by physicians themselves should also be reported. Retain all evidence of misconduct. While many physicians retain their licenses even with clear evidence of failing their responsibilities and even after convictions for drug misuse, your complaint will be registered and will be on that doctor's record for public scrutiny. Your complaint may contribute to the physician curtailing the abuse.

Likewise report to the pharmacy board any pharmacist who dispenses addictive medications without an authorized prescribed prescription or honors an obviously falsified prescription.

These measures are intended to help prevent prescription addiction or prevent addicts from easily getting inappropriate prescriptions filled. The harder it is to continue addictive behavior, the more likely the addict is to turn to treatment for relief. The goal is to make it easier to get treatment than to get the drugs to feed the addiction.

Just as I have found great satisfaction and, hopefully, have made a difference by spreading the word about prescription addiction, so you can help by being aware of the problem, understanding that addiction of any kind is an illness that affects people physically and psychologically. Telling all who will listen that treatment is available and recovery is possible is worth the effort. To all those who are fighting to recover, I send congratulations. I hope you will reach out to other addicts who need your guidance and understanding in order to take the first step toward recovery.

---

**Rx** FOR ALL DOCTORS AND PRESCRIPTION ADDICTS

Healthy Choices: Make them and live by them!

Directions: Use every day; believe in yourself.

Refills: A lifetime

Individuals recovering from chemical or substance abuse, <u>do not</u> use caution while on this prescription.

Reported side effects: Happiness, growth, and serenity.

—Signed and approved by all who have listened and learned.

# Appendix 1
## Questions and Answers

The National Institute on Drug Abuse says about 48 million people (ages 12 and older) have used prescription drugs for non-medical reasons in their lifetime. That figure means a staggering 20% of the U.S. population has at least one time abused prescription drugs. Many of them have become addicted. Over the years, recovering pill addicts and families in recovery have asked me many questions. Most of the answers can be found in this book, but I've found that people often don't absorb general information directly into their own context; they need to ask about their individual situations. I hope the following questions I've been asked along with my answers will address some of your concerns.

First, here are some questions frequently asked by an addict's family members and loved ones.

## Concerns of Friends and Families of Prescription Addicts

**Q:** I've been married to this person for years; I should have known there was something wrong, shouldn't I have?

**A:** No. Some addicts can be the best actors in the world. Despite the perfect vision of hindsight, if you are not already aware of the dangers or the signs, it is easy to miss addiction. Just as you wouldn't see a disease like cancer coming, neither would you see the disease of addiction. Don't feel guilty about not knowing. However, do learn all you can about addiction and recovery now.

**Q:** I have a friend I believe is hooked on pills. We are close, but she has never told me about any problem with drugs or alcohol. Suppose one day she tells me about her addictions and voluntarily asks me for help. Does this ever happen? My answer of course would be, "*I will help you*," but what should I say next?

**A:** When someone says, "I need help," ask, "Do you really want help?" This question jolts the person. It also makes her say, "Yes, I need help" again as an affirmation of commitment. You respond, "Let's make an appointment today and go see a doctor who can give you referral options for treatment." Take your friend there yourself and constantly reassure her that things will get better, and you will be there to support her through this difficult time.

**Q:** My family wants to do an intervention as soon as possible with our addicted father. What are the chances we can do this without an intervention professional?

**A:** Addiction, as I have said many times, is a family disease. The behavior of family members has revolved around the addiction, to some extent, even if they have not known about the addiction until recently. The intervention will shake up everyone's life, not just the addict's. Preparation for an intervention with a professional might act as the first session of therapy for the family. That would definitely be a positive thing. Everyone would be starting with the same information and the same strategy.

The danger of going into intervention without professional counseling is that some family problems could come out during the intervention that would distract everyone from the main purpose. The result would be a breakdown in the family's united front. For example, if a family member who went along with the plan suddenly blurted out that he didn't think the problem was that bad anyway, an argument might ensue, letting the addict off the hook. Or, if one family member blamed another for the problem, someone else might defend the accused person and suddenly everyone is taking sides. Such a situation would not help the addicted person at all and would only make matters worse for him or her and the entire family. A trained professional experienced in intervention could handle the discord and lead you all to more productive behavior.

If you must do an intervention without help, practice what each person is going to say ahead of time, and find out what the feelings of each person are so that problematic issues have been brought out in the open and dealt with ahead of time. You may get a feeling during practice about whether these people are going to work together well or not. Furthermore, if you feel you "have to" do the intervention without professional help, that suggests you are trying to keep the whole matter hidden. Such a need for secrecy doesn't speak well for the overall healthy approach to a problem whose solution requires complete and open honesty. Addiction is a disease, so get professional help.

**Q:** Our daughter is addicted to controlled substances and over-the-counter pills. We have sent her to therapy and even had her in treatment once. We've given her money, support, housing, food, and clothes. At this point what else can we do?

**A:** At some point you have to get on with your life, too. This disease will take the family down if you allow it. If you have done all you can do without destroying the rest of the family, tell your daughter that you will always love her, but that you can't let her live with you and you can't give her money, clothes, etc. Giving material things to her is like rewarding bad behavior. Tell her you hope she will recover and seek treatment. Withdrawing support may even jolt her into getting serious about recovery. In the meantime, you may need family counseling to help you with this tough love approach. You do have to take care of yourself, too, just as the addict has to take care of herself.

Those who stand on the sidelines and wish they could do something to save their friend, partner, or family member from self-destruction eventually realize that no matter how many good intentions, wishes, and earnest efforts they have for a loved one, ultimately it's entirely and exclusively up to the addicted person to make choices for change. As one family member said to me, "You can't will someone to live any more that you can will someone to die." This is a "family dis-ease" that will either heal or destroy if left unspoken or untreated.

**Q:** I think we will be able to get our son taken to a hospital or rehab facility for treatment when he is very sick, but you say the addict has to want to recover. Our son doesn't seem to want to recover as much as we want him to. So will forcing him into treatment work, or will it just be a waste of our time and money?

**A:** It is true that someone who is forced to face his addiction by police, his family, or his friends may not really be facing it; instead, he goes through treatment to please others, not because he is really committed to change. He will have trouble complying with treatment and have difficulty opening up because he can't open his mind to the possibilities that he has an illness or serious addiction that warrants going to a hospital or rehab. For him, there is a high risk of relapse and less likelihood that he will stay in treatment. Even so, treatment to which a person is not open at first may open a door that has previously been closed. Plenty of people have sincerely faced their illness after detoxing in a treatment center; they have accepted help and gone on to recover. No one can say if your son will open his heart to recovery and take responsibility or not. The only sure thing is that he will probably never recover if he does not go to a treatment center or work with an addiction therapist or recovery coach. Use your best judgment and, if you feel he is in danger or harming himself or someone else, call 911 immediately.

**Q:** Our bills are never paid on time. Important appointments are never kept. Promises to our children are always broken. Pills have become a more important part of my husband's life than his family. There's no sign of changing behavior and he's become verbally abusive. I don't want to endure everything you have to go through to get a person to recover. I want to leave him. What do you say to someone like me who just isn't willing to stick it out?

**A:** Only you can decide what you are willing to go through to assist the recovery of a loved one who refuses to listen or has no desire to stop abusing pills. If you have something between you that you feel is worth saving, get support through treatment counseling, enlist the help from an Addiction Recovery Coach, or try a professional interventionist. You can say to your husband that you will leave if he doesn't get treatment. Or, if you are not willing to see it through, you can say that you are leaving anyway and you hope he gets treatment. Either way, you have given your husband a shot at sobriety. You have let him know that life cannot go on as before. It is your decision. I recommend you seek professional therapy for yourself and your children no matter what your husband decides to do.

**Q:** My mother died of pill addiction and alcohol. Our family is left with so many "what if"s and "if only"s that we wish could have been answered before it was too late. How can we deal with this?

**A:** I am very sorry about your great loss. Maybe you could have done something differently and it would have saved your mother's life, but maybe not. Recovery starts with the individual that is asking for help and ready for change. You cannot make someone recover even if you do all the right things. We all wish we had done some things differently in life. We don't get many "do-overs" in life. If you are consumed with guilt, please get counseling for yourself and anyone directly involved with your mother's addiction, and attend family support group meetings at Al-Anon and bereavement support groups. If you want a way to "do something" about it now, help publicize the dangers of misusing and abusing prescription drugs, be available to talk to other families, and speak at schools about your experience with your mother to inspire others to seek help before it's too late and they lose someone they love.

## Concerns of People in Recovery

**Q:** I've finally admitted I'm addicted to my pills and cannot control my behavior. I just cannot face admitting this to my family, so I am putting off getting help. How can I get the courage to tell them?

**A:** Many families are relieved to hear an announcement such as yours because they already knew or had some idea. There's a good chance they will be very supportive. However, I understand your fear. Ironically, your family is probably also dealing with a lot of their own fear about how to approach you with their concerns. They may fear you are going to blame them. They may exclaim, "How could this happen to you!" Or they might try to minimize your addiction, complaining that they can't understand why you can't simply follow the instructions on the bottle and take your medicines as directed. They may say you can recover on your own; you don't need psychiatrists and treatment centers. What they are really telling you when they say these things is that they are afraid, too. If you go into treatment, your addiction will be out in the open, and they may fear shame and embarrassment. Furthermore, they may have adapted to your addiction, whether in a healthy manner or not. They have developed a routine. Even so, most families will be ready to hear what you have to say and will be very supportive in your decision to get help. Families fear change because it means they may need to change their behavior in order to help you during and after recovery. They may have been enabling you in your helplessness; now they are going to have to support you in a different, yet equally difficult venture.

Knowing family members may be acting out of fear as great as yours may help you face their reactions. Explain to them that you need to make this change with the help from addiction therapy, and you must put your struggle first—even before them. Tell them you may need to maintain some distance from your family and friends for a time. Ask for their support without judgment or criticism. To their accusing "How could you?" simply say, "I have to learn about pill addiction first before I can explain it to you." Once you have decided to put recovery first, you cannot worry about them. Whether you decide to admit yourself into a drug treatment facility or hire an Addiction Recovery Coach at home; commit yourself to stopping your addiction and change past behavior. In the end, those around you will benefit from your recovery. And in the end, you can reconnect with loved ones. You will be able to explain addiction and recovery to them or, if you prefer, you can do this at a family counseling session together with a professional to help guide you and offer further explanation about addiction. In the end, you'll be showing them daily the wonderful changes you've made in yourself, and you will rebuild trust again without addiction.

**Q:** How can I get in touch with Prescriptions Anonymous and Addiction Recovery Coaching?

**A:** The best way to get in contact with me for additional information, answers to questions about national treatment facility resources, or to schedule an appointment with an Addiction Recovery Coach is to go to:

www.prescriptionsanonymous.com. Leave a message on this site, and someone will be in contact with you the same day or within 24 hours, using your preferences for contact via email, online chat, Skype, text, or a phone call.

**Q:** I have been through detox and feel that I still need help. I haven't prayed very much in my life. I don't know how to start. Is there a prayer you could give me that can help remind me everyday that I'm not alone.

**A:** Prayer doesn't work unless you believe in a higher power and want recovery to work. The God or the higher power you have in your heart and believe in can be a powerful help to keep you in recovery and offer you peace when you need it the most. A prayer or chant can get you in the right frame of mind to do what you have to do. The following is a well-known prayer that was adapted with permission from Alcoholics Anonymous for Prescriptions Anonymous network meetings.

*God, grant me the* **Courage** *to admit that I am powerless over my addiction to any mood altering substance and co-occurring illnesses, the* **Wisdom** *that I gain through support groups, sponsors, and prayer, so that I may share with others who still suffer, and the* **Serenity** *that comes from within, which can be felt not only by me, but by those I choose to have in my life.*

**Q:** How do I find doctors and treatment centers that understand pill addiction?

**A:** Get recommendations from other recovering addicts you meet, Prescriptions Anonymous, internet research for treatment rehabilitation facilities, and the resource listing in my book in Appendix II.

**Q:** How do I keep myself from relapse and depression?

**A:** Here are some things you can do to stay honest and positive with yourself:

**Keep a journal** in which you record feelings, moods, and anger-provoking situations as they arise. Include a note about the intensity of your feelings and how you dealt with them. This record helps you track your mood changes over time so that you can learn from them and share your findings with your addiction recovery coach, therapist, or sponsor.

**Talk about your guilt and shame.** Addicts often feel extremely guilty and shameful about a disease over which they have no control. They may feel guilty over things said in anger to their families, spouses, children, coworkers, even a loss that impacted their lives. In recovery, they may feel guilty about not paying more attention to others instead of focusing all their energy on themselves. They are ashamed of their failings. If you are experiencing these feelings, discuss them in treatment, with your recovery coach, and at support group meetings. The understanding you receive from them gives you the support you need to deal with many emotional feelings.

**Learn to forgive yourself.** For most addicts this is one of the toughest steps to take. Forgiving myself and others from my accident in 1973 involving the death of a pedestrian took me years to forgive myself, but in time and therapy it does become a lighter burden to carry. Forgiving yourself is a process that doesn't happen overnight but gradually feeling peace and forgiveness from within feels satisfying. While you are not responsible for your disease, you are responsible for your recovery. You can't forget your past and may not be able to make amends to all those you have harmed, but you do have control over your future. If you're doing all the right things to change your behavior, you will become happier and healthier, and, if you keep recovery first in your life, time will heal you, and you will be able to forgive yourself and others.

**Identify feelings of loss.** Some people have a strong sense of loss or grief after stopping their abuse of pills. They become depressed and withdrawn as if they had lost a loved one or a job. In a sense you really have lost something that was once close to you, something that gave you a sense of security. Share your feelings of loss and depression with your addiction recovery coach, therapist, or group support meetings. Soon, a healthier life and positive behaviors will be more fulfilling than pills and will replace your loss.

**Q:** Before I got clean, I had some friends who used illegal drugs and abuse alcohol. I still like them, and I wish they were in recovery, too. I hate to cut them off when they call me. Do you have to give up your friends? That makes recovery hard and difficult.

**A:** Friends are indeed valuable. You need friends more now than ever before. However, most people in recovery cannot keep the same friends they had when they were abusing drugs because those friends may have been as ill as the addicts were. Remember, changing old behaviors isn't easy. If you go back to your old friends, you will be tempted to go back to your old ways. Staying in recovery comes first, always, above all else.

Yes, you will need friends. New friends. You need the healing powers of a good friend, someone you feel comfortable with, someone who will listen without judgment or criticism. You need someone who won't lie to you, but, more importantly, who won't allow you to lie to him. Friendships keep you planted solidly on the ground and help you to feel peace. Choosing a friend is very important, especially in recovery. Choose wisely someone who will be a benefit to you, someone who does not abuse or mis-use controlled substances or over-the-counter medicines. Many of us meet these new friends in support groups, church, or community fellowships.

Tell the old friends who call and who still abuse or misuse mind-altering substance that your recovery is the main priority in your life and you cannot be associated with them for a while, if ever. Tell them you hope they, too, will get help through an Addiction Recovery Coach, treatment center, or individual therapy and that you will do all you can to encourage them when that time comes. Maybe your recovery will inspire them to follow suit. That is surely the best way for you to show your friendship. But for now, it's best to stay away.

**Q:** Is there some easy way to know when I am in danger of relapse? I seem to get too down in the dumps before I realize what's happening. I need to recognize danger sooner.

**A:** In Chapter 9 there are lists of situations which will help you recognize the triggers for relapse. I suggest you read over the list every week or so to help you recognize what's happening in your life. Also, a popular tool in the recovery world is the acronym: H.A.L.T. It means: Hurt, Angry, Lonely, Tired. These states of mind will trigger compulsive actions. When you feel hurt, angry, lonely, or tired, change your behavior and surroundings. Do something soothing to take your mind off your trigger, call a friend, sponsor, recovery coach, therapist, or go for a walk, read this book again, and get some rest.

**Q:** I thought if I took one or two extra pills for my stress that I would feel better more quickly and wouldn't have to think about my problems. That is ruining my life. I've finally given up the pills and now my problems seem worse than ever. What can I do besides start taking more pills again?

**A:** You will need to work with your therapist on both the addiction and the original problem that you were trying to mask through pills. At least half of all prescription addicts have a dual diagnosis of addiction and depression or some other psychological problem. Find a therapist who understands both addiction and other psychological disorders. Hire an Addiction Recovery Coach for relapse prevention. Find support in recovery groups where you will find peers who understand your situation and who will share stories with you that validate your feelings while offering their views of what worked for them in their situations similar to yours.

**Q:** On top of all the other painful emotions I had before, I now have the shame of knowing how badly I hurt the people I care about while I was on prescription drugs. That's just one more thing to worry about in recovery. How can I face the people I've hurt?

**A:** You've already hurt these people, and your relationships probably can't get much worse. The only thing you can do is improve yourself. Think through what you honestly feel now that you have taken responsibility for your behavior. Rehearse your speech and prepare to listen to their responses without defensiveness. Your therapist or Addiction Recovery Coach can help you plan your approach. Tell them that you now realize and regret how much you have hurt them. Speak calmly, no matter what. Almost always the hurt person's response is better than you expected. It almost always helps your relationship enormously. Moreover, when you take responsibility for what you did, the other person often volunteers that he realizes he had a part in the original problem, too. In any case, both of you will feel better when you reach out honestly and contritely to those you have hurt. You will probably find they are on your side more than ever before.

**Q:** I am sober and supposedly in recovery. I still feel like killing myself sometimes. I think I'll never make it. Is it really worth the struggle?

**A:** Yes, you are worth it. The early part of recovery is never easy or a quick fix. Please call 911 whenever you're feeling suicidal or in danger of hurting yourself or someone else. Call your psychiatrist or licensed addictionologist, who can help you with not only your addiction but your struggle with emotional problems and make any helpful adjustments with your prescribed medication.

**Q:** I was diagnosed with addiction and depression. How can my doctor take away my pills without making my depression worse?

**A:** You are right that doing without your pills may leave you depressed and anxious. You are also right that depression may require medication similar to the pills to which you were addicted. However, the new treatment will include prescriptions for non-addictive drugs at much lower doses, which will be effective now that you are detoxed. Any healthcare professionals you consult must be ones who understand addiction, and you must inform them that you have an addictive personality and that you are in recovery from controlled substance addiction. Doctors will appreciate your honesty and will closely monitor your medications prescribing only non-addictive medicines.

**Q:** Can over-the-counter medications really be addictive? Which ones can I take that would be low risk?

**A:** Yes, over-the-counter medicines can be addictive. Some contain addictive components similar to what is in prescription medication, just in much lower doses. Refer to Chapter 9 for a list of over-the-counter medications considered low risk by a pharmacist. For more information about over-the-counter addiction research www.addictioncenter.com and www.ridgeviewinstitute.com for Safe Drug Use for the Recovering Addict or Alcoholic.

**Q:** I can't talk to my family or friends; they don't believe I have a disease called *prescription addiction*. How can I make them understand that my addiction is real and just as potentially deadly as any other addiction?

**A:** It's difficult for anyone to stop abusing drugs, learn new skills, change lifestyle, and at the same time educate your family and convince disbelieving relatives that the problem you have is not just sleazy behavior. Don't try. Tell your family once, repeat it once more if necessary, and then let them be. To overcome addiction, you have to concentrate on you and your life. You have to let what others say slide and leave convincing them for another day. This is a time when others who know about prescription addiction from experience should become your confidants and friends. This is one reason support groups are so important. When family begin to see a positive turn around in you, they might then begin to listen and ask about the changes you've made. When they're ready to listen; share with them more about your addiction, suggest family support groups such as Al-Anon, and recommend they read this book. Listening is a two-way street, so be prepared to answer their questions respectfully, and be sensitive to their concerns while they learn about addiction.

**Q:** My husband and I are having difficulty talking to each other about my addiction. He doesn't trust me. Where do we go from here?

**A:** Of course he doesn't trust you. You've probably lied to him a hundred times to hide your addiction and emotions. Now, you must say what you need to say, being open and truthful and brave; then don't worry about what he says back. Don't try to talk him into trust, that will come back naturally the longer you're in recovery and not abusing pills and alcohol. Your focus needs to be on you. In time, your changed behavior will convince him that you are becoming worthy of his trust again. He might even be interested in learning more about addiction and the effects it has had on you and on you both as a couple.

**Q:** I am truly sorry for how I have hurt my family, and I want to make amends. I am terrified and don't know what to say.

**A:** Start with the short statement, "I am very sorry for how I have hurt you." Just that simple apology is a release and sometimes is enough to reestablish comfort and repair broken bonds. As an example, consider what I told my father when I tried to make amends. I had hurt his feelings. I had stopped showing respect, and I wasn't talking to him. When I finally found the courage to try to repair our relationship, I said, "I am really sorry I have hurt you." I also said that he had hurt me, and I had to deal with that. He replied, "I do feel badly. I didn't handle things as well as I should have." That made me feel that I didn't bear the whole burden of our estrangement and reconciliation. We were both sorry, and we wanted to reconnect. My father and I were very fortunate that we were able to repair our relationship before his passing. He told me he was very proud of me, my recovery, and how I now help others living with addiction.

**Q:** My husband and I are planning our first trip since I have been in recovery. I am worried that, since our routine will be different for a few days, I won't be able to handle it. There will be tensions and temptations. Is there anything I can do to make this trip safer for me?

**A:** As with any successful vacation or trip, planning ahead is essential. You will likely plan your itinerary, activities, and visits with friends and family. Why not include planning ahead for scheduled support meetings to attend as well? You can search on the internet for support group meetings such as those of Dual Recovery Anonymous, Alcoholics Anonymous, or Narcotics Anonymous. Prescriptions Anonymous, the organization I founded, is a national, non-traditional and 12-step program, virtual network-based Addiction Recovery Coaching program available through Skype, phone, email and chat for individuals and families. Call these wonderful helpers and ask about the locations closest to where you will be vacationing, or schedule a virtual meeting with Prescriptions Anonymous anywhere you go on vacation. I promise you that people in support groups will be just as receptive, kind, and welcoming as your own support group at home.

Prescriptions Anonymous Recovery Coaches offer Sober Companion services to attend special events, meetings and vacations when you need us the most for relapse prevention.

**Q:** How do I act when I go back to work? What do I say about my absence?

**A:** If no one at work knows of your addiction, you have options. You could simply state that you had gotten addicted to prescription drugs your doctor prescribed, and you needed to take some time to recover. That would help to keep communication with you and co-workers open and lessen any false rumors around the office. If you think it would be to your advantage to keep your addiction private, or if you just choose to do so, tell people you have had a health problem, give a few details that could apply to any illness, such as that you "felt really bad," and your doctor gave you some medication and recommended you take time off from work to rest. Then stick to this account. To any additional questions, say, "I'm trying to put my illness behind me, and I'd feel better if I didn't talk about it." Your behavior and skills at work, no longer subject to the effects of inappropriate drugs, will build your colleagues' trust in your competence. If, on the other hand, some people know about your addiction, you can still tell them whatever truth you want about the addiction, or you can still say, "I'm trying to put my illness behind me now that I have recovered, so I'd prefer to not talk about it."

Additionally, if your work was stressful before treatment and recovery, seriously consider seeking a new job that would make you happier and be less stressful. A better job might mean more routine or more variety, more action or a slower pace, whatever will not tempt you to medicate for stress. It is better to earn less and be at peace than to earn more and never know when you will feel the desire to take a mind-altering substance to help you "get through a crisis."

**Q:** I have been in recovery for a year, and therefore I'm eligible to be a sponsor. I have been asked to be a sponsor by others in my support group. I don't know if I am ready for this or if I even want to do it. What are the pros and cons of agreeing to sponsor others?

**A:** People who have been in recovery for a year or more often find they enjoy becoming a peer sponsor and facilitator at support groups. They also feel sponsoring someone else helps them continue their recovery more easily. The following comments of sponsors I know address this question:

"Newcomers remind me where I was, and being a sponsor reinforces my own recovery."

"It keeps me tuned-in and aware of my own problems as well as my own progress."

"Listening to newcomers reminds me I can be right back to where they are at any time. No one is immune to relapse."

"I found being a sponsor to be very rewarding and a great way to give back the lessons I learned in my own recovery."

As you teach and listen to newly sober people, you are reinforcing the lessons you need to remember forever yourself. Helping people also gives you a good feeling and helps your own self-esteem. I personally have as strong an urge today as I did in 1998 to continue my efforts to reach out to others with our disease. Writing this book was another way for me to reach millions searching for addiction resources and treatment options. If you don't have this desire, that's okay too. The option to sponsor if and when you're ready can be done any time or not at all. Sponsorship isn't for everyone; your own recovery is your first priority.

**Q:** I am in recovery, and I know I must remember that I am still a recovering addict so I won't relapse. But I'm so tired of my life revolving around being as addict/alcoholic and always thinking about codependency and enabling and trying not to be part of a dysfunctional family. Is there ever any other way of looking at it?

**A:** I agree that so much attention must be given to the dysfunction of the family and so much is said about the disease that you forget you can eventually be a part of a healthy family.

Someday you will get beyond these troubled times. Then you will need to change your mind-set. You will no longer have a dysfunctional family but a "functional" family. To encourage "another way of looking at it," Prescriptions Anonymous network group members came up with the following acronym with its positive elaboration. Perhaps this acronym will help you look at the brighter side:

## FUNCTIONAL

**F:** *Freedom of expression*: Each of us holds the power and right to perceive, to want and desire, to exhibit emotion, to make choices and to change.

**U:** *Uninterrupted attention* given to each other: Couples need to set aside time to listen to each other without interruption.

**N:** *Negotiated differences*: To negotiate differences there must first be the desire to cooperate and a willingness to hear other viewpoints and concerns.

**C:** *Communication*: Clear communication requires respect for one's self and others as well as effort and skill.

**T:** *Trust:* Trust is created by honesty. Express yourself honestly. Sharing emotion, thoughts, and fears is more important than agreement.

**I:** *Individuality:* Individual differences between members of the family should be encouraged. Families often learn from one another. Our own uniqueness should be honored.

**O:** *Open-mindedness:* Family members should be open-minded and flexible with each other so that each person can be spontaneous without fear, guilt, or shame.

**N:** *Needs fulfilled:* Couples and families that get their needs met feel respected, loved, important, and happy. Express your needs and your appreciation when they are met.

**A:** *Accountability:* You each (through treatment, recovery coaching or therapy) know what your part in recovery is. Be responsible for your part and acknowledge when you have made mistakes.

**L:** *Love:* Love is allowing loved ones to make mistakes and find solutions for themselves. Love is patient, kind, and forgiving.

This last question is the one I'm asked most often. I hope my answer will reassure you.

**Q:** Will I ever be happy again?

**A:** Yes, when you've been in recovery for a while and you've learned the essential steps and personal goals of recovery, you will be happier than you ever were before. No one can give a time frame for when you'll feel happy, but just know it does happen for anyone who is "sick and tired of being sick and tired" and willing to go to any lengths to get there. I am living proof—and I have many friends who are living proof that recovery is worth all that you go through to get to the other side and achieve a happy life. Clean and sober opens a new world of possibilities and accomplishments. The process of recovery helps you grow, have confidence in yourself, set goals, learn new skills and relate to people in a healthier way. Recovery allows you to find your purpose, plan for the future, and move on with your life holding your head high.

You deserve all that recovery offers; I'm pulling for you.

# APPENDIX 2
## *Resources*

This section contains a list of resources for drug and alcohol addicts, families, and their loved ones. Included are support groups, national government agencies, and state addiction prevention programs. These groups and organizations can provide answers to questions or direct you to other appropriate sources.

## SUPPORT GROUPS

Prescriptions Anonymous (RxA)
Naples, FL 34109
www.prescriptionsanonymous.com
(239) 451-3441

Prescriptions Anonymous is a national non-traditional program for prescription, over-the-counter addictions, and other cross-addictions for individuals and families who are currently active in addiction, relapse, or post treatment coaching for aftercare relapse prevention at home. Addiction recovery coaching services for individuals and families in recovery include sober companions for safe travel transports and special events. Recovery Coaching services can be done in person or by phone, email, on-line chat, or virtual recovery meetings by Skype with an addiction recovery coach.

Pillars Recovery
Newport Beach, CA 92663
www.pillarsrecovery.com
(844) 262-8853

Pillars Recovery is a non-traditional boutique rehabilitation program located at Newport Beach for men and Laguna Beach for women in Orange County, California providing inpatient residential and outpatient aftercare programs for drug and alcohol rehabilitation, relapse prevention and dual diagnosis counseling.

Dual Recovery Anonymous
Brentwood, TN 37027
www.dualdiagnosis.org
(866) 998-3750

Dual Recovery Anonymous is a 12-step, self-help program that is based on the principles of A.A. and the experiences of men and women in recovery with a dual diagnosis. The DRA program helps us recover from both our chemical dependency and our emotional or psychiatric illness by focusing on relapse prevention and actively improving the quality of our lives.

Narcotics Anonymous (NA)
Van Nuys, CA 91409
www.na.org
(818) 773-9999

Members learn to live drug free through the 12 steps and 12 traditions adapted from Alcoholics Anonymous World Services. They focus on all drug addictions rather than specified or co-occurring illnesses. NA is a nonprofit, international, community-based organization.

Alcoholics Anonymous (AA)
New York, NY 10163
www.aa.org
(212) 870-3400

Alcoholics Anonymous, a worldwide organization 12-step recovery program, is a fellowship of women and men who share with each other their experiences, strengths and hope in order to help each other in recovery from alcoholism. The focus is primarily on alcohol recovery, support meetings and sponsorship.

Al-Anon Family Groups (Headquarter)
Virginia Beach, VA 23454
www.wso@al-anon.org
(757) 563-1600

Al-Anon is a worldwide organization that offers a 12-step program of recovery for the families and friends of alcoholics and those with other addictions whether or not the loved one seeks help. Members offer comfort and understanding that binds individuals and groups together through mutual exchanges of experiences, strengths, and hopes.

## INFORMATIONAL AGENCIES

Substance Abuse and Mental Health Services Administration (SAMHSA)
5600 Fishers Lane
Rockville, MD 20857
www.samhsa.gov
(877) 726-4727

The Substance Abuse and Mental Health Services Administration (SAMHSA) is the agency within the U.S. Department of Health and Human Services that leads public health efforts to advance the behavioral health of the nation. SAMHSA's mission is to reduce the impact of substance abuse and mental illness on America's communities.

American Pharmaceutical Association
2215 Constitution Avenue, NW
Washington, DC 20037
infocenter@aphanet.org
(800) 237-2742

APHA Foundation distributes health information to the general public and offers continuing education programs for pharmacists. APHA is a professional organization of pharmacists and specialists who understand the correct use of medicines. Pharmacists dispense drugs according to prescriptions from healthcare providers and can answer questions about non-prescription products sold in pharmacies.

American Psychiatric Association
800 Maine Avenue, S.W., Suite 900
Washington, DC 20024
apa@psych.org
202-559-3900

APA is a professional society of psychiatrists and medical doctors who specialize in treating individuals with mental or emotional disorders. The association continues to research and improve the diagnosis, treatment and rehabilitation of individuals through continued education programs for psychiatrists. Individuals can contact the Association to locate a psychiatrist in their area for consultation.

Center for Substance Abuse Prevention (CSAP)
5600 Fishers Lane
Rockville, MD 20857
www.samhsa.gov
240-276-2420

The Center for Substance Abuse Prevention (CSAP) works with federal, state, public, and private organizations to develop comprehensive prevention systems by:
Providing national leadership in the development of policies, programs, and services to prevent the onset of illegal drug use, prescription drug misuse and abuse, alcohol misuse and abuse, and underage alcohol and tobacco use.
Promoting effective substance abuse prevention practices that enable states, communities, and other organizations to apply prevention knowledge effectively.

National Institute on Drug Abuse (NIDA)
6001 Executive Boulevard
Bethesda, Maryland 20892
www.nida.nih.gov
301-443-1124

NIDA is a federal government agency developing effective strategies to deal with problems and issues associated with alcohol and drug abuse. They provide information to healthcare professionals and the public on the risks and consequences of drug and alcohol abuse. Researchers funded by the Institute work to identify new ways to prevent substance abuse.

## STATE PROGRAMS FOR SUBSTANCE ABUSE AND MENTAL HEALTH SERVICES

**Alabama**
Substance Abuse Division
100 N. Union Street, Suite 402
Montgomery, AL 36130
(334) 242-3218

**Alaska**
**Division of Behavioral Health, Mental Health Central Office**
Alaska Department of Health and Social Services
3601 C Street, Suite 878
Anchorage, AK 99503
(907) 269-5948

**Arizona**
Arizona Health Care Cost Containment System
801 East Jefferson
Phoenix, AZ 85034
(602) 417-4711

**Arkansas**
Division of Behavioral Health Services
Arkansas Department of Human Services
305 South Palm Street
Little Rock, AR 72205
(501) 686-9981

**California**
California Department of Health Care Services
1501 Capitol Avenue,
Sacramento, CA 95389
(916) 440-7400

**Colorado**
Office of Behavioral Health
Colorado Department of Human Services
3824 West Princeton Circle
Denver, CO 80236
(303) 866-7400

**Connecticut**
Connecticut Department of Mental Health and Addiction Services
410 Capitol Avenue
Hartford, CT 06134
(860) 418-8650

**Delaware**
Division of Substance Abuse and Mental Health
Delaware Health and Social Services
Main Building, 1st Floor
1901 North DuPont Highway
New Castle, DE 19720
(302) 255-9657

**Florida**
Substance Abuse and Mental Health
Florida Department of Children and Families
Building 6, Room 275
1317 Winewood Boulevard
Tallahassee, FL 32399-0700
(850) 717-4322

**Georgia**
Georgia Department of Behavioral Health and Developmental Disabilities
Office of Addictive Diseases
2 Peachtree Street, Northwest, Suite 22-273
Atlanta, GA 30303
(404) 657-2331

**Hawaii**
Alcohol and Drug Abuse Division
Hawaii Department of Health
Kakuhhewa Building, Room 360
601 Kamokila Boulevard
Kapolei, HI 96707
(808) 692-7510

**Idaho**
Division of Behavioral Health
Idaho Department of Health and Welfare
Cenarrusa Building, 3rd Floor
450 West State Street
Boise, ID 83720-0036
(208) 334-0642

**Illinois**
Division of Alcoholism and Substance Abuse
Illinois Department of Human Services
401 South Clinton Street, 2nd Floor
Chicago, IL 60607
(312) 814-2300

**Indiana**
Division of Mental Health and Addiction
Indiana Family and Social Services Administration
Indiana Government Building, Room W353
402 West Washington Street
Indianapolis, IN 46204
(317) 232-7845

**Iowa**
Division of Behavioral Health
Iowa Department of Public Health
Lucas State Office Building, 4th Floor
321 East 12th Street
Des Moines, IA 50319-0075
(515) 281-4417

**Kansas**
Behavioral Health and Addiction Services
Kansas Department for Aging and Disability Services
503 South Kansas Avenue
Topeka, KS 66603
(785) 296-6495

**Kentucky**
Health and Family Services
275 East Main Street 4W-G
Frankfort, KY 40621
(502)-782-6173

**Louisiana**
Department of Behavioral Health and Hospitals
Bienville Building
628 North 4th Street
Baton Rouge, LA 70821
(225) 342- 8916

**Maine**
Substance Abuse and Mental Health Services
Maine Department of Health and Human Services
11 State House Station
41 Anthony Avenue
Augusta, ME 04333
(207) 287-2595

**Maryland**
Behavioral Health Administration
Spring Grove Hospital Center
55 Wade Avenue
Catonsville, MD 21228
(410)-402-8452

**Massachusetts**
Bureau of Substance Abuse Services
Massachusetts Department of Public Health
250 Washington Street, 3rd Floor
Boston, MA 02108-4609
(617) 624-5151

**Michigan**
Bureau of Substance Abuse Services
Massachusetts Department of Public Health
250 Washington Street, 3rd Floor
Boston, MA 02108
(617) 624-5151

**Michigan**
Bureau of Community Based Services
Behavioral Health and Developmental Disabilities Administration
Michigan Department of Community Health
Lewis Cass Building
320 South Walnut Street
Lansing, MI 48913
(517) 373-2576

**Minnesota**
Alcohol and Drug Abuse Division
Minnesota Department of Human Services
St. Paul, MN 5516428 Alcohol and Drug Abuse Division
Minnesota Department of Human Services
St. Paul, MN 55164
(651) 431-4928

**Mississippi**
Bureau of Alcohol and Drug Abuse Services
Mississippi Department of Mental Health
1101 Robert E. Lee Building
239 North Lamar Street
Jackson, MS 39201
(601) 359-5198

**Missouri**
Division of Alcohol and Drug Abuse
Missouri Department of Mental Health
1706 East Elm Street
Jefferson City, MO 65102
(573) 751-9499

**Montana**
Chemical Dependency Bureau
Addictive and Mental Disorders Division
Montana Department of Public Health and Human Services
Helena, MT 59620
(406) 444-7157

**Nebraska**
Nebraska Department of Behavioral Health and Human Services
Nebraska State Office Building
301 Centennial Mall South
Lincoln, NE 68509
(402) 471-855-3402

**Nevada**
Division of Public and Behavioral Health
Nevada Department of Health and Human Services
4150 Technology Way, Suite 300
Carson City, NV 89706
(775) 684-4200

**New Hampshire**
Bureau of Drug and Alcohol Services
New Hampshire Department of Health and Human Services
105 Pleasant Street, 3rd Floor North
Concord, NH 03301
(603) 271-6110

**New Jersey**
Division of Mental Health and Addictions Services
New Jersey Department of Human Services
222 South Warren Street, 3rd Floor
Trenton, NJ 08602
(609) 777-0711

**New Mexico**
Behavioral Health Services Division
New Mexico Human Services Department
37 Plaza la Prensa
Santa Fe, NM 87504
(505) 476-9295

**New York**
State Office of Alcoholism and Substance Abuse Services
1450 Western Avenue
Albany, NY 12203-3526
(518) 457-2061

**North Carolina**
Division of Mental Health, Developmental Disabilities and Substance Abuse
3007 Mail Service Center
Raleigh, NC 27699
(919) 733-4670

**North Dakota**
Department of Behavioral Health and Human Services
Prairie Hills Plaza
1237 West Divide Avenue, Suite 1C
Bismarck, ND 58501
(701) 328-8824

## Ohio
Mental Health and Addiction Services
30 East Broad Street, 36th Floor
Columbus, OH 43215
(614) 466-2596 or 1-877-275-6364

## Oklahoma
Mental Health and Substance Abuse Services
1200 North East 13th Street
Oklahoma City, OK 73152
(405) 522-3877

## Oregon
Behavioral Health Policy and Analytics
500 Summer Street, NE
Salem, OR 97301
(503) 367-0479

## Pennsylvania
Department of Drug and Alcohol Programs
Health and Welfare Building
625 Forster Street, Room 903
Harrisburg, PA 17120
(717) 214-1937

## Rhode Island
Department of Behavioral Healthcare
14 Harrington Road, Barry Hall #52
Cranston, RI 02920
(401) 462-0917

**South Carolina**
Department of Alcohol and Other Drug Abuse Services
2414 Bull Street, Suite 301
Columbia, SC 29202
(803) 896-8371

**South Dakota**
Department of Social Services
Division of Behavioral Health
Kneip Building c/o 700 Governors Drive
Pierre, SD 57501
(605) 367-5078, (800) 265-9684

**Tennessee**
Mental Health and Substance Abuse Services
6th Floor Andrew Jackson Building
500 Deaderick Street
Nashville, TN 37243
(615) 532-6500

**Texas**
**Mental and Social Services, Behavioral Health**
909 West 45th Street
Austin, TX 78751
(512) 206-4500

**Utah**
Substance Abuse & Mental Health Services
195 North 1950 West
Salt Lake City, UT 84116
(801) 538-4298

**Vermont**
Alcohol and Drug Abuse Programs Division
Department of Health
108 Cherry Street
Burlington, VT 05402
(802) 951-1258

**Virginia**
Behavioral Health and Developmental Services
1220 Bank Street, 13th Floor
Richmond, VA 23219
(804) 786-3921

**Washington**
Behavioral Health and Recovery
Department of Social and Health Services
Olympia, WA 98504
(360) 725-3700

**West Virginia**
Behavioral Health and Health Facilities
Department of Health and Human Services
350 Capitol Street-Room 350
Charleston, WV 25301
(304) 356-4798

**Wisconsin**
Bureau of Prevention Treatment and Recovery
Department of Health Services
1 West Wilson Street, Room 850
Madison, WI 53703
(608) 266-1351

**Wyoming**
Behavioral Health Division
6101 Yellowstone Road, Suite 220
Cheyenne, WY 82002
(307) 777-6494

## ADDITIONAL NETWORK RESOURCES

**District of Columbia**
Department of Behavioral Health
64 New York Avenue, NE. 3rd Floor
Washington, DC 20002
(202) 671-2200

**COMMONWEALTH OF PUERTO RICO**
Mental Health Services Administration and Addiction
Highway #2, Km. 8.2
Prior Mepsi Center Bo. Juan Domingo
Bayamon, PR 00958
(787) 764-3670

**UNITED STATES VIRGIN ISLANDS**
Division of Mental Health, Alcoholism, and Drug Dependency Services
3500 Estate Richmond, Charles Harwood Complex
Christiansted, VI 00820
(340) 718-1311

**RED LAKE BAND OF THE CHIPPEWA INDIANS**
Indian Health Service Headquarters
5600 Fishers Lane
Rockville, MD 20857
(406) 745-2411
Red Lake Tribal Government Center
Highway #1 East
Red Lake, MN 56671
(218) 679-3341

**AMERICAN SAMOA**
Department of Human and Social Services
997534 Utulei Street, Suite 302
Pago, AS 9679
(684) 633-7506

**FEDERATED STATES OF MICRONESIA**
Department of Health and Social Affairs
Federated States of Micronesia
P.O. Box PS 70 Palikir
Pohnpei, FM 96941
(691) 320-2619

**COMMONWEALTH OF THE NORTHERN MARIANA ISLANDS**
Commonwealth Healthcare Corporation
1 Lower Navy Hill Road
P.O. Box 500409 CK
Navy Hill, Saipan, MP 96950-0409
(670) 236-8201

**GUAM**
Department of Mental Health and Substance Abuse
Government of Guam
790 Governor Carlos G. Camacho Road
Tamuning, GU 96913
(671) 647-5330

**REPUBLIC OF THE MARSHALL ISLANDS**
Republic of the Marshall Islands Ministry of Health
Capital Building, 2nd Floor
Amata Kabua Avenue
P.O. Box 16
Majuro MH 96960
Telephone: 011(692) 625-3399

**REPUBLIC OF PALAU**
Bureau of Public Health
Ministry of Health
P.O. Box 6027
Koror, PW 96940
Telephone: 680-488-4573

www.ingramcontent.com/pod-product-compliance
Lightning Source LLC
Chambersburg PA
CBHW071343290426
44108CB00014B/1421